The Hollow Crown

THE
HOLLOW CROWN

A LIFE OF RICHARD II

BY

Harold F. Hutchison

for within the hollow crown
That rounds the mortal temples of a king
Keeps Death his court . . .
Richard II, Act 3, Scene 2

THE JOHN DAY COMPANY
NEW YORK

FIRST AMERICAN EDITION, 1961

Library of Congress Catalogue
Card Number: 61-12719

MANUFACTURED IN THE UNITED STATES OF AMERICA

TO MY SON

ANDREW MURRAY HUTCHISON

AND, IN GRATITUDE, TO

T. MALCOLM KNOX

PRINCIPAL OF THE UNIVERSITY OF ST ANDREWS

Contents

Illustrations

Following Page 142.

The following acknowledgments for the illustrations are due: to Mr F. L. Kennet for his photograph of the Richard II effigy; to Mr A. F. Kersting for his photograph of the Edward III effigy; to Mr Herbert Felton for his photographs of the Edward, Prince of Wales effigy, and the effigy of Henry IV; to the Bursar of All Souls College, Oxford for the portrait of John of Gaunt; to the Dean of Westminster for the portrait of the young Richard II; to the Warburg Institute for the effigy of Anne of Bohemia; to Dr H. Zincam for the photographs of the roof of Westminster Hall. Richard II's signature on p. 240 is Crown Copyright; reproduced by permission of the Controller of H.M. Stationery Office.

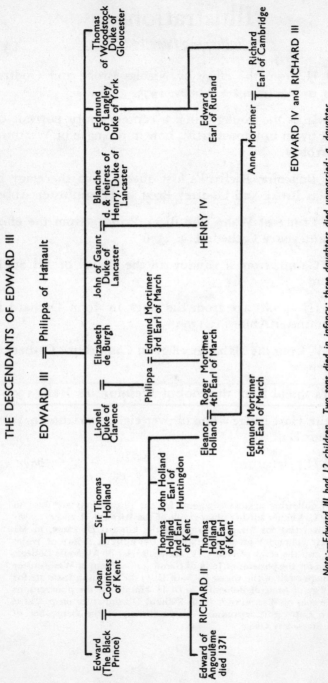

THE DESCENDANTS OF EDWARD III

EDWARD III = Philippa of Hainault

Note:—Edward III had 12 children. Two sons died in infancy; three daughters died unmarried; a daughter Isabella married into the Coucy family; another daughter Mary married into the Montfort family.

THE DESCENDANTS OF JOHN OF GAUNT

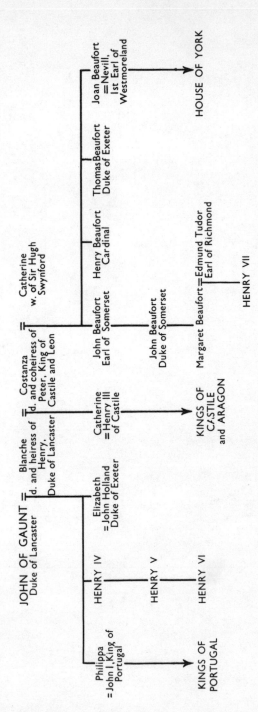

FOREWORD

THE STORY OF Richard II is usually quoted as a classic example of a prince who as a young King displayed the greatest promise, and who deservedly lost his throne because of his own folly and an almost insane lust for tyranny. Shakespeare's *Tragedy of King Richard II* is generally accepted as the authentic history of a despot who deserved his fate, and who is only rescued from our contempt by the pathos of his abdication and the bravery of his end.

Most of us have two other memories of Richard II. We remember clearly a handsome fourteen-year-old who faced Wat Tyler's mob at Smithfield alone and unafraid. We have a more confused recollection of a group of Richard's barons known for obscure reasons as the Lords Appellant, whom we are for ever mixing up with another group of barons known as the Lords Ordainers. Neither Shakespeare nor our text books have done much to clarify our confusions or to reconcile that brave fourteen-year-old with the pathetic neurotic he is usually supposed to have become, and, lacking evidence to the contrary, most of us have continued to assume that our greatest dramatist was also a reasonably reliable historian.

This is not fair to Shakespeare. Shakespeare was a poet creating a drama on the fall of a monarch; and he saw nothing strange in the theory of the Divine Right of Kings. His play deals only with the last two years of a reign of twenty years – it therefore tells us nothing of Wat Tyler or the Lords Appellant – and it was planned as the first of a tetralogy which had for its consistent theme the Nemesis that overtakes usurpation. In introducing this theme, Shakespeare took liberties with history. The scene in which Richard is disgracefully cruel to the dying Gaunt has no basis in fact; the political background to the Lists of Coventry is much too subtle for his dramatic simplification; the description of Gloucester as that 'plain well-meaning soul' is a travesty; the story of the abdication has been radically revised by modern research; Richard's Queen was a child and not a woman in 1399; Richard's death scene has no warranty; and all the playwright's sources were rooted in Lancastrian prejudices and distortions. But what may be excused to the dramatist should be corrected by the historian. Shakespeare wrote a great drama on Richard's end as the beginning to succeeding tragedies. It is the historian's function to reconcile Richard's tragic end with its own fair beginnings.

The facts of Richard's reign are for the most part now well established, thanks to the painstaking researches of modern scholars, a careful reassessment of the French sources for the period, and the discovery in recent times of English chronicles written without a Lancastrian usurper looking over their authors' shoulders. The Shakespearian version nevertheless still commands general belief. As long ago as 1867, a great French scholar, H. Wallon, wrote a better-balanced history of Richard II, which has never even been translated into English. Since then, at the Universities, lecturers and scholars have warned students against accepting the Lancastrian Shakespearian versions of Richard's life and death without question – but the general public are rarely students. Only one biography of Richard II has been published in English – by Anthony Steel in 1941 – but, although scholarly and brilliant, it is, in its author's own words, 'limited to Richard in his political function'. For the rest, modern revisions have been confined to the limits of monographs and articles addressed to specialist scholars, and the average enthusiast's queries, as the final curtain falls on Shakespeare's *Tragedy*, are still for the most part unanswered. Only a dramatist of our own time has essayed a revised version. In 1932, the play *Richard of Bordeaux* by Gordon Daviot was first produced in London, and that it was an immediate and lasting success is proof not only of its dramatic power but also of the historical gap it partly filled.

My book is an attempt to rescue Richard from the innocent libels of our greatest dramatist, and, in the light of modern research, to present a fairer version of the life and death of Richard for general consumption. It tries to show Richard in his period, and to avoid the anachronistic approach of liberal historians who have too often looked at mediaeval history through Whig glasses. It depicts the history of Richard's thirty-three years as a mirror to Chivalry in brilliant decline, to the Middle Ages in middle age, and to the English renaissance in embryo. It has to report the first emergence of the English people in violent mood, the first stirrings of the English Reformation, and the first flowerings of the English literature and of the native arts and crafts. But, above all, it has to explain the drama of a King with great gifts, who summed up so much of the mediaeval past and who anticipated not a little of its future, who suffered tragically from his elders and successfully worked out his own calculated revenge, yet who finally made possible his own downfall.

I have tried to offer explanation without distorting fact, and without easy surrender to any theory of madness. We can still look at Richard II in portrait and effigy in Westminster Abbey, and it is the thesis of this book that we see there the likeness of a fascinating King who was also a rational, if unlucky, human being.

I wish to pay tribute to all those professional scholars without whose toil this book could never have been attempted and whose works are referred to in the Notes. I also wish to record my thanks to my wife, and to my secretary Miss G. I. Long, for typing from my handwriting, and to my friend and colleague A. Bryce Beaumont for his invaluable help at the proof-reading stage.

HAROLD F. HUTCHISON

The Monk of Evesham (14th cent.). 'He was of the common stature
. . . abrupt and stammering in his speech . . . prodigal . . .
extravagantly splendid . . . timid and unsuccessful in Foreign
War . . . arrogant, rapacious . . . remaining sometimes till
morning in drinking and other excesses that are not to be
named . . .'

Froissart (14th cent.). 'Some had on him pity and some none, but
said he had long deserved death.'

Wallon (1864). 'Il ne's était pas montré indigne du sang qui coulait
dans ses veines . . . ce sont les fautes de Richard qu'ont preparé
mais c'est surtout l'ambition de Henri qui a consommé la
révolution.'

Stubbs (1873). '. . . whether the result was obtained by long waiting
for an opportunity . . . combined with unscrupulous craft and
unflinching promptitude of action, or whether it was, like
the cunning of a madman, a violent and reckless attempt to
surprise the unwary nation . . . it is hard to say.'

J. R. Green (1874). 'The brilliant abilities which Richard shared
with the rest of the Plantagenets were marred by a fitful in-
constancy, an insane pride, and a craving for absolute power.'

Trevelyan (1899). 'He fought and fell to free the King's counsels
from the thraldom of an intensive and domineering aristocracy,
and in his youth Lords and Commons gained a grip they never
lost.'

Vickers (1913). 'To attribute to him a long planned scheme of
revenge is to accept too lightly the accusation of his none too
acute opponents and to ascribe to him a strength of character
which he did not possess or a gift of perceptive cunning only
to be explained by incipient insanity.'

Oman (1920). 'There was method in his madness. His attacks on
the constitution were carried out with cunning and ingenuity
. . . he fooled away the crown.'

Clarke (1930). '. . . the official story of the revolution carried no more weight than any other tainted and partisan contemporary evidence.'

Cambridge Mediaeval History (1932). 'Richard's worst handicap was his own temperament . . . he too often postured as if he were the tragic hero of a melodrama.'

Steel (1941). '. . . a mumbling neurotic sinking rapidly into a state of acute melancholia.'

McKisack (1959). 'He rode roughshod over common right; and the nation at last repudiated him for the tyrant that he was . . . Richard II had become dangerous, perhaps dangerously mad.'

PART I

Boyhood, Tutelage and Revolt

I

BOYHOOD

RICHARD THE SECOND was born at three o'clock on the
morning of Twelfth Day, Wednesday, January 6th, 1367,[1]
in the abbey of Bordeaux. One can make what one will of
Froissart's surprising precision; it is of greater significance that
he was born the second son of that Prince Edward of England
who has been known since Elizabethan times as the Black Prince,[2]
that his grandfather was King Edward III, the most spectacular
English king of the Middle Ages, and that he was born in Bordeaux.
The future heir to the English throne was not born on English
soil. He was by birth and place of birth a Plantagenet, and therefore inherited an escutcheon which quartered the leopards[3] of
England with the lilies of France; and it is part of the fascination
of Richard's story that he was to outgrow this continental heritage
and become so English a king of England.

It is a modern fashion to seek for guidance to character in the
influences of heredity, but, in dealing with evidence which is
chiefly concerned with matters of fact, and which in subtler
matters is both scanty and unreliable, it is a dangerous fashion.[4]
On the other hand, what information is available as to the
characters of Richard's forbears is entitled to its full if not very
heavy weight.

Richard's mother, Princess Joan, was, in the equivocal judgment of the courtly Froissart, '*la plus belle et la plus amoureuse*' of
ladies, and her early matrimonial adventures[5] were to have a
bearing on the final phases of Richard's reign. Her first marriage
(to Sir Thomas Holland) had only been legitimized by papal
decree, and her second marriage (to the Black Prince) had not
only been preceded by a liaison but had also needed an indulgent
Pope to set aside the difficulties of the prohibited degrees. Thus,
when Richard's future throne was in jeopardy, potential usurpers

3

were to be presented by his mother with a twofold possibility of questioning his hereditary title. To her contemporaries, however, Princess Joan was the 'Fair Maid of Kent'. She remained popular enough to be treated with rude affection by the rebels of Kent when they met her litter as they marched to the sack of London in 1381,[1] throughout Richard's boyhood she was a devoted and attentive mother, and when he reached manhood she was frequently a wise peacemaker. From Richard's ninth birthday she was his only parent, and, until he lost her when he was a mature eighteen, she was constantly at his side. The effect of what was apparently a strong, kindly and warm personality is impossible to assess accurately at this distance of time, but it would be a mistake to underestimate it or to ignore it. Richard had a generous endowment of normal passions and affections from a mother he knew and loved well.

Of Richard's father more is known and more must be said; but the fact that Richard saw very little of him, and that he died when Richard was only nine, does not lessen his possible influence – the traditions of the dead can be even more exacting than the precepts of the living. As a mere boy the Black Prince had won his spurs at Crécy, as a young man he had been commander-in-chief at the victory of Poitiers, in the prime of life he was to win the battle of Nájera; and even the ruthlessness he sanctioned and witnessed later at the sack of Limoges did not prevent the shocked Froissart from summing him up as the 'flower of Chivalry'.[2] The fame of Richard's father as a brilliant soldier and knight was even wider than Christendom. He was celebrated not only for his personal bravery and successful generalship but for his lavish and chivalrous hospitality to captive kings and barons, and, although the unemotional judgment of history has dimmed his pristine glamour, there is no question that in the eyes of his contemporaries he was all that Froissart wrote of him. His fame was a measuring rod by which his son was to be judged by many critics, and found sadly lacking. On the other hand, in all that is known of the Black Prince there is nothing to suggest that he could have faced the problems which were to beset Richard with any better qualifications for success; yet his reputation as a general and knight could give to every feudal swashbuckler an easy taunt against a king who was to use war only as an instrument of policy, and never for its own sake or merely for the sake of booty and ransoms, and who in any event much preferred the arts of peace . . .

From his mother, Richard received kindly help and restraining experience; from the father he scarcely knew, he received a heritage of military glory which was a handicap rather than a stimulus; from both his parents he inherited his good looks, and, if we are to judge by effigy and portraits, a physique which suggests the aesthete rather than the athlete, the scholar rather than the knight. It is bad logic to assume that a reign without famous military victories was due to a king with only average physical endowment, but the son of the greatest knight and the grandson of the most brilliant king of the fourteenth century was to be burdened all his life with ancestors whose ghostly scorn could support the unthinking taunts of contemporary enemies.

When Richard was three days old he was christened in the cathedral of Bordeaux. Round the font were kings, princes and knights not many of whom had more than a few words of the English tongue, and none of whom could have guessed that they were christening a child who within ten years would be King of England – Richard's elder brother Edward of Angoulême was the Black Prince's heir and favourite. Richard's sponsors and the attendant courtiers were witnessing a ceremony of no great significance which was delaying much weightier matters – they were in Bordeaux not to celebrate a royal birth but to cement a feudal alliance, and to begin a campaign which was to rival those of Crécy and Poitiers, and achieve victory as brilliant and as barren. The expedition, which ended in the Rout of Nájera, illustrates well the fourteenth-century conception of princely duty which Richard inherited from both his father and his grandfather and which he finally modified; it reveals its apparent pointlessness to modern eyes and its obvious fascination for mediaeval onlookers; it is a useful guide[1] to the environment into which Richard was born.

The Black Prince was Lord of Aquitaine, and he was as convinced that he would one day be King of France as he was certain that he would soon be King of England. His hereditary enemy was the king who reigned in Paris, and whose father he had captured at Poitiers and held to ransom. This Charles V of France was

5

supporting in Spain one Henry of Trastamara, a bastard usurper of the Castilian throne who had succeeded in exiling the legitimate king, known to history books by the unpleasant title of Pedro the Cruel but known to his subjects as the first King of Castile who had attempted to curb the violence and lawlessness of a brutal baronage. Pedro had appealed to the Lord of Aquitaine for help in regaining his kingdom, and the Black Prince had three good reasons for agreeing: first, it was in the interests of every rightful heir to a throne to support every other rightful heir whose authority was in question; second, it might be possible to strike a useful blow against the French by defeating them on Spanish soil; third, the unemployed and embarrassing 'free companies' [1] could be diverted from their lawlessness in Aquitaine by the prospect of ransoms and loot in Spain. The first was a summons to his chivalry and knight errantry, the second and third were temptations to his shrewdness, and all three were appeals to his passion for military glory and to the normal instincts of a mediaeval prince.

The Black Prince's feudal array from Aquitaine, and many of the 'free companies', supplied and led by his younger brother John of Gaunt, therefore became the mercenaries of Pedro in the cause of legitimacy, and of mediaeval glory. They invaded Spain through the famous pass of Roncesvalles, where the Paladin Roland had been slain, to restore a legitimate monarch to his throne, but they were also looking forward to the fulfilment of Pedro's promises of handsome rewards and rich booty. Meanwhile, Henry of Trastamara had been reinforced not only with knights and men-at-arms from the French King but also with the genius of the Breton Bertrand du Guesclin, the greatest professional soldier of the age. The rival armies met on April 3rd, 1367, at Nájera half-way between Burgos and Pampeluna, and, as at Créçy and Poitiers, the archery of the English foot decided the day. The Black Prince, ably assisted by his brother, John of Gaunt, destroyed the best feudal arrays of France and Castile, and even took prisoner the famed du Guesclin.

But, overwhelming as the victory of Nájera was, it bore no rich fruits. Henry of Trastamara had escaped the slaughter, and lived to fight again. The restored Pedro broke every promise he had made to his allies, and the Black Prince's armies were compelled to plunder and forage in order to survive. By August, the victorious allies were struggling wearily back across the Pyrenees. Some brilliant pages had been added to the chronicles of Froissart, of Chandos' Herald, and of Ayala. John of Gaunt had learnt something of soldiering, and much of the darker side of diplomacy. The Black Prince had added more laurels to his brow, but he had also contracted the dysentery which was speedily to wreck his life. To modern eyes, Nájera was just another episode in that catastrophic Hundred Years War which saddled Europe for three centuries with the scourge of the mercenary soldier, and a plundering militarism which delayed peaceful and fruitful progress. Yet, by every contemporary standard, the campaign was justified. When Froissart tells us with what acclamation and popular rejoicing the news of the victory was received in Aquitaine and in England, there is no reason to doubt his word. If nurse Mundina Danos of Aquitaine,[1] as she rocked the cradle of the baby Richard, could sing him to sleep with ballads of Crécy and Poitiers, her successors, his knightly tutors, could try to rouse him to envy with the tales of his father and eldest uncle at the Rout of Nájera. It was not yet the time for wisdom to deplore the never-ending war with France, and for an English King to seek glory within the limits of his own islands.

Nájera was the greatest of the Black Prince's victories, but it was also his last. His private campaigning against the French continued with varying but no final success; his dysentery became worse, and, three years later, 1370, he sullied his great name by that massacre at Limoges which must have been fearful indeed[2] – the Middle Ages were not easily shocked. In January of the following year, Edward of Augoulême suddenly died, and the Black Prince's cup of bitterness was overfilled. Richard of Bordeaux, who had been living with his mother in Bordeaux and Cognac, had at four years of age every prospect of becoming heir to the most magnificent throne in western Europe – he had become the most important of royal infants round whom swirled the intrigues of courtiers, and over whom the clouds which darkened the closing years of the reign of Edward III threatened to break in a deluge. When the Fair Maid of Kent landed with her son near Plymouth in the year 1371 and set out for her manor of Berkhamsted, she could look back on years of unsurpassed success and good fortune, but the future was gloomy. It was true that they received a tumultuous welcome from the Londoners as they passed through the capital, but her husband was now doomed to an early and painful death, her father-in-law had sunk into dishonourable dotage, and her only surviving child was a son whose inheritance might easily be threatened by uncles and barons neither scrupulous nor unambitious.

On reaching home, the Black Prince was compelled by his illness to entrust the tuition of his son to others, and he chose two of his favourite companions in arms – Sir Guichard d'Angle and Sir Simon Burley. For a mediaeval prince with his record of action this was no bad choice. Froissart, who knew them well, refers to Sir Guichard as 'the gentle knight',[1] while Sir Simon was not merely a faithful old soldier but a man of some culture – we still have an inventory of his library which contained twenty-one books in an age when very few persons outside the cloister possessed even one.[2] Richard seems to have been fond of both these knightly tutors. At his coronation, he was to ennoble Sir Guichard, and in later years he even risked his throne in a vain attempt to save Burley from the scaffold. If Richard loved and honoured his tutors it can be assumed that he found little fault with their teaching, and that his father's orders that he should be 'instructed in noble virtues' were carried out in the orthodox manner to be expected from such orthodox teachers. A fourteenth-century manuscript in the British Museum[3] gives an illuminating picture of what such an education involved. At the age of four, the son of a mediaeval knight was taught his letters, at six he was set to learn a foreign language and his table manners, at ten or twelve to learn dancing, singing and conversation, at fourteen to cultivate bravery in hunting and intelligence in the tracking of game, and at sixteen (when he was considered fully grown) to begin his career of jouster, rider, besieger of castles, skirmisher, and 'knight' in the full Chaucerian sense of that word. In Richard's day there was a natural bias towards the arts of war because the mediaeval notion of knighthood connoted generalship and personal bravery; there was a natural under-emphasis on scholarship because the mediaeval scholar was assumed to be a priest; but there was also a liberal allotment of time and energy to the graces if not to the arts of living – it was an apprenticeship rather than an education, vocational rather than cultural training. In Chaucer's 'Prologue' to his *Canterbury Tales* we find a good description of a knight, the finished product of such a training. Chaucer's knight was an admirable and real person and not merely a moralist's impression of an unrealized ideal. Richard's education was to produce a knight true to his period, and at the same time a king with some ideas well in advance of his time: it could not have done more.

There is no evidence to suggest that Richard's tutors were an unfortunate influence, and there is no reliable support for the story that Richard suffered permanent moral harm from his boyhood companions. It has been suggested that his two half-brothers, Thomas and John Holland,[1] were the corruptors of his most impressionable years; yet it has never been proved that either was evil. It is known that Thomas was a distinguished soldier and that John was a great jouster and a man of hasty temper, but the one was seventeen and the other fifteen years older than Richard – they could scarcely therefore have been his playmates. Richard was apparently always on the best of terms with both of them, they both supported him loyally throughout his life, and Thomas's son became a specially intimate friend. In later years, when the fury of John Holland resulted in murder, Richard rightly punished him, but took the earliest opportunity of forgiving him and restoring him to his patrimony. These half-brothers may have had only one bad effect on Richard – their prowess in arms may have silently reminded him too often of his inability, or refusal, to live up to the military traditions of his father who was also their step-father and hero.

It would not be wise to blame Richard's parents and tutors, or his boyhood friends and companions, for the faults he was to display as King, but neither would it be fair to attribute to them all the credit for the merits he was also to reveal. Richard was the child of his environment, but his was a childhood of much loneliness, with few elders he could trust and few companions of his own age to whom he could turn – his struggle to make his own mark in his own way was to reveal not a few traces of true originality.

To the contemporary chroniclers, the next five years were years of gloomy foreboding. Both King Edward III and the Black Prince were dying. The old King, whose earlier years had given Froissart some of his most enthusiastic and colourful pages, was now dominated by his mistress, Alice Perrers, who was formidable enough even to overawe the King's judges. Outside the intimate royal circle, effective power was in the hands of John of Gaunt,

Duke of Lancaster, whose motives and ambitions were already suspect. The Church was under attack from both lay and clerical critics, and in danger from baronial jealousy of its status and privileges. The Nájera campaign had brought no substantial gains, and Edward's claim to the throne of France was as far from realization as ever. The sun of mediaeval England seemed to be setting in grey storm clouds.

Richard spent most of this period with his parents and tutors at Berkhamsted, and nothing is recorded of these boyhood years. But of the year 1376 this history must take note – it saw that famous session of Parliament known even in the fourteenth century as the 'Good Parliament',[1] it had to record the lamented death of the Black Prince, and it watched Richard's grandfather slipping rapidly to an inglorious end. Richard was only nine years old. But the age of nine in mediaeval times was nearer the age of twelve or fourteen in modern times – it was a highly impressionable and critical age, and, if Richard's later acts as King are to be fully understood, it is necessary to study the events of this fateful year in some detail – they reveal forces which were already at work, and which were to mark Richard's future reign as the watershed to so many storms, economic, religious, social and political, and they reveal his mother and his tutors almost overdoing their duty in so rapidly producing a King out of a boy . . .

At this crucial period of English history, many familiar words bore a connotation for the chroniclers very different from their significance to modern students, who must constantly be on guard against the attractive vice of reading history backwards. The young Richard, as he watched the proceedings of the Good Parliament of 1376, was not watching 'democracy' at work, even if with a historical microscope a modern historian can see it germinating. He was about to become the head of a mediaeval monarchy with a vast but ill-defined royal prerogative, the apex of the majestic feudal pyramid, and by heredity the fountain of all justice. A fourteenth-century Parliament[2] was neither constitutional nor unconstitutional, because there was then no sense of any law of the constitution. Its 'Commons' formed an *ad hoc* committee of spokesmen for various 'communities', and had no conception of sovereignty and still less of popular government.[3] Government was the special function of the monarch aided by those clerical and baronial advisers whom he chose to summon to his Council; a *plenum parliamentum* was a full public session of that Council enlarged to include representatives of communities who could provide the sinews of war and the necessities of peace; the 'Commons' was a body of petitioners few enough to be accommodated comfortably in the Chapter House of Westminster Abbey, and directly representing not 'the people' but the new classes whose influence came from trade and merchandise, and the new power of those who had learned something of government and justice in their local borough and shire moots.

In the spring of 1376, Edward III 'held his Parliament' at the palace of Westminster some two miles south-west of the city walls of London. All the great barons, including 'magnates' [1] of the Church, were summoned to his Council, and, in addition, the knights from every shire and two burgesses from every borough. After a day's wait for late arrivals, the proceedings opened on April 28th with the Chancellor announcing why Parliament had been summoned. The reason rarely varied – it was to make provision for the safety of the realm by supplying the means by which the business of the realm could be carried on. The representatives of the 'communities' of England were becoming difficult – they represented that new wealth which was not in lands but in the profits of commerce, the price of wool-fells, and in that mysterious and theoretically sinful trick by which money bred money; and this was an occasion when they were determined to apply the principle, which has since become one of the foundations of all free government, that 'redress of grievances must precede supply'. But they were not elected representatives of the people sitting in a sovereign House of Commons, they were lesser but monied interests asked to join a Great Council of the great in order that a feudal monarchy might have the wherewithal to govern. It was a natural but significant step for the knights and burgesses to retire to discuss the Chancellor's request for financial help, and they retired to the Chapter House of Westminster Abbey. [2] There emerged from their debates a speaker who outshone all his contemporaries in the vigour of his language, the logic of his purpose, and the strength of his leadership. His name was Peter de la Mare. He was no rustic or menial but a businessman of some position – steward to that Earl of March whose son (after Richard's accession) was to become heir presumptive to the throne by virtue of his descent from Edward III.

11

What grievances was de la Mare voicing on behalf of the 74 knights of the shires and perhaps 200 burgesses of the towns of mediaeval England? Before he would pledge his friends to give of their wealth, he demanded three things: that the King should 'live of his own', that the 'staple' [1] (which canalized the wool-trade through one outlet to the looms of Flanders) should be restored to Calais, and that two fraudulent officers of the Crown should be punished and the King's mistress dismissed. He was stating problems which it took centuries to solve, he was revealing the fact that the Middle Ages were almost totally ignorant of the principles of economics, and he was questioning the authority of the monarch by attacking not only the misdemeanours of his ministers but the scandal of his private life. But this was not an attack by a House of Commons on the Divine Right of Kings or on the hereditary privileges of a House of Lords. De la Mare represented monied interests using their power to obtain more power, and well aware of their weakness against the solid strength of feudalism. He held the purse-strings of the 'Commons' firmly enough to be able to face feudal barons calmly, to be able to insist that all the 'Commons' should be present before he addressed the Lords on their behalf, and to be able to keep the Lords waiting until the late-comers had been rounded up, and, finally, with a touch of genius, he asked for a committee of twelve 'magnates' to help them in their deliberations. It is at this stage that the Commons '*par commune assent par cause qe le dite sire Peirs de la Mare fuit si bien parlaunt et si sagement rehersaunt les maters et purpose de ses compaignons . . . prierent a luy qil vodroit prendre la charge pur eux davoir la sovereinte de pronuncier lour voluntes en le graunt parlement*', [2] and Peter de la Mare's name henceforth heads the roll of Speakers of the House of Commons, or, as they said in 1376, '*prolocutor*', '*commune-parlour*', or '*vant-parlour*'. The baronial committee was sanctioned by the King, and went to work with the Commons in the Chapter House. When their joint deliberations – they lasted over a week – were concluded, they all reported back, with de la Mare to speak for them, and '*ses profrerent dentrer en parlement et vendrent al huse de parlement*'. When that early 'House of Commons' was sitting it was not *in* Parliament at all – it was a financial joint committee huddled in a convenient corner of the nearest church.

De la Mare's success was impressive and immediate – the fraudulent ministers were punished, the 'staple' was restored to

Calais, the King's expenditure was to be checked by a permanent committee of Lords, and, even more astonishing, de la Mare's personal attack on the King's extravagant mistress was rewarded by her instant disgrace and dismissal. True, in the next Parliament most of these gains were lost, but for the first time in English history the independent voice of the Commons had been heard and obeyed, and that this voice was also in part the voice of the people is witnessed by the many traces in contemporary sermons[1] and songs of the principles and grievances first proclaimed by Peter de la Mare.

If Richard was too young to have comprehended the implications of the rhetoric of de la Mare, at least it should have been clear to his elders that there was a new power to be reckoned with outside court and castle, whose Speaker could achieve so much, and who could even remind the King that he was expected to live on his feudal and legal revenues and only to depend on subsidies from the Commons at a price. Of what that price was finally to be, no fourteenth-century prince, baron, or commoner could have had the remotest conception.

The Good Parliament lasted until July 6th, but in the middle of the proceedings, on June 8th, the Black Prince – who is supposed to have been sympathetic to the demands for reform – died at the age of forty-six at Berkhamsted. The notion of hereditary monarchy was well established in England, but the tradition of primogeniture was still not quite taken for granted, and might well be questioned when the presumed heir was a child. So, on the Black Prince's death, it did not automatically follow that Richard would be heir to the throne; he did not even automatically inherit his father's titles of Prince of Wales, Duke of Cornwall and Earl of Chester. The chroniclers give moving descriptions of the Black Prince's untimely end,[2] and throughout can be seen the fear of a father that his son might be cheated of his full inheritance, and the emotions of those who dreaded that the throne of England was about to be occupied by a boy, and was perhaps in the gravest danger of usurpation. On his deathbed, the Black Prince entrusted Richard to the personal protection of the old King, and, although his own titles could not be handed on immediately, he naturally showered on his only surviving child the major part of his property accompanied by a father's curse should he ever give it away. The pathetic mood of the final scene, the sense of tragedy which accompanied the high solemnities of the subsequent funeral in Canterbury Cathedral, and the knowledge that soon he must follow his grandfather's cortège too – this was the boy Richard's gloomy introduction to his heritage.

One of the shadows which now darkened the throne of England was the shadow of Richard's eldest uncle John of Gaunt,[1] Duke of Lancaster; and both contemporary chroniclers and modern historians have found it difficult to decide whether John of Gaunt was a benevolent or a wicked uncle, a noble protector of the young prince, or a scheming baron determined to win a throne if not in Spain then in England itself. To a chronicler like Knighton, whose monastery owed so much to the House of Lancaster, Gaunt was always '*Pius Dux*'; to a chronicler like Walsingham, who suspected Gaunt of coveting the wealth of the Church and conniving at heresy, he was an arch-criminal. Most of the other English chroniclers are suspect of bias because they were alive to edit and amend diplomatically when Gaunt's eldest son had finally founded the royal House of Lancaster. On the other hand, the Black Prince bore Gaunt no ill-will – he appointed his 'very dear and well-beloved brother of Spain' as his first executor, and his widow remained Gaunt's faithful friend till death. Fortunately, time enables exaggerated praise to be set off against excessive blame and discovers when a dispassionate historian is superseded by a sycophantic courtier, and the final portrait which emerges is that of a typical mediaeval baron with great ambitions, some skill as a general but no luck as a campaigner, an exact regard for the highest traditions of chivalry, and, on the whole, a wise sense of responsibility and duty to his young nephew Richard. To expect more than that, to lament that Gaunt was not a 'defender of the constitution' as understood by a Jacobean lawyer, or to be disappointed that he was no friend of the first Speaker of the Commons, is to condemn a baron for being true to his period and less politically advanced than his distant descendants. John of Gaunt has suffered, as Richard was to suffer, from the greater glamour which surrounded the Black Prince, and in modern times he has been unfairly judged because of the habit of expecting mediaeval barons to be fathers of democracy. John of Gaunt lived almost to the end of Richard's reign, and there seems to be no good evidence that at any time he was guilty of treason either in fact or intent.

On the other hand, there is no doubt that in this year of 1376 he was very much suspected – the 'time-honour'd Lancaster' of Shakespeare's day was now the villain of the piece, and the Commons of England, and especially the Londoners, had conceived a suspicion of him which continued into the coming reign and was to culminate in the sack of his palace of Savoy by the rebels of Essex and Kent in 1381 . . .

On June 25th, 1376 the last act of the Commons of the Good Parliament was to insist on having Prince Richard brought to Parliament in order 'that they might see and honour him as the very heir-apparent'.[1] It was clearly intended as a warning that the Commons thought the worst of Gaunt, but for the youthful heir to the throne it was an impressive scene – his hereditary claims were now reinforced by the bold voice of the Commons of England, he was soon to be mightier than his mighty uncle, and to rule the great realm of England as undisputed monarch. It was heady wine for one so young . . .

Seen from the twentieth century, this Good Parliament appears to have anticipated some of the basic principles of a parliamentary democracy; seen in its own context, it was an empty gesture and an immediate failure. Before the year 1376 was out, most of its work was deliberately undone, and its only substantial result was the reestablishment of Calais as the seat of the 'staple' – the London merchants depended for much of their fortunes and their power on a wool-trade which could thus be controlled and taxed more profitably in their interests. John of Gaunt had been virtual Regent throughout the proceedings – Edward III was nearing his end – and Gaunt, although suspicions of his own intentions had clearly been the background to much of the Good Parliament's work, had had the wisdom not to thwart it while it sat. But, as soon as the knights and burgesses had ridden back to their manors or their account books, Gaunt took speedy steps to summon a Council which forthwith declared most of the acts of the Good Parliament invalid, set the fraudulent ministers free, imprisoned the heroic Peter de la Mare without charge or trial in Gaunt's own castle at Nottingham, and deprived Bishop William of Wykeham (whose benefactions to Winchester and Oxford will be remembered long after his work as a time-serving priest-administrator has been forgotten) of his property because he had dared to side with the Commons. Contemporaries saw in these high-handed acts of John

15

of Gaunt clear evidence that the wicked uncle was planning and plotting the usurpation of his young nephew's patrimony. There is no justification for seeing in them anything more than a mediaeval baron reacting typically and ruthlessly to an attack on the age-old privileges of his peers. There is rather the evidence that Gaunt seems to have been defending the mediaeval idea of 'regality', and to have gone out of his way to be pleasant and helpful to the young heir to the throne. In November 1376 he raised no objections not only to the creation of Richard as Prince of Wales, Duke of Cornwall and Earl of Chester, but also to his receiving the confiscated property of William of Wykeham. Gaunt was quite ready to wreck the work of a so-called Good Parliament; he was not planning to seize the throne.

On Christmas Day of this same fateful year, another great occasion faced the young Richard. Froissart[1] tells us the story of how in Westminster Palace

> 'the King of England made to be known to his sons, the Duke of Lancaster, the Earl of Cambridge, and to the Lord Thomas the youngest, and to all the barons, earls, prelates and knights of England, how the young Richard should be king after his decease, and so caused them all to swear solemnly to maintain him. And on Christmas Day the King made him to sit at his table above all his own children in great estate representing that he should be king after his decease.'

At nine years of age to be feasted with such pomp and ceremony by a grandfather whose rather disreputable old age could not dull all the lustre of Sluys, Crécy and Poitiers, to be paid homage by uncles who owned more than half England between them, and to be acknowledged as rightful heir by the great prelates of the Church and the representatives of the baronage and knighthood of England – here was more heady wine. A year before Richard received his crown he could appreciate something of its weight.

Did the dying Edward III share the common suspicion that Gaunt might plead Richard's youth as excuse for claiming not merely a regency but the throne itself? This Christmas Day banquet is not sufficiently convincing proof – it can be taken simply as the natural declaration by a dying mediaeval monarch that he wished his direct heir to succeed him. His anxiety for his grandson did not necessarily implicate his son. But when, at the end of January 1377, a new Parliament was to meet, Edward insisted that Richard should open it in his stead. The Londoners seized upon this opportunity to stake their claims to future royal favour by organizing a magnificent civic welcome to Richard. The chronicles present a charming picture of mediaeval politics.[1] There were fountains of wine in Cheapside, there was a great civic banquet, there were mummers and dancers, there were presentations, and, a pretty touch, games in which dice were loaded so that the young Richard always won. But Gaunt was not to be so easily outdone – we are told by one chronicler that it was at Gaunt's special instigation that Richard acted as the King's Lieutenant,[2] and that he showed Richard special deference and honour at the ceremony of welcome. It must have been something of an ordeal for a youth of but ten years of age, and there is a wealth of pathos in the chronicler's dry note 'his mother had care of him'.

On an afternoon in February of this same year, 1377, Prince Richard was staying with his mother at the palace of Kennington. Sounds of tumult could be heard in the city of London round the bend of the river, and soon the barge of John of Gaunt was seen making for the palace. Gaunt was fleeing for his life from the anger of a London mob, and he sought safety where his enemies alleged he planned treachery. What was the explanation of this riot and this flight? The answer goes back to the roots of the English Church and forward to the first blossoms of its Reformation. John of Gaunt was fleeing from the citizenry ostensibly because he had acted as protector to John Wyclif, at this time on trial for heresy before the heads of the Church. What was the true significance of so strange an alliance between saint and sinner? It is clear from a later incident, which also involved Wyclif, that Richard's mother was favourably inclined towards the reforming doctrines of Wyclif (and, with much less evidence in support, it has been said that even the Black Prince had the makings of a Lollard in him), but no one has ever suggested that the alliance of the cynical Gaunt with the scholarly Wyclif had any other basis than political opportunism on the part of Gaunt. The great landed nobility, of which Gaunt was the head, had been irritated and frightened by the rising influence of clerical administrators who owed little or nothing to their birth but everything to their brains. Of this class of what we would now call self-made civil servants, William of Wykeham, Bishop of Winchester, was typical, and Gaunt had already shown what he thought of him. One of the commonest methods of rewarding such a useful administrator was to present him not with an earldom (which meant some sacrifice of royal revenue) but with a bishopric, which carried its own emoluments. Wykeham had begun as a mere struggling clerk-of-the-works, and had even become Chancellor before he was finally rewarded with his bishopric – he was therefore detested as an interloper by the old nobility, and had at the same time incurred the criticism of a religious reformer like Wyclif, who preached and pamphleteered against the sins of 'Caesarean clergy' and urged the need for a priesthood which kept to its vows of poverty. Gaunt, the jealous and able baron whose power had been challenged by an alliance between the Commons and this chancellor-bishop, had found a useful ally in Wyclif, whose re-forming doctrines could easily be twisted from a call for Franciscan poverty into a demand that bishops should look after their bishoprics, and even into justification for bare-faced robbery and confiscation. Meanwhile, the orthodox clergy had at last appreci-ated the revolutionary implications of Wyclif's doctrines of civil and divine 'dominion', and the papal court had also urged stringent repression. But it was not until Gaunt had used Wyclif to support his attack on Wykeham that the bishops had dared to summon Wyclif to London to answer for his teaching before the assembled heads of the church in St Paul's Cathedral. Gaunt had provided Wyclif with expert ecclesiastical defenders, and, when the case was opened, added the additional pressure of the actual presence of himself and Henry Percy, the Earl Marshal, together with their armed retainers. The place of trial was unwisely chosen. Though Wyclif had a strong following among the Londoners, Gaunt was hated and distrusted by all, and the presence of the baronial men-at-arms was naturally resented. The bishops were divided between those who admired the scholar, who so calmly faced the storm, and those whose temper had all the bigotry of an Inquisition; but they were united in opposition to baronial inter-ference. Gaunt and Percy were anxious to ensure a fair trial with, if possible, the defeat of the orthodox clericals. In such an ex-plosive atmosphere, the high handedness of Percy, who angered the citizens by presuming to exercise his Marshal's authority within the 'liberties' [1] of the city, and the haughty temper of Gaunt, who found it difficult to argue with anyone but his feudal equals, soon provoked a riot. The trial broke up in pandemonium, and the two Lords were forced to flee for their lives. The Marshalsea fortress prison was sacked, and Gaunt escaped in his barge and made for the safety of the royal palace at Kennington. Wyclif in the general confusion quietly slipped away to Oxford, but his scholarly retirement was to be twice more disturbed – his doctrines touched both lay and clerical affairs – before he finally retired to the peace of Lutterworth rectory. Prince Richard could have understood nothing of the implications of this turbulent day, but his mother must have been sick at heart – the world she knew was beginning to rock on its foundations, and her son was all too soon to inherit the governance of a realm in which the standards and axioms of centuries were to be in question.

Edward III was now sinking rapidly, and John of Gaunt was still the effective head of state. If there is little ground for suspicion of intended treason in Gaunt's conduct at this critical time, it is nevertheless a fact that he did not hesitate to use his influence with the dying King to reward himself most handsomely for his loyalty. By royal charters dated February 28th, 1377,[2] Gaunt's Dukedom of Lancaster was declared a Palatinate for his lifetime. It was no empty change of title. As Gaunt's biographer puts it, 'for the life of the Duke, England is dismembered. For all purposes of justice finance and administration the County of Lancaster is severed from the body politic. Within its limits the King is dethroned; the Count Palatine is set up in his place.' [3] Gaunt was granted an 'imperium in imperio' and, in addition to the income from feudal rents and dues, he received that 'magnum emolumentum' which was the notorious accompaniment of mediaeval 'justitia'. One of Edward III's last acts was to give away half his kingdom. But a great baron seizing the opportunity to obtain what his ancestor had also obtained, though it is clear evidence of great ambition, is not proof of treason. It was only when these colossal palatinate powers and privileges became hereditary thirteen years later, and when the heir to them was Henry Bolingbroke, that this generous gesture of the dying Edward III is seen to be so pregnant with drama.

The last ceremonial act of which the King was capable was to preside on St George's Day, April 23rd, 1377, at a great festival in Windsor Castle, where Prince Richard was inducted with lavish ceremony as a Knight of the Garter.[1] But behind the accompanying festivities and rejoicings was the prevailing pessimism which prompted the chronicler of the scene to add 'and unfortunate thynges and unprofytable harmes, with many evle, began for to sprynge, and, the more harm is, conteyned longe tyme after'.[2]

And on Sunday, June 21st, 1377 Edward III at last died in Sheen Palace, over whose site the royal borough of Richmond now sprawls. It was the day of his jubilee, and a bitter commentary on the glories of war.[3] The victor of Sluys and Crécy died deserted by what few friends he had left, a dishonoured dotard. His mistress, for whom he had latterly sacrificed so much of his good name, is said to have robbed his corpse even of the royal rings. Yet the fame of Edward III in his prime was great enough finally to banish the unpleasant memories of his closing years. A fortnight later his funeral was celebrated with great pomp, and, as he lay beside his Queen in their beautiful tomb in Westminster Abbey, his ghost was ready to be invoked, together with that of his equally famous son, to accuse a grandson of different metal. Richard of Bordeaux at ten years of age was to be crowned King of England and France and Lord of Ireland – heir to a heritage which might have intimidated an experienced prince of three times his age.

The coronation ceremony was arranged for July 16th – there were obvious reasons for speed in ensuring a smooth succession – and all parties seem to have gone out of their way to settle their differences for a time, and to launch the new ship of state with a favouring wind even though the seas beyond might be rough and the cross-currents dangerous.

Prince Richard and his mother were staying at Kingston-on-Thames, and, just before the actual death of Edward III but as soon as his desperate condition was known, the citizens of London had sent a deputation to Richard proclaiming their loyalty, and begging him to go to London to settle the quarrel between the greatest baron and the greatest city in the land. Richard had been wisely advised. He had sent a gracious reply, and, on the following day, despatched four knights (including his tutor Burley) to give London the official news of his grandfather's death, together with his own greetings, and notice that he himself would come to

London very soon to settle the dispute with Lancaster. The embassy pointed out that Gaunt had already submitted himself without reserve to the new King's will, and invited the Londoners to follow suit. After some suspicious argument, the citizens swallowed their pride and sent a deputation to Richard at Sheen, where, in front of his mother and the assembled court, Richard reconciled Londoners to Lancaster, and both sides swore loyalty and devotion to himself. The chroniclers[1] are loud in their pious thanksgivings for a scene which reeks of hypocrisy; the enmity of the feudal lord and the city merchant was deeper than a personal brawl, and not to be cured by a formal kiss of peace. But, for the moment, a façade of good will and reconciliation was the due of a slim youth who was now to be crowned their King, this Richard who was the only surviving son of their renowned and beloved Black Prince.

The last political act of the late King had been to restore William of Wykeham to his privileges and property as Bishop of Winchester, an act of justice that was no less just because it came at the instigation of Alice Perrers. Only one more act of reconciliation and justice therefore remained to be done. Peter de la Mare was still a prisoner in Nottingham Castle. Gaunt's pride now had to acquiesce in the instant release of the bold Speaker who had defied him, and, even more galling, to hear of the triumphal procession which brought de la Mare back to London a hero and martyr.

A week remained before the coronation was due. Gaunt as Earl of Leicester had the right to act as High Steward of England, as Duke of Lancaster to bear the sword 'Curtana' on coronation day, and as Earl of Lincoln to carve before the King at the coronation feast. He decided to carry out all these duties and then retire from the court at least for a while. In all his actions at this time there was clearly an anxiety to disarm suspicions which twisted his simplest duties into sinister plots and his genuine help to his young nephew into diabolical perfidy. He spent that week in deciding as Steward the claims of those who wished to perform the traditional ceremonial services, and he seems to have carried out a thankless task with adroitness. There were two significant innovations which he sanctioned: first, a minor, Robert de Vere, Earl of Oxford, was permitted to act as the King's Chamberlain – it is the first appearance of the young noble who later became

21

Richard's closest friend: second, the Mayor of London was to be allowed to serve Richard with a golden cup, and chosen citizens were to serve in the butlery. There was an almost desperate anxiety on every hand that peace between all factions should be a publicized reality . . .

As Richard rode out from the Tower of London on the day before his coronation, there was no sign of the disunity, suspicion and distrust which were seething below the surface. The barons and their liveried retainers with the Mayor of London and the sheriffs, accompanied by the blare of trumpets and the cheers of the citizens, escorted Richard to his palace at Westminster close to the Abbey. Now citizen seemed reconciled to duke. Now even a Gaunt and a Percy, who a little while before had been running for their lives, were cheered by those who had hunted them, and it is from this day of civic welcome and mutual rejoicing that some of the nobility satirically referred to Richard as the 'Londoners' King'.[1] There were fountains of wine to add to the revelry, cloth of gold, all the heraldry of Chivalry, and all the brilliance of the city guilds to add to the enthusiasm of the scene – and there was a slim boy of great beauty and but ten years of age to add to its pathos . . .

The chroniclers have handed down a very detailed description of the magnificent ceremonial of Richard's coronation day.[2] It is impossible to read it without wondering how a boy so young was able to stand its physical strain, still less to understand its spiritual and traditional symbolism. The ceremony in Westminster Abbey included mass, a sermon, the taking of the royal oath, the presentation to and acceptance by the people, the blessing, the anointing, the robing, vesting and arming, the enthronement, the crowning, the offering, the confession, the absolution, and finally the dramatic appearance of the King's champion, Sir John Dymmock, in full armour at the Abbey doors to offer mortal combat to any opposition. No wonder that Richard was exhausted and had to be carried on the broad shoulders of his tutor, Sir Simon Burley, back to the palace for rest before the great coronation banquet which ended a stupendous day. Richard lost a slipper as he went, but we have the word of an eye-witness that even amid so much splendour and magnificence he played his part nobly in all the beauty of his youth.

Before the banquet began, the new King created four new earls. His youngest uncle, Thomas of Woodstock, he made Earl of Buckingham; Sir Thomas Mowbray, a companion of his own age, he made Earl of Nottingham; Sir Henry Percy he made Earl of Northumberland; and his tutor, Sir Guichard d'Angle, he made Earl of Huntingdon – it was a well-advised mixture of family correctness, feudal influence, and personal preference. The banquet itself was of gargantuan proportions, and once again the revelling Londoners were regaled with fountains of wine. And even then the celebrations were not over. On the following day, a state procession to St Paul's gave the assembled citizens a closer view of Richard and in a sermon by the Bishop of Rochester they were urged to compose their differences with their Lords. In all fields, appeasement was the order of the day.

In an age when the taking of an oath was even more binding than the sealing of a bond, and when the mysticism of the Christian church was a vivid part of the life of ordinary men, and perhaps even more vivid to those in higher places, the words of Richard's coronation oath,[1] and the basis of his claim to the crown as proclaimed to his witnesses, have great significance. He swore before Lords, prelates and people first, that he would allow the Church to enjoy her liberties; second, that he would see that the good laws of the land were kept everywhere; and third, that he would judge fairly between man and man: and he was crowned King of England, King of France and Lord of Ireland by heredi- tary right, and it was only a glossing chronicler who added 'and also by the will of the people'.[2]

A visitor today to that bleak Westminster Hall, where the coronation feast was held, can have little conception of the colour and pageantry which must have entranced even an exhausted Richard, and the scraped gloom of our modern Westminster Abbey can give no idea of the impressive glory of that full mediaeval coronation ritual which may have planted deep in the adolescent Richard a sense not merely of his own importance as King but of his mystic grace and the subtleties of divine unction. At this distance, the atmospheric conditions which surrounded a throne so celebrated amongst the laity and so hallowed by the Church can only be guessed, but that they were charged with meaning for Richard we know from his references to them twenty years later.

23

THE HOLLOW CROWN

Richard of Bordeaux now sat on the throne which his father or his elder brother should have inherited, and which his grandfather had made so famous and so feared. No Regency was declared. From the day of his coronation at the age of eleven he was the proud possessor of his own great seal, privy seal and signet. Richard the Second had no boyhood – he was the King of a troubled kingdom before he reached his teens.

II

TUTELAGE

THE EXTRAVAGANCES OF London's welcome to Richard, the 'long and looked forward to' celebrations of the corona- tion,[1] the emphasis which the chroniclers put on the hopes of contemporaries that a brighter day had dawned, all bear witness to an underlying fear that to have entrusted so great a kingdom at so difficult a time to so young a boy – however beautiful – was tempting Providence. Adam of Usk was voicing what many thought when he quoted the words of the Preacher 'Woe to thee O land, when thy King is a child'.[2] An England which had basked too long in the glories of Sluys, Crécy, Poitiers and Nájera awoke to the chilling realization that the realm was on the verge of disaster.

Froissart reports[3] that the news of the old King's death, and the accession of his youthful grandson, was kept as long as possible from the French so that measures could be taken for the safety of England. There were strong reasons for such precaution. Behind the brilliant façade of a chivalry artificially enriched with booty from France and Spain there was a populace threatened at any moment with yet another outbreak of that Black Death which only twenty-five years before had wiped out a third of the popula- tion – the threat of pestilence[4] was as frightening and as real as the threat of a French invasion. In the ranks of those burgesses and knights of the shire who were beginning to challenge the rule of a feudal oligarchy there was even more cause for fear. Knights who had gloried in and profited from the victories of Edward III were now impotent and ashamed at the news that, while London made holiday, the fleets of France and Castile were sweeping the Channel unchallenged.[5] The Isle of Wight was overrun, some south coast ports were harried, the martial Prior of Lewes was taken prisoner, and the Londoners could see the smoke pall from burning Graves- end. In the north, the Scots were over the Border again; and across

25

the Channel, as Froissart sadly noted, England was losing all her great captains one by one.[1] A general paralysis seems to have struck the leaders of England, and their only activity was both pointless and misdirected – ordering the walls of Oxford to be put in repair,[2] and the castles of the Welsh marches to be fully garrisoned. If news had travelled faster in the fourteenth century, or if its primitive censorship had been less effective, a full-scale invasion of England by the French at this juncture might have given a curious twist to English history.

Who were the real rulers of England at this time? Froissart, observing from across the Channel, states that 'the Duke of Lancaster had the government of the kingdom'. A modern historian – Trevelyan – judges that the Queen Mother wielded more personal influence than anyone. Froissart, of course, was not stating a fact, he was overstating an opinion – but his opinions were always shrewd. Trevelyan also is guessing, and equally shrewdly but with the advantage of longer perspective.[3] It was clearly necessary for some authority to be acknowledged while Richard was so young, and, as Gaunt was suspect, the only alternative was a group of lesser men who would represent the major interests involved. On the day following the coronation, a Great Council speedily appointed a continual Council of twelve (soon reduced to eight) which was in effect a Council of Regency. In a difficult situation it was a fair attempt at an honest compromise – a coalition whose only ulterior motive was to thwart the suspected ambition of Lancaster. Gaunt and both his brothers – Edmund of Langley, Earl of Cambridge and future Duke of York, and Thomas of Woodstock, Earl of Buckingham and future Duke of Gloucester – were excluded, but Gaunt's influence was represented in the person of his Chancellor the Bishop of Salisbury, and at first by his friend Lord Latimer. The Earl of Cambridge was represented by Richard Fitzalan, Earl of Arundel, and the Earl of Buckingham by Courtenay, Bishop of London. The Queen Mother was represented by Lord Cobham, and Edmund Mortimer, Earl of March, was included presumably because he had married Gaunt's elder brother Lionel's daughter Philippa, and was therefore father to the heir presumptive if strict heredity were to be followed. Some of the chroniclers do not hesitate to affirm that the whole plan was merely a manœuvre to screen Gaunt's treasonable purposes,[4] but, in a situation where his birth,

26

his experience and his power left him vulnerable to such obvious slanders, Gaunt acted with the greatest discretion – he retired for the time being to his estates. At the same time, his ally Henry Percy, Earl of Northumberland, also retired, surrendering his post of Earl Marshal to Sir John Arundell, brother to the Earl of Arundel and a friend of the Earl of Buckingham. Both Froissart and Trevelyan are right – the influences of Gaunt and the Queen Mother were obviously paramount behind the scenes, but, for the next five years, the actual governance of England was in the official hands of a very ill-assorted team – a coalition of rival interests which, however well intentioned, resulted in a policy of drift in matters both of peace and of war, and was to leave England totally unprepared to face one of the gravest crises of the Middle Ages – the Peasants' Revolt of 1381 . . .

The first Parliament of the new reign met at Westminster in October 1377. The customary opening address by the Archbishop of Canterbury contained a passage of some significance which proves how long a journey there was to go before mediaeval monarchy could be replaced by constitutional democracy. He referred Richard to 'the noble grace which God has given you, neither by election, nor by other such way, but only by right succession of heritage'.[1] The 'Divine Right of Kings' thus early hinted at was not yet to influence practical politics, but, before the reign was out, the boy who heard this address at his first Parliament was to prove that it had not fallen on deaf ears.

As usual, the real reason for the summoning of a full Parliament was that the Council needed money. Twenty-three of the seventy-four knights of the shire who attended were veterans of the Good Parliament, and the Speaker was again the redoubtable Peter de la Mare.[2] It was the Commons who secured the final dismissal and disgrace of Alice Perrers, and again they attempted to limit court extravagance, and to obtain efficient control of public income and expenditure. Before they had begun their usual programme of debating and petitioning, they had repeated the experiment of suggesting that a committee of the greater baronage should assist them, and, revealing how anxious all men were for at least a show of unity, they headed their list of possible advisers with the hated name 'the King of Castile and Duke of Lancaster'.

John of Gaunt had no intention of accepting so cynical a nomination, but he did seize this excellent opportunity to issue a dramatic challenge to whisperers and slanderers. In full Parliament, he fell on his knees before the young Richard, begged him to listen, and, in a speech both dignified and boldly spoken,[1] offered to defend his honour with his life, and challenged his secret accusers to come into the open and face the judgment of Chivalry. Lords, prelates and Commons crowded round the throne to pacify the slandered duke, and to proclaim their innocence of any suspicions of his conduct. Gaunt gracefully allowed himself to be appeased, and as soon as possible again departed from Westminster for his beloved deer-forests and the care of his vast properties. When leadership was so badly needed it was a misfortune that the most powerful noble and ablest remaining leader was thus forced into retirement – the balance of power he refused personally to join was in effect an inefficient compromise between irreconcilable private interests, the King was still powerless, and his nearest guardian was a Queen Mother living on her memories.

But this first Parliament of the reign was at least aware of the desperate state of the country's finances; so much so that it sought the advice of the ablest cleric of the age in an attempt to find an easy way out of its financial embarrassment. Once again John Wyclif was summoned to London. Richard knew of him as the great scholar whom his uncle Gaunt had protected at the risk of his life against the angry Londoners; now he was to meet him face to face. At so impressionable an age it is very probable that this meeting had profound effects – effects which would naturally escape the notice of chroniclers in their scriptoria, but which are clearer the more Richard is studied in relation to the great movements of his period. That is why a life of Richard II must take some cognizance of the teachings of John Wyclif, and especially of these early years when John Wyclif was the scholar, diplomat and political scientist rather than the theologian, missionary and near heretic he subsequently became.

There is a misleading view of English history which sees pre-Reformation England as orthodox romanist and post-Reformation England as wholly protestant, and forgets that the river of any history, though it may have indeterminate sources and many tributaries, nevertheless has a main stream and a decisive flow.

The opening of Richard's reign coincided with the confluence of two tributary movements – the new awareness of England as a national entity, and the long tradition that the English Church, while remaining Catholic and apostolic, could also be national in its acceptance or rejection of much of the authority of Rome. Like Luther after him, Wyclif lived and died a Catholic.[1] It was unthinkable for any sane European in the Middle Ages to be anything but a Catholic, and the idea of founding a new Church outside the one community of Rome would never have occurred to anyone in his right mind. But this did not exclude efforts at reforming and improving the Church, and, in so doing, it involved the risk of being condemned as a heretic by those whose orthodoxy prohibited reform. The Church in England was geographically and spiritually always on the outer perimeter of the Roman dominion, and, from the days of the Conqueror onwards, her relations with the head of the Church in St Peter's were subject not only to the views of princes but also to the growing grievances of a very insular flock. True, the pilgrimage to the Canterbury shrine of that St Thomas who had defied a king in the interests of Rome was a national custom, but folk-pride also remembered that the submission of King John to the Pope had coincided with the loss of Normandy. Knights of the shire and burgesses of the cities were well aware of the treasure which year by year was sent out of the country to enrich the papal court. All men could criticize plurality of livings and the non-residence of foreign ecclesiastics, and, since 1305, when the Pope had moved to Avignon and exchanged the imperial traditions of Rome for the parochial convenience of what was called 'the Babylonish Captivity', all Englishmen could readily suspect that Peter's Pence were probably now a contribution to the exchequer of the national enemy in Paris. At home, the Church was satirized as much by the worldly Chaucer as by the puritanical Langland, and was soon to be attacked more directly even by the conventional and orthodox Gower. Her bishops might be good scholars and efficient government officials but they were therefore the poorer shepherds to their flocks; her monks were not so much licentious as useless; her friars could use the confessional as an aid to seduction and the Doom of Hell's Mouth as an aid to extortion; her vicars were frequently both poor and ignorant; her rectors were often both pluralists and absentees. And a large proportion of the population by claiming that 'benefit of clergy' which meant the easier justice of special ecclesiastical courts, and by abusing the ancient rights of sanctuary, could avoid civil justice – the lesser degrees of clergy covered clerks and undergraduates and almost every man with even the rudiments of the Latin tongue, and therefore a multitude of sins and sinners. Throughout the fourteenth century, it is clear from statutes, ordinances and parliamentary petitions, as well as from popular literature and pamphlets, that there was a crescendo of feeling in favour of church reform, and opposed at least to the financial claims of the papal court; and John Wyclif had already added all the weight of his learning, all the skill of his pen and tongue, and all the prestige of his sincerity and saintliness to the more worldly and more selfish criticisms of lay clamour.[1] It was therefore quite natural that, when the Council discovered the country in so parlous a state and the treasury empty, it cast covetous eyes on the untouched wealth of the Church, and asked Wyclif's considered advice as to the lawfulness of withholding papal dues in order to provide for the defence of the kingdom. Wyclif's answer was definitely in the affirmative, and it has come down to us in a document[2] which, like most of his writings, is a masterpiece of precise argument and mediaeval logic, and which also deserves examination because of implications which have a significant bearing on the kingship of Richard. Although it was surprisingly outspoken it was not a revolutionary document; it was not even an original thesis, it was a brilliant summing up of the teachings of some of his most radical predecessors and contemporaries. His championship of the temporal power was part of a European movement which was seriously undermining the established tenets of Thomas Aquinas, who, writing when the Emperor Frederick II had lost his final struggle against the Pope, had justified the papal supremacy and prepared the way for the Bull 'Unam Sanctam', which made it a necessary article of faith that every human being must be subject to the Roman pontiff.[3] That aggressive Bull was a sign of inner weakness – it could not hope to survive a 'Babylonish Captivity' – and its basis had been attacked with increasing vehemence and authority from within and without the Church. Dante's ideal was the universal sovereignty of two co-ordinate powers of Christendom, both alike receiving authority direct from God without any question of the subordination of one power to the other. Franciscans had put forward the upsetting view that, as neither Christ nor his apostles had possessed property, Pope John XXII, who had amassed a fortune of 25 million gold crowns, was perhaps in error. Marsilius of Padua, in one of the most original of mediaeval treatises,[1] had pointed out that the Church meant the whole Christian community, and it was therefore intolerable that one section of the Church – the priests – should usurp the prerogatives of the whole Church, and that, though in their spiritual office priests had special functions, the word 'spiritual' could scarcely cover matters of income, property and taxation, and therefore could not exempt them from legal obligations which other members of the community had to bear. William of Ockham[2] had written boldly against the doctrine of papal infallibility and the temporal power of the Church. Richard Fitz Ralph,[3] Archbishop of Armagh and a Fellow of Balliol (where Wyclif himself became Master), had made a vigorous attack on the whole official ecclesiastical position and from him Wyclif borrowed much of the inspiration which created the famous theory of 'Dominion'. It was this theory which was summarized in his affirmative answer to Parliament.[4] Lordship and service were corresponding terms. Might must be balanced by Right, or, as Wyclif summed it up, 'Dominion is founded on Grace'. All 'dominion' was conferred by God in return for service, and no man in mortal sin had any right to any gift of God. All men held their 'dominion' directly from God by virtue of 'grace' – the priesthood was therefore deprived of its privileged position as sole intermediary. In such theories – elaborated with all the subtlety of the Schoolmen – there is implicit the future philosophy of the protestant Reformation, but, for the moment, Wyclif's answer gave a theoretical justification to what many less subtle minds most desired. The Pope and his representatives might not be in a state of grace, and they therefore could err. If any act of a Pope was wrong, it was invalid, and it was then the duty of every Christian to disobey. The superfluous wealth of the Church was clearly the evil fruit of error, and the remedy was for the State to appropriate it, and so obtain some relief from the increasing burden of necessary taxation. This was the answer that Wyclif's questioners wanted – the honest theorist is so often too ready, in his innocence, to supply principles to men of no principle. The Council of 1378 was faced with an urgent and immediate financial crisis, and it was indeed fortunate in having so saintly a character

31

as Wyclif to cloak its expediency; but the immediate effects on parliamentary legislation were small – the logical conclusion to Wyclif's premises was not drawn until over a hundred and fifty years later. On the other hand, Richard had heard Wyclif exalt the 'dominion' of Kings as against the 'dominion' of pontiffs, he had heard him urge obedience even to tyrants,[1] so great was his respect for properly constituted civil authority, and he had heard him express a profound distrust of popular elections because the 'electing community is often in greater part infected with crime'. The weakness of Wyclif's theory was the difficulty of deciding precisely when a particular 'dominion' lacked 'grace'. That problem was not solved – if it has ever been solved – until barons had killed off baronage, until a king had been dethroned and executed, until Parliament had worked out its own sovereignty and established its own Church. For the time being, the young King could contemplate his inherited regality – his own 'dominion' – with a new interest and perhaps a new ambition.[2]

In the early spring of the following year, 1378, Wyclif for the second time was summoned to the bar of the Church which he had been rash enough to criticize, and whose special privileges he had been brave enough to attack in open Parliament. The English hierarchy acting on their own initiative had failed to press home their attack on Wyclif – in the brawl between Gaunt and the Londoners 'the Devil had known how to save his own' as the orthodox chronicler put it – and they had subsequently called in the direct reinforcement of the Pope himself. Five papal Bulls had been addressed to the King of England urging the condemnation and imprisonment of Wyclif, but their receipt had coincided with the death of Edward III, and there had been unavoidable delay before Wyclif was at last summoned to Lambeth to face an ecclesiastical commission. The detailed history of this Lambeth Conference of 1378 is obscure, but its conclusion is dramatically clear. Again, Wycliff was saved; but this time by the direct intervention of Richard's mother,[3] who sent a knight of her household, Sir Lewis Clifford, to forbid Wyclif's condemnation. If Princess Joan could take so bold a course, she must have been not only a very confirmed Wyclifite but reasonably sure of popular support. The Lambeth Conference was abandoned, but for form's sake Wyclif was forbidden to lecture on or to preach about his recently formulated doctrines. Richard had had an impressive demonstration of the power of personal regality even as against the express wishes of the papal see.

In August 1378 a storm blew up suddenly in this atmosphere charged with so many conflicting forces and so much dangerous tension – it is known as the Westminster Sacrilege,[1] and contains in its details much that is illuminating in a dark and confused period.

Two of the Black Prince's esquires – Robert Hawley and John Shakell – had captured a Count of Denia in the Nájera campaign, and naturally had hoped to make considerable profit from his ransom. The knights of Chivalry in the late fourteenth century had become hard-headed fortune seekers rather than knights errant looking for dragons. The Count had been released on parole in order to make arrangements for providing the ransom money, and his son had been retained as hostage and security. For ten years, the English squires had been hoping for their money, and in the meantime they had treated their hostage with every kindness. At last the Count of Denia had sent representatives to England with a portion of the ransom, and orders to negotiate full final payment and the release of his son. It was at this point that the Council stepped in, and, having seen an opportunity of acquiring easy money, ordered the squires to surrender their hostage to it. They refused, on the intelligible ground that they might, after waiting so long, find their personal reward diverted to the coffers of the State in its time of need. Their refusal was met by their committal to the Tower for contumacy. As they had committed no crime they had been reasonably well treated, and had even been allowed to take one servant with them. They had been imprisoned since November 1377 but, being men of considerable spirit, they had steadfastly refused all information as to the whereabouts of their young hostage. In the August of 1378, they escaped from the Tower, and found sanctuary at Westminster Abbey. The Constable of the Tower pursued them, and, accompanied by an armed retinue, approached the sacred precincts. A trick succeeded in trapping Shakell, but Hawley retreated into the Abbey where mass was being celebrated. The Constable and his men forced their way in, murdered a sacristan who opposed them, and despatched the resisting Hawley on the steps of the high altar. In the King's name, sanctuary had been appallingly broken, and a double murder committed at the most sacred shrine in the kingdom.

This Westminster Sacrilege is a revealing incident – it exposes so much of contemporary life in its true colours. The Church was insulted at a time when all its special privileges were in question, and when popular feeling was mounting against her on every side. But churchmen have never lacked courage, and, after some thoughtful delay, the Bishop of London excommunicated all concerned, and, in spite of royal letters urging discretion, he boldly repeated the sentence of Holy Church three days a week, and even added a rider which, by specifically excluding the King, the Queen Mother and John of Gaunt, implicitly connected all three with responsibility for the crime. The Constable and his men happened to be followers of Gaunt and had clearly exceeded their duty, but on the other hand the right of sanctuary had been abused in order to thwart the civil authority. The rival claims of Church and State were now involved. The Council summoned the Bishop of London to Windsor to appear before it and explain his high-handed actions. But the bishop refused the summons. Meanwhile Gaunt himself took a hand, and, in promising support to the Constable, threatened physical violence against the contumacy of the 'ribald knaves of London'.[1] The storm blew over, and the incident was finally closed by a gift of lands to Shakell in exchange for his hostage, and the promise of a chantry for the souls of its victims. It is the appendix to this story of murder and bickering which is so revealing. It was discovered that the hostage was none other than the servant who had been allowed to accompany Shakell and Hawley to the Tower. In the best traditions of a dying age, the young Spanish nobleman had kept faith with his captors, and had preferred service as a menial in a fortress to a betrayal which would have besmirched his escutcheon. On every hand, sordid motives were poisoning the fountains of Chivalry, but the sequel to the Westminster Sacrilege proves that the most brutal disrespect for law and order had not altogether destroyed the original idealism of the European Order of Knighthood.

In September of this same confused year, 1378, there occurred in Italy an event which, apart from shocking all good Christians, had profound effects on international politics.[2] Christendom had already been embarrassed by the 'Babylonish Captivity', it now had to face the tragic spectacle of two Popes each claiming to be the rightful heir to St Peter and sole regent of God on earth. The details of this fateful episode are outside the scope of this book, but some of its consequences are not. Official Roman Catholicism has not yet given a definite decision as to which Pope was the true Pope, or faced clearly the implications of such indecision; it is not therefore surprising if contemporary lay thought treated the Great Schism cynically and took sides in accordance with political expediency. England's decision was due for discussion at Richard's second Parliament, which was held at Gloucester in October 1378. It is supposed that Gloucester was its meeting place because Westminster was still uncleansed of the stain of sacrilege, and it is witness to England's comparative parochialism that the affair of Shakell and Hawley took precedence over the Great Schism. For the last time John Wyclif received a royal summons to appear before Parliament – to advise on that right of sanctuary which had so recently been both abused and overridden. He and other Doctors of Theology and Civil Law gave their verdict in favour of a change, and a year later the law was altered to exclude from sanctuary the person and property of fraudulent debtors. A mountain of discontent had produced a mouse of reform; but it was a beginning. The Parliament only then gave its attention to the rival claims of the two Popes, and, to men who still regarded the King of England as the rightful King of France, French merchants as their greatest competitors in the Flemish wool markets, and the French people as their natural and hereditary enemies, there could be no doubt as to which Pope was the true Pope. Urban VI was an Italian Pope at Rome, Clement VII was a French Pope at Avignon; the enemies of France must clearly be Urbanists. England henceforth was Urbanist because France was Clementist, just as Flanders, Portugal and the Empire became Urbanist while Scotland and Christian Spain became Clementist. The Great Schism helped to decide the diplomatic bias of all European States until the Reformation, and gave the English claims against the French monarchy the semblance of a crusade against an anti-Pope. From the young King of England's point of view it was to give him his bride – the league of Urbanist powers against Clementist France was to make the choice of a daughter of the Urbanist Emperor as Queen of England an obvious move in the plans of a ruthless mediaeval diplomacy.

Richard's first months on the throne may seem dull and uneventful because they lack the colour of dramatic action, but for Richard himself, and even more for his mother, his advisers and his guardians, they were months of anxious crisis. A sacrilege in Westminster Abbey, a scholar on trial, an uncle under a cloud, these may seem small matters; but the split of Christendom was a portentous event, a crack in the dykes of the Church was a sign of disturbance everywhere and might eventually release a flood.

Meanwhile the war with France was not over. What was the son of the Black Prince learning from the prowess on the battlefield of his elders, while he himself remained in tutelage?

The Hundred Years War[1] had begun partly as a dynastic quarrel, based on that claim of Richard's grandfather to the throne of France which quartered the lilies with the leopards in the royal escutcheons of England down to the nineteenth century. But, like all wars, it had deeper as well as proximate causes, and results both good and evil. To Richard's contemporaries, war with France was considered right and necessary – it was only criticized when it was unsuccessful. The fourteenth and fifteenth centuries were centuries of violence, they accepted war as natural, and pacifism was an undreamt-of creed.[2] It was the unquestioned duty of every lay man to be able to defend himself at arms – the knight with his lance, the yeoman with his longbow, the burgher with his short sword or 'anlace', even the villein with his billhook. It was the unquestioned duty of every layman to answer a summons to fight for his King, Lord or city, and this mediaeval militarism was as old as the Saxon fyrd. The Hundred Years War can only be understood if it is studied as the first major war fought by the English people outside their own islands not as unwilling conscripts or mercenaries but as Englishmen who were rapidly learning to hate the foreigner. Froissart, who knew and respected the English as well as he knew his compatriots, stated a plain if unpalatable truth: –

'The English will never love or honour their King unless he be victorious and a lover of arms and war against their neighbours, especially against such as are greater and richer than themselves. Their land is more fulfilled of riches and all manner of goods when they are at war than in times of peace. They take delight and solace in battles and slaughter. Covetous and envious are they above measure of other men's wealth.'

There is no mention here of the dynastic motive, and the truth is that Edward III had cloaked a feudal war for aggrandisement in the guise of a war for hereditary right. He was the rightful and acknowledged heir to the Angevin empire, but his ambition had soared to the illegitimate conquest of the whole of what was soon to be France. During his long reign, England had won four great victories – the naval battle off Sluys which gave her only temporary command of the Channel, and the battles of Crécy, Poitiers and Nájera, which had produced little but glory and booty. By the Treaty of Brétigny (1360) England had retained her bridgehead of Calais, and owned half France by right of title and conquest combined. But there was a clause in that treaty which obliged Edward III to surrender his claim to the throne of France, and Charles V to surrender his claim to the suzerainty of Aquitaine. Neither King kept his word, and Edward's reign had closed in military stalemate.

How were these famous victories won, and were they as barren as they now seem? Feudalism in the thirteenth century was as wide and un-national as Christendom, but in England it had been wedded to the traditions of free Saxons, and, when the Hundred Years War began, it had developed into something very different from the French system. English feudalism had married the militarism of knight and tenant with the free native institutions of folk-moot and shire-moot, and could produce an army at need which was a rough cross-section of the nation.[1] Continental feudalism created a wide gulf between knight and serf, and had not yet achieved a unity. France was only nominally a kingdom; its royal writ did not run unquestioned into the great duchies which hedged in the comparatively tiny Ile de France round Paris. Her army was a temporary alliance of independent nobles hiring mercenaries, whereas an English King could call on the ancient virtues of the Saxon host. Moreover, the English had perfected a new technique of fighting in their wars against the Scots, and in this technique, as contrasted with the French system, was the secret of their success and an expression of national progress. At Falkirk, the 'hammer of the Scots' had discovered the weapon of victory in the longbow drawn by free swordsmen protected by knights, who were not ashamed to dismount and fight shoulder to shoulder with their social inferiors. At the defeat of Bannockburn, the English had learnt the bitter lesson that sturdy

37

spearmen could defeat the cavalry charge of armoured knights. And at Neville's Cross the northern militia and the longbow had again brought victory. These lessons were well learned, and had made certain of the overwhelming victories of Edward III and his son. The only reply which the French could make was heavier armour for mounted knights, and therefore even less mobility than before. But these were victories of tactics, and the French had at last produced a strategist. After Poitiers, the great Bertrand du Guesclin had out-generalled the English. He had realized that the English technique could only win when fighting a defensive battle on chosen ground; if the archers could be compelled to become mobile, they were less easy to protect, and easier to ride down. He therefore counselled the Fabian principles of avoiding pitched battles, harassing stragglers, and besieging fortresses, where French superiority in mining, in the use of gunpowder, and in military engineering generally was pronounced. The English could win battles, but the French could avoid them, and the truce of Brétigny had been necessary for both sides to take stock of the position. It was an uneasy truce, and, through the last years of Edward's reign, raiding across the Channel by the French and raiding into France from Calais and Aquitaine by the English, were part of a normal summer routine – the French war had smouldered on.

But at home the victories of Crécy and Poitiers had greater significance than in France. They were the glorious victories of English bowmen protected by English knights led by that pattern of chivalry, the Black Prince. Soldiers, selected by commissions of array to fight overseas, returned not only with tales of glory and valour but with appreciable booty. Knights returned with noble captives whose ransoms made chivalry worth while, and whose continental tastes added a polish to the comparatively rude manners and habits of the islanders. The great merchants of London, as financiers of war and purveyors to fleets and armies, increased their wealth, power and indispensability. By the time Richard had left boyhood behind, not a few Englishmen of all classes were looking back with envy to the glorious days of Edward III, when they had waxed fat on the loot of France, and lord and commoner, yeoman and labourer, burgher and apprentice, were beginning to be conscious of that mixture of tradition, race, emotion and geography which was becoming England.

There was, of course, another side to this picture. Luxury based on plunder was not a sound basis for permanent prosperity – still less for national morality. Although the victors of Crécy and Poitiers were English, they were not all strictly 'soldiers of the king' – the loyalty of many of them was primarily to their lords, and the idea of allowing the king to have a *standing* army was not yet even mooted. The Hundred Years War glorified the idea of kingship and stimulated the growth of what is called 'nationality', but it also gave overmuch encouragement to great barons to support their power with armed retainers. The King could hire men through their lords, and, by commissions of array, he could create something approaching an English national army; but he could not summon all men directly to his service as a Saxon king could call out his 'fyrd'. The struggle for final sovereignty between king and barons was still to be fought out, and the Hundred Years War was only a prelude to the Wars of the Roses. And, when victories were few, the Commons of England were not slow to point out that, as the French war was supposed to be a war to establish the King's hereditary claim to the crown of France, then the King should finance it from his own resources and without recourse to new and onerous methods of taxation.

In the wars of Chivalry, the sordid motives of personal gain and the factors of economics are as clearly visible as the knight errantry and the growing national sentiment. The wealth of England was in its wool. English pastures, largely out of reach of marauding pirates and pillaging armies, produced fleeces which were the envy of Europe, and the necessary raw material for the looms of the thriving cities of the Low Countries. The fact that the Lord Chancellor still sits on a woolsack in the House of Lords, is a reminder that in the fourteenth century the wealth of both Church and State was for the most part dependent on the wool markets in Flanders; the trade with Aquitaine was useful, but less important. The flourishing market and industrial cities of Ghent, Bruges, Antwerp and Ypres were naturally coveted by the King of France – and here was yet another reason why the Hundred Years War was more than dynastic. As Richard studied the diplomacy of his day, his tutors could not have had much difficulty in impressing upon him that to fight the power of France was not only a glorious tradition but a necessary duty – to save the wine trade with Gascony and to safeguard the wool trade

39

with Flanders, and through Flanders with Central Europe and the Mediterranean. That his elders were failing in both duties is quite clear to modern observers, but, though this may have been suspected by some contemporaries, the causes of this failure must have been obscure to all. The reign had scarcely begun before the French and Spanish fleets had attacked the Channel ports from the Isle of Wight to Gravesend, and it was not until the following year that the English were ready to make reprisal. From 1378 to 1381, the story of the French war is a dreary catalogue of ineptitudes, only relieved here and there by the unco-ordinated exploits of a few individuals. And the ineptitude was not one-sided – the French were unable to profit from English inefficiency. Of creditable individual exploits, the story of Sir Hugh Calverley is notable. Of disgraceful incidents, the expedition of Sir John Arundell is typical. As an example of unprofitable campaigning, the military career of the luckless John of Gaunt is outstanding. In a brief outline of all three is a summing up of that '*damnosa hereditas*' with which Richard had been presented willy nilly on his accession . . .

Sir Hugh Calverley was one of the most distinguished of the Black Prince's knights, and a great hero to the chivalrous Froissart. When the Truce of Brétigny had lapsed, he was the Warden of Calais, that gateway into France which Froissart pointed out as 'most convenient'. The French could have command of the Narrow Seas and take fire and sword to the south coasts of England; Calverley could answer with fierce sorties from his safe base in Calais. He hired a mercenary force, razed Boulogne, and took a rich booty when he advanced further and sacked the great Fair of Etaples. Later in the same year, he used the same marauding tactics to sack and raze Merk. Although its abbey was a main objective, and its riches the best part of the spoil, it is an illustration of how nationalism was superseding an international Christianity that the Monk of St Albans praised the deed 'because God was with him and directed all his works'.[1] In the following year, Calverley was promoted to the post of *Admiralis Maris* – in the warfare of this period ships were merely merchantmen with cargoes of soldiers, and naval tactics were as simple and as military as the tactics of Salamis. Calverley was called upon to aid the Duke of Brittany, who was trapped in the harbour of St Malo by the French under Du Guesclin, and this minor clash has a special

40

interest – Calverley was relying on his archers whereas the French were trying the effect of certain 'missiles called guns'.[1] For the moment, the hail of arrows defeated ill-directed and unreliable shot, and Calverley's personal bravery earned the unstinted praise of the great Du Guesclin who watched the fighting from across the harbour. Calverley's soldiering, even when he raided an abbey, was in the best if curious traditions of the perfect Chaucerian knight, but it was quite incapable of winning a war because it was without direction from any co-ordinated plan of campaign.

The story of the death of Sir John Arundell,[2] on the other hand, is a sinister sidelight on that Chivalry of which the life of Calverley is on the whole so admirable an example. In 1379 he was appointed one of the commanders of an expedition to Brittany, which had the blessing of the Urbanist Archbishop of Cashel, who had arrived in England to promote war against all adherents of Pope Clement. When a proclamation of Charles V announced that all Urbanists would be executed, the Brittany expedition became almost a crusade. Sir John Arundell gathered his men and marched towards the coast, where, delayed for lack of favourable winds, he amused his troops by leading them to the sack of a neighbouring nunnery. In a lawless and violent age this even shocked contemporaries, but the sequel gave them the satisfaction of pointing a moral. Arundell sailed too soon with his loot and some of the ravished nuns on board, and in a terrible storm his whole fleet was wrecked and Arundell drowned. It was the judgment of God,[3] and from the strategic point of view a major disaster, for once again England lost command of the Narrow Seas.

Meanwhile, John of Gaunt had not been wholly content in his diplomatic retirement, and, as the campaigning season (May to October) of 1378 drew near, he had again been anxious to add his weight to the perennial struggle with France. He had a double motive. By his second marriage, 1371, to Costanza the daughter of Don Pedro, he had become the legitimate King of Castile, whereas Charles V of France was still supporting the usurper Henry of Trastamara. Gaunt was proposing to fight for his personal throne as well as for the glory of his young nephew's. After some debate – which again revealed the general suspicion as to his motives – Gaunt was given command of an expedition to France, but, while preparations were being made, the chroniclers tell of another of those smaller incidents which illuminate the greater

41

scene. A Scottish knight – Sir John Mercer – was imprisoned in England. His son, in revenge, was harrying English shipping as far away as Cherbourg, and doing it to some purpose. John Philpot,[1] one of that new class of merchant financiers which the city of London was now producing, fitted, equipped and manned a fleet from his own resources, and captured the young Mercer in a brilliant Channel fight. It was naturally a highly popular victory with the Londoners, but it brought heavy censure from nobles who still believed that they had a monopoly of leadership. But, at last, Gaunt sailed. Opposing him was the French Admiral, Jean de Vienne – a great sailor and an able strategist. Obedient to the policy of his King, de Vienne avoided trouble at sea as cleverly as Du Guesclin avoided it on land. Gaunt was compelled to give up his search for an elusive foe, and, afraid to return home without something to show, he foolishly attempted to besiege the well-protected fortress of St Malo. This involved the dreary method of mining operations in which Gaunt, under the Black Prince, had shown considerable skill at the siege of Limoges. When all seemed to be going well, a sortie surprised the Earl of Arundel, who at that moment had charge of the mine; the mine collapsed, and with it Gaunt's hopes of fame and glory. Gaunt was compelled to return to England a disappointed and now even despised failure. The 'ribald' Londoners, who cursed Gaunt as the murderer of Hawley, were also expressing their disappointment at the non-arrival of booty, and comparing the failure of a subsidized duke with the independent success of a London citizen.

These dreary years of ineffective fighting provide obvious morals for those who are judges long after the event. It seems obvious that, though the longbows of yeomen could pierce the plate and mail of French knights, a brilliant battle was no substitute for a sound policy, and that, if archers had no target, campaigns became mere marauding route marches. It seems obvious that if an expedition to Brittany was compelled to attack via Calais, then the primary essential to the success of the French war was a navy in un-questioned command of the Channel. It seems obvious that divided forces were dissipating the advantages of a ring of bridge-heads which included Calais, Cherbourg, Brest, Bordeaux and Bayonne, and that there was no hope of final victory without a large-scale and concentrated invasion. But none of these deduc-tions were drawn at the time, because large-scale war required money, and the citizens who had the money were not yet sufficiently at one with nobles and King to think their money well spent in financing a ruling class which despised them.[1] The Commons were glad enough to enjoy the fruits of victory, they were not so eager to advance the needs of dynastic or baronial wars or even to provide the means for economic war, largely because it was not yet established that those who supplied means should also have control of ends.

In this cruel process which was hammering out nations on the anvils of war, there was a constant stirring of those in authority to find some simple way out of the complicated financial *impasse* which always resulted, and in the story of the experiments and expedients to which the Exchequer resorted is the story of the prelude to the Peasants' Revolt of 1381. In appreciating this story, modern conceptions of governmental duties must be set aside.[2] A modern government needs taxation not merely for defence and offence but for a very wide range of social services. A mediaeval oligarchy needed taxation in order to supplement the private wealth of the monarchy (the royal income from the revenues of crown lands, the fees of feudalism and the fines of justice) and to provide enough cash to meet royal expenses, and especially the expenses of waging war. Social service as a function of government was quite alien to mediaeval thought – its substitute was the mutual self-help of communities, whether those communities were monasteries, manors, townships, or wards and guilds of a city. A mediaeval tax was therefore in essence a forced payment whose return was the uncertain bounty of booty and the vague advantages of military glory; it was therefore always granted grudgingly and coupled with the vain hope that, in the words of Parliament after Parliament, the King might 'live of his own resources and carry on his war'. When 'his' war did not bring victory and booty, a new group of Lords might oust the unsuccessful leaders, and the Commons, who usually supplied the hard cash, might be bold enough to demand the production of accounts, and even at times the impeachment of the unsuccessful. But the Commons were not the people, and even a full Parliament was not yet a true mirror of the nation. The people – Langland's 'folk' and Gaunt's 'knaves' – were villeins still tied to the feudal obligations of work or villeins who had bought their release, free labourers who worked for the highest bidders, free yeomen who had prospered enough to become

43

successful farmers, the artisans, craftsmen, journeymen and small tradesmen of the towns, and the retainers and men-at-arms in the pay of landed Lords. None of these classes, except the yeomen, paid or expected to pay direct taxes.

During the fourteenth century, the traditional methods of financing the Exchequer had become stabilized. When the King and his Council required additional funds, they were usually granted an export tax on the wool trade, collected by means of that 'staple' system which ensured that prices, quality and tax could be efficiently supervised and controlled, together with a subsidy or tax on all movable property. There were two other sources of public revenue – first, the Church, which wisely followed the lead of the Commons and in its own Convocations granted equivalent contributions, and second, the foreign merchants, with whom the King's officials had formerly made private bargains at 'colloquies of merchants', and whose payments were now authorized by parliamentary sanction at a rate roughly fifty per cent in excess of the rate for native merchants. In addition to these revenues, the King had the financial benefits of his position at the head of the feudal system, as its chief landowner and the recipient of the fines of royal justice.

It was, therefore, a complicated and not very satisfactory financial system in which the borders between private and public purse were as ill-defined as the borders between private and national war, and in which the comparatively simple obligations of the feudal pyramid were becoming hopelessly involved with the complex bonds of trade and industry. Furthermore, it had ceased to provide sufficient revenue for the needs of continental war. It was a problem which had been worrying the servants of the royal household for some time – including those political clergy whom Wyclif had denounced – and, in the last year of Edward III's reign, they had devised an experiment to overcome their difficulties. They had invented the poll-tax. Every adult – defined as over fourteen years of age – except the beggar, was to pay a groat (4d.) to the royal Exchequer. From the point of view of its inventors, it was a simple method of bringing the whole nation within the obligation of contributing to the glory and stability of the realm as a whole – or, as later centuries put it, 'broadening the basis of taxation'. Its obvious injustice was that it assessed all men equally – the poor paid exactly the same as the

44

rich; but, as hitherto the poor had never paid anything, and as the rich still supplied the traditional revenues as well, there was a case for a tax which took a little from everybody. On the other hand, there was the more relevant objection that not everybody had consented to the tax – the poor were not represented in Parliament. In the event, the first poll-tax of 1377 (also called the 'tallage of groats') while naturally rousing much resentment, produced but meagre returns – there was as yet no trained bureaucracy to make tax collecting either fair or productive.

Two years later, the inventors of the first poll-tax tried again. In a Great Council held in February 1379, the Lords had adopted the significant course of raising loans by compulsion[1] on a large scale from many of the landowners, monasteries and towns – so desperate were the financial needs of the Exchequer. It was a drastic method of which much more was to be heard in later years, and it was followed by presenting the Parliament called to Westminster at Easter with the necessity of repaying the loans. The anger of the Commons was only appeased by the voluntary production of accounts which proved the desperate need for funds, and as a result the second poll-tax was agreed. '*Quod omnes tangit ab omnibus approbetur*' was an accepted legal maxim, but it was not yet carried to its logical conclusion – the people were still to be taxed by the Commons. But this time there was a very interesting attempt to apply a sliding scale[2] to the payments demanded. The definition of an adult was altered to read 'over sixteen', and, where the poorest were to pay a groat, the Duke of Lancaster and the Archbishops of Canterbury and York were to pay ten marks, and between these two extremes a graduated scale of payments was fixed for the different classes of laymen and clerics. Again the resentment was widespread and the results disappointing – a tax estimated to yield £50,000 in fact raised only £27,000.

In the following year, 1380, the last and most notorious third poll-tax[3] was agreed by a Parliament which met at Northampton. There were dark reasons for a meeting so far away from the capital in a town with poor communications and not over supplied with hostelries and lodgings. London was again in turmoil; but this time over a question of trade rivalry. A rich merchant from Genoa had been murdered,[4] and John de Kyrkby, a Londoner, was one of those charged with the crime. It is clear from the

45

chronicles that this was a sordid quarrel between monopolists and interlopers. The city merchants were jealous of foreign merchants who could tempt court and baronage with rarer luxuries than those within the scope of English traders, and whose prices could not be controlled in the interests of the city rings. The chronicler Walsingham remarks that the Genoese's chief crime was that he proposed to sell pepper at a mere 4d. the pound! At the same time, the news of the war was disheartening – a Breton expedition led by the Earl of Buckingham was not going well, and an expedition of Gaunt to Scotland was as unpopular as Gaunt himself. At Northampton, the Commons might be more amenable – they could be faced with the realities of the financial situation, and urged to provide the means for a solution. A sum of £160,000 was demanded – a staggering figure to mediaeval eyes. It was determined that £100,000 was a fairer target, and the Parliament agreed to find two-thirds of this sum providing the clergy supplied the remainder. The method of assessment to which the Commons agreed was that of the first poll-tax. The manifest injustice of this method had been to a certain degree corrected by the sliding scale of the second poll-tax, but this lesson was ignored, and the injustice trebled in weight by a flat-rate tax at treble the rate – every adult had to pay three groats, but this time an adult was re-defined as anyone over fifteen. Trebling the rate was arrived at by a simple arithmetic which argued that, as the first poll-tax had supplied £22,000, a tax of three times the rate would produce £66,000. The only concession made in view of the objections to the first two poll-taxes was the suggestion that the rich should help the poor – but this was only a pious hope because no machinery was provided for carrying it into effect, and a subordinate clause went far to nullify what small effects it had – no man and wife together were to pay more than twenty shillings, a restriction which applied to the generous rich as well as to the mean. It is difficult to understand why the Council persisted in this savage and crude experiment. True, the times demanded desperate remedies: the Treasury was empty, and to the debts due to unpaid soldiery were now added the un-settled debts on account of the forced loans of the previous year, and there was no sign of warfare ending either in truce or still less in victory. There is perhaps a clue to the reasons behind this act of folly in the remark of one chronicler who states, incidentally but categorically as an accepted fact, that 'all the wealth of the kingdom was in the hands of artisans and labourers'. Ever since the Black Death there had been a growing belief among the feudal landowners that the lower orders were becoming not only too independent but too well-off, and in the towns the earnings of the free journeymen were similarly begrudged by the older established rings who controlled civic government and representation. Here was hitherto untouched wealth ready for the tapping. To differentiate between rich and poor, and between prosperous and struggling areas, never occurred to men who were oversure of their power and tragically unaware of the strength of new forces about to emerge.

The first four years of Richard's reign provided him with an uninspiring and dismal tutelage. His uncles and his peers could only sink treasure in losing command of the Narrow Seas, and fritter away subsidies and reputations in fruitless expeditions which could never find the enemy save when he was safe behind fortifications. Perhaps England would rally one day to the leadership of a son of the Black Prince and fare better? His guardians, whether feudal lords or clerical administrators of long experience, seemed incapable of managing the national finances either to the satisfaction of the tax payers or to the benefit of the Exchequer. His churchmen were harassed by the schism in the very seat of their authority, and divided between conservatives who would fight for the *status quo* and reformers ready to try new techniques in a revival of true Christianity where it seemed so badly needed. Was it to be wondered at that, in a Parliament held in London in the winter of 1380, the Commons in desperation urged the King 'now that he had reached years of discretion' – the ripe age of thirteen – to take over his full regal powers? His mentors and regents were too wise – and perhaps too jealous – to permit it, but the request would not pass unnoticed by an adolescent whose sense of kingship had been so early roused by relatives and by circumstance. Richard's tutelage could only have taught him one bitter lesson – that there was little hope of help in his future responsibilities from those who were his elders, and for the time being his masters. The following year was to reveal the bankruptcy of England's baronial oligarchy contrasted with the potentialities of its youthful King.

III

REVOLT

SIR JOHN FROISSART, who watched the events of the year 1381 from his detached and cosmopolitan vantage point across the Channel, was in no doubt as to their importance; 'There fell in England,' he writes, 'great mischief and rebellion of moving of the common people, by which deed England was at a point to have been lost without recovery.' [1] It was a just comment, and time has not questioned his judgment, though it has softened his condemnation. In retrospect the year 1381 can be deemed worthy to rank with the famous years of 1215, 1649 and 1688 as a very significant date [2] in the long history of the English people's march to freedom. And to appreciate the full contemporary significance of the Peasants' Revolt of 1381, and especially its effects on the ruling classes and on Richard, it is necessary first to glance at the social structure of the day . . .

The English people [3] were living under what has since been described as the 'manorial system'. It is a phrase that covers a wide variety of agriculture, but broadly it describes a way of life based on the holding of land and work on the land, and a system of military and social service also based on the land, which had been developed to suit the needs of a military oligarchy and an agricultural society slowly establishing prosperity against the handicaps of bog, heath and forest. [4] The invasion of the Norman knights had superimposed on a mixed society of free Saxons and Danes (with a sprinkling of submerged British slaves) a feudalism which enforced some kind of service on high and low, but which left a small land-holding aristocracy in almost absolute power over the common folk, who tilled the land, and who were neither wholly bond nor wholly free but 'villeins' tied to the soil owning, as a fourteenth-century abbot of Burton put it, 'nothing but their bellies'. The villeins formed the backbone of the Peasants' Revolt. [5] Why?

48

Froissart's answer comes pat – because of 'the ease and riches that the common people were of',[1] and the researches of economic historians since have gone a long way to support this paradox. The villein ancestors were not starved into bitter rebellion, they were loyal to their King, and, in their own half-blind way, striking blows for freedom; certainly, they were not whining for bread. The 'manorial system' had many faults, but, if it secured luxury only to the few, it also ensured a bare sufficiency to the many. So long as a villein could work he was sure of livelihood; trouble only arose when he also wanted to be free. The 'custom of the manor' bound him to his ancestral holding, and to those feudal bonds which were never suffered gladly by a peasantry with dim folk-memories of sea-roving freedom, and which became more and more irksome as the common people slowly responded to new ambitions. For several days each week, the villein was a lesser human being not very much more valuable than his Lord's oxen, and what seems to modern eyes mere labour slavery was to a feudal lord an equitable system of levying rent in hours of work, where cash was sometimes a suspect and always a rare and risky medium of exchange.

This 'great servage', which Froissart noticed in England, had many local variations, and was never quite as rigid as later analysis makes it appear; but, from the end of the eleventh to the end of the fifteenth centuries, the economy of rural England was carried on with reasonable efficiency by this system. In the year 1349, this economy had been shattered by a visitation of a plague which, though always a likely danger in so insanitary a civilization, had at this time reached the proportions of a continental calamity. The Black Death[2] within a year had carried off at least a third of the total population of England. Its immediate effect was a dearth of villein labourers and of free labourers. The free labourers who survived could claim a scarcity price for their labour, the villein labourers who survived schemed for a freedom which was no mere theoretical change of status but an obvious gateway to comparative prosperity. And, with campaigning close at hand, the Lords needed money more than ever. The final effects of the Black Death and the needs of the Hundred Years War accelerated the process of 'commutation'[3] and gave freed men a privileged position in that wage-bargaining which is at the root of economics. In a static agricultural community, when

49

a third of the available labourers are killed, the produce from the land will be significantly less and the prices for that produce will be higher; money will decline in purchasing power. That was the justification for the higher wages the labourers demanded – and the need of the manors was so great that in many places the labourers were given what they asked – and the explanation of that economic spiral with which Statutes of Labourers[1] (attempting to limit wages, to peg prices, and to prevent the mobility of labour) tried in vain to contend. A villein had only to be bold enough to escape to the next shire, and his own ready tongue would be passport enough to the status of a free labourer, when the hirer was desperate for workers and without the machinery which nowadays tabulates life from birth to the grave. But not every villein was bold enough to be an adventurer: the bulk remained as they had always been but with still greater envy of the freedom they lacked, needing to scrape and save still more if they were to be able one day to afford the increased price of 'commutation', and becoming more and more resentful of those bond services which were a perpetual reminder of semi-servitude.

To expect the military landowners, who were lords of most of the manors of England, to find the right solution to a social problem of such great complexity is to expect too much. The knights and the burgesses, who represented a new kind of oligarchy from shire and town in the central assemblies of the King's Parliament, should have been better able to understand the economic problems of their day, yet in petition after petition they clamoured for stricter enforcement of the Statutes of Labourers. They demanded the fixing of wages at rates paid in 1346 (before the Black Death), and they obtained branding as part of the punishment of those who sought wages in excess of such niggardly rates. There was no individual and no group in a fourteenth-century Parliament to represent the masses of the population – either rural or urban: economic government was rarely therefore in the interests of the governed, it was entirely on the side of the lords of the manors and the oligarchies of the towns. If villeins in the country and free labourers in the towns were to improve their respective lots, their only means of expression was that assembly which their masters would call a mob, that demonstration which the authorities would try to suppress as a riot, and that combination which the King's Council would try to crush as treason. There is ample

50

evidence that, long before the third poll-tax finally caused a conflagration, there were 'confederacies' of villeins to make resistance to their Lords. In the preamble to the very first Statute of Richard's reign[1] are these revealing words,

> 'the villeins and land-tennants in villeinage, who owe services and customs to their said Lords, have now late withdrawn, and do daily withdraw their services and customs due to their said Lords, by comfort and procurement of other their counsellors maintainers and abbettors in the country, which hath taken hire and profit of the said villeins and land-tennants, by colour of certain exemplifications made out of the book of Doomsday of the manors and towns where they have been dwelling, and by virtue of the same exemplifications, and their evil interpretations of the same, they affirm them to be quite and utterly discharged of all manner servage, due as well of their body as of their said tenure, and will not suffer any distress or other justice, to be made upon them, but do menace the ministers of their Lords of life and member, and (which the more is) gather themselves together in great routs, and agree by such confederacy, that everyone shall aid other to resist their Lords with strong hand: and much other harm they do in sundry manner, to the great damage of their said Lords, and evil example to other to begin such riots: so that if due remedy be not the rather provided upon the same rebels, greater mischief (which God prohibit) may thereof spring through the realm . . .'

The only remedy that could be thought of was repression; but there was no police force, and not even a standing army, to enforce suppression; and there were many of the landowners ready to disregard their own Statutes in a race to corner whatever free labour was available at any price it asked.

In considering revolutions which spring from below, it is often pointless to look for that careful organization and secret plotting which are more typical of palace revolutions and governmental *coups d'état*. The story of the Peasants' Revolt, for example, is a story of spontaneous combustion. Moving up and down the country through town and manor was that wayfaring life which M. Jusserand[2] uncovered from the dust of the past – the life of vagabonds, chapmen, beggars, tumblers, players and pilgrims capping one good story of grievances with a better over their

51

drinks, linking manor to manor, town to town, and uniting isolated injustices and separate indignities into one great chorus of resistance. The efficiency with which messages can be passed from mouth to mouth in all primitive communities is astonishing to civilizations which rely on newspapers, telegraph and radio. And the power of the spoken word – magnified by the art and presence of the born storyteller – has frequently proved the most effective of all methods of propaganda. In a truly revolutionary situation it needs only a few men of a courage well above the ordinary to sound the tocsin, and they quickly find a mass of malcontents at their back.

There was another kind of verbal stimulus to the general dissatisfaction. Very few townsfolk could read, and very few villeins needed to, but they all had ears and memory for those tales and ballads which have been summed up in the legend of Robin Hood – the good yeoman who took to the greenwood as an outlaw, and who robbed the rich to give to the poor. Robin Hood may have been a wish-fulfilment dream of the manorial villein, and stories, which today are only acceptable as prizes for children, were in 1381 part of an unorganized yet inflammatory propaganda which finally drove peasant, labourer and ordinary working man to the capture and sack of London itself. For the few who could read – and who could use their knowledge in order to recite to others – there was in fact an actual literature of revolt. There still exist forty-five contemporary manuscripts of *Piers Plowman*, and, even though Langland himself wrote from the point of view of a conservative chantry priest, there was more than enough castigation of Idle Rich and Grasping Greedy in his poem to give ample ammunition to agitators who would not hesitate to quote the most apt passages out of their contexts.

But there was an even more powerful and more far-reaching agency which worked up to the climax of 1381 – the propaganda of the parson. Every manor in the England of the Peasants' Revolt had its priest – and the priests were for the most part as discontented as their congregations. The great wealth of the Church was in the abbeys, cathedrals and monasteries, and there was very little to spare for the parish priest, who was frequently merely a poor curate to some rich monastery to which the rector-ship had been appropriated. When Chaucer's Poor Parson preached, he spoke as a man of the people summoning God's wrath, as portrayed in the dooms painted on the church wall,[1] against those who oppressed the people and misused their wealth. The itinerant friars, who spoke so well and who frequently stole the congregations of the parson by their eloquence in the churchyard, were just as condemnatory of an aristocracy out of touch with the needs and aspirations of those on whose labour they were so dependent. If all parsons were not as admirable as Chaucer's, and, like Wyclif's, if they 'haunted taverns out of all measure, and stirred lewd men to drunkenness, idleness, and cursed swearing, and chiding and fighting', it is not necessary to look far to find instigators of revolt – the priest in the taproom, as the history of Ireland can illustrate, is perhaps more effective than the priest in the pulpit. It is not surprising that, when the outbreak came, many priests were with the rebels, and one of them – John Ball – became a leader, one of whose famous sermons has come down to us in the chronicles of both Froissart and Walsingham. To him is usually attributed the couplet:

> '*When Adam delf and Eve span*
> *Who was thaune a gentilman?*'

However, a modern scholar[2] has shown that Ball was probably merely quoting a catchphrase in common circulation. That Wyclif's Poor Preachers and the Lollards were also instigators of revolt has never been proved, though in later years ecclesiastical orthodox chroniclers were only too ready to blame them. Wyclif himself could not have approved of civil rebellion, however much he disapproved of upper class immorality – whether lay or clerical. On the other hand, it is likely that the priest who eventually became a Lollard might well have begun as one of those poor parsons who certainly marched with the men of Essex and Kent in 1381.

The growing anti-clericalism of the laity and the bitter criticisms of Wyclif were presented with telling justification by the visit of Cardinal Pileo di Prata to England just before the Revolt broke out. He came to negotiate a marriage between Richard and the Emperor's sister, and the orthodox Walsingham is as outspoken as the more heterodox Adam of Usk in complaints against the profits the Cardinal made during his visit from the sale of papal indulgences and chaplaincies. Silver was not good enough for him, he demanded gold; and Walsingham alleges with wrathful exaggeration that Pileo took out of England more money than was ever raised by tax or tallage.[1] Luther was to be preceded by Texel, and it is a legitimate guess that the indignation against Pileo, common amongst the orthodox, was even more exaggerated amongst the more radical.

Although to all history books the revolt of 1381 is known as the Peasants' Revolt the name is inaccurate. A better name would be the 'People's Revolt', because it was a revolt of those common folk of 1381 who had no say whatsoever in the government of their country, and it was therefore as much an artisans' as a peasants' revolt.[2] The cities of England in the fourteenth century were flourishing communities. They were not large by twentieth-century standards – ranging from such cities as Norwich with about 5,000 inhabitants to London with its 40,000 – but they were thriving, thanks chiefly to the great wool trade with the Low Countries. The city authorities were the heads of the various merchant guilds, who shared power in accordance with local jealousies, and who had developed their guilds into wealthy monopolies enforcing high standards, making the most of a 'just price', and refusing any share of power to the artisans, craftsmen and labourers who took their wages. The jealousies of the powerful merchants were soon to unite with the grievances of suppressed wage earners, and hand over even the city of London to the invading peasants. The cities and towns added yet another class to the side of the rebels.

In most towns, too, there were men-at-arms returned from the French wars, broken and frequently embittered men. The promises of good pay had not been fulfilled, the prospects of rich booty had faded, and, while men-at-arms slew and were slain, knights in armour preferred a Chivalry which, in the taking and ransoming of wealthy prisoners, had found a profitable alternative to mortal combat. The common soldier in all ages has had a share of glory while he fights, but, when discharged, his one privilege of grumbling has frequently been fanned into the flame of revolt, his knowledge of arms proving a useful ally to the civilians, and his aptitude for looting often transforming an orderly protest into a raging mob. The ex-soldiers of 1381 had not even had the laurels of victory in compensation. They had suffered from the incompetence of the barons, and, in the hour of revolt, many of them gladly joined peasants and artisans who, even if untrained in the finer arts of war, at least knew how to draw a bow, and were now to draw it to some purpose.

When the rebels began to march, therefore, their ranks included not merely villeins of every degree from near serf to near freeman, but poor priests, discontented artisans, idle soldiery, yeomen and free farm labourers, wage earners and craftsmen, and every man with a grievance against those in power, the law of the land, the custom of the manor, the encroachments of sheep-farming lords, the privileges of foreign merchants and the craft secrets of foreign workers. They were marching for the most part for freedom[1] – for a new kind of social freedom, and not for that 'liberty' which in Magna Carta meant special privilege. They were not traitors in the service of a dynastic plot – their banners were the banners of St George, their oath was to King Richard; their special care was the guarding of the coasts, and their special hatred was against ministers (who had betrayed not only the Commons but the King) and foreigners in Church and trade who were robbing the country.

It has been well said that in 1381 'England was full of inflammable material and at the mercy of a spark' [2] – the necessary spark was the poll-tax of 1380. A tax which demanded a shilling from every adult in the land, whether he were duke or villein, alderman or apprentice, maid-of-honour or dairy-maid, joined a thousand discontented grievances in one united crescendo of protest from those to whom a shilling was the equivalent of a month's wages. But actual revolt did not come immediately, and when it did come it was not a national rising; it was a sporadic outbreak with little cohesion save in the neighbouring counties of Essex and Kent. Apart from the evidence of the Statute already quoted, the chroniclers do make mention of a 'Great Society' [3] and the stirrings of revolt some years before 1381, but this is only evidence of that mass of discontent, that 'revolutionary situation', which demanded a much more sophisticated leadership and planning than could be supplied by the oppressed classes of the day if it were to achieve any lasting success. Just as it is absurd to expect a mediaeval baron to have had a social conscience, it is equally absurd to expect a mediaeval villein to have displayed the technique of a Cromwell, a Danton or a Lenin. The men of Essex and Kent made attempts to create a national movement; but they were over-handicapped by the comparative isolation of life at that time, their lack of any efficient organizing machinery, and their total ignorance of affairs of state.

In the spring of 1381 it was clear that the third and most hated poll-tax was likely to be a failure. There had been widespread attempts at resistance to the tax, and there were many, even among the 'Lords and Commons', who, in the words of the best chronicler of the Revolt, considered that the tax was levied unfairly on the poor and with 'great profit and advantage to the collectors who defrauded King and Commons'.[1] Swindling on the part of the collectors had combined with evasion and fraud on the part of the tax-payers to produce lists of adults totalling far less than the lists of 1377, and the Exchequer determined to correct the assessments. Commissions of revision were sent into sixteen counties, and it is significant that these were the counties of the Revolt, and that the author of the revision scheme – the sergeant John Legge – was one of the Revolt's early victims. No doubt these Commissions were justifiable on grounds of efficiency – but to the new tax-payers they appeared to be instruments of a tyranny, which, having received the tax once, was attempting to reimpose it, and so cover up its own miscalculations and dishonesty. The authorities knew that the countryside was in an explosive mood, they must have been aware of their own unpopularity, they could not divert grumbling at home affairs by reference to victories abroad, and we have Froissart's word that 'the rebellion was well known to the King's court or any of the people began to stir',[2] yet those in power persisted in adding exasperation to exaction, regardless of the consequences. They had not only miscalculated their tax, they had miscalculated the temper of the common folk of England.

Armed rebellion actually began at the end of May in Essex. A certain Thomas Brampton had been appointed a commissioner to collect the poll-tax in Essex on revised assessments, and at Brentwood he summoned the inhabitants of three Thames-side villages to his judgment. They came, and showed him by their tallies that they had already paid the tax. Brampton refused to recognize these tallies as full quittance on the ground of fraudulent assessment, and he insisted on a revision. He was rudely told that he would receive nothing more, and, as the proceedings began to develop into tumult, he ordered his guard of two men-at-arms to make arrests. The crowd of villein labourers and fisherfolk rose in fury and chased Brampton and his men out of the town. The common folk of the otherwise unheard of Essex villages of Fobbing, Corringham and Stanford-le-Hope on that day of May 1381 wrote these names on a very significant page of English history.

Brampton rode hard for London to report rebellion, the rebels took to the comparative safety of the 'greenwood', and it is at this stage that we find traces of an attempt at a concerted and organized revolt. Some of the picturesque slogans, watchwords and signal catchphrases have come down to us in the chronicles.[1] There is the John Schep, a priest of Colchester, who 'greeteth well John Nameless and John the Miller and John Carter and biddeth them beware of guile in borough, and stand together in God's name and biddeth Piers Plowman go to his work and chastise Hob the Robber'; there is the Jack Miller who urges that 'with right and with might, with skill and with will, let might help right and skill go before will and right before might, then goeth our milne aright'; there is the Jack Trueman who 'doth you to understand that falseness and guile have reigned too long'; and the cryptic message from John Ball, who 'greeteth you well all and doth you to understand that he hath rungen your bell'. Such a simple and primitive code of revolt sped along the trackways and the muddy roads of that mediaeval world – handed on from tapster to wayfarer, palmer to priest, villein to villein – and found ready interpreters in every outlaw of the forest. The tinder, littered over that part of England which lay south-east of a line drawn from Scarborough through Chester and down to Plymouth, was never gathered into one colossal blaze but it was fired now here now there; it burst into a roar of flame in the capital, and it continued to splutter in the provinces when the central flames had died down.

Brampton's news produced an immediate response from the authorities. However helpless and feeble they seem later, their first reactions were determined and speedy. They despatched Robert Belknap, a Chief Justice, into Essex armed with a commission of 'trailbaston' – the word means 'cudgel carrier' and represented the mediaeval equivalent of the modern Riot Act – to restore order. But the villagers of Thames-side had roused the countryside. They drove back the Chief Justice as they had driven back Brampton, and now they drew first blood. His jurors were beheaded summarily, and three of Brampton's clerks were given the same short shrift; their heads on pikes were the first grisly standards of revolt. But, even at this early stage, it is clear that here was no French 'Jacquerie'.[1] This was not the revolt of impoverished serfs murdering, violating, robbing, and mutilating every member, dependent and scion of a master class. The men of Essex were protesting against what they considered an illegal tax in the only way which was open to them, and they were pushed to such extreme measures by an accumulation of social grievances which could find no other outlet. In Essex, the rebels included not only villeins but also artisans and quite a number of well-to-do landholders – the movement was respectable enough to win the immediate support of some of the aldermen of London itself. The motives of the landholders are obscure, the motives of the aldermen are more plainly motives of civic jealousy and self interest, the motives of the villeins and artisans were clear even to contemporaries – they were not rebels to King Richard, they were attempting to save him from corrupt administrators, and, in the words of so conservative a critic as Walsingham, they had risen 'for freedom, to be made equal to their Lords, and never again to be held in servitude to any man'.[2]

It is not surprising that the revolt in Essex was closely synchronized with the revolt in Kent. To the Essex fisherfolk, who were the first to resort to arms, the coast of Kent was more easily reached than London or Norwich – the estuary was less difficult and dangerous than the road. By June 2nd, the men of Kent began to assemble at Erith. They were for the most part men who had already won their freedom, they were therefore very jealous of it, and exasperated like the rest of the Commons of England at an unfair poll-tax now apparently to be re-imposed. Discontent broke into open revolt at Gravesend. There the representatives of the King's tutor – Sir Simon Burley – were reclaiming an escaped villein they had detected, and, when the people went to the villein's aid with an offer to buy his freedom, they were met with the impossible price of £300. The villein was recaptured by Burley's men and flung into Rochester Castle. The Kentish revolt began.

The chronicler tells us nothing at this stage of 'Wat Tyler'. In fact, he is at pains to make it clear that the Kentish revolt had 'neither head nor chieftain'[3] – it was a mass rising with a certain

58

sense of responsibility which seems lacking in the less advanced shires. The rebels came to Dartford to make plans, and their first act was to ordain that no man was wanted who lived within twelve leagues of the sea – *their* duty was to guard that vital coast against the King's enemies, and, the chronicler emphasizes, 'they did not wish to have any King other than King Richard'.

Meanwhile, exactly as in Essex, opposition to the tax had been met by a commission of trailbaston, and John Legge, and one of the King's justices, had been despatched into Kent. They hoped to hold their Assize in Canterbury, but its citizens were already in revolt and refused them entry.

Within a week, the men of Kent won startling victories. On June 6th they captured Rochester Castle, freed Burley's villein, and took the governor, Sir John Newton, as hostage. On June 7th Maidstone was in their hands, and John Ball released from its gaol. On June 10th they were welcomed into Canterbury by the citizens who had rejected the King's Justice, broke into the cathedral (interrupting the mass in their search for Archbishop Sudbury, who as Chancellor carried most of the odium of the poll-tax) and forced the mayor to take their oath of loyalty 'to King Richard and the loyal Commons of England'. Three unnamed 'traitors' were handed over to the rebels' rough justice and immediately executed, fifty citizens were taken hostage, and arrangements were made for civic government while the main body of the Kentish men marched towards London.

At this stage, the names of leaders appear in the chronicles; but the most earnest research has not discovered very much about their personalities or previous history, and there are even grave doubts about some of their names. The Kentish rising threw up two famous men. First, priest John Ball, and, second, Wat Tyler of Maidstone. Ball had been a priest in York and perhaps also in Colchester. He had been preaching on the village greens, and outside the village churches, for over twenty years before the Revolt, and his attacks on all established clergy and their property had earned him the love of the common folk,[1] the condemnation of several archbishops, and finally, at the hands of the mildest and most ill-fated of them, an ecclesiastical prison. He proposed to have only one archbishop – himself; to abolish all lords, archbishops, bishops, abbots and priors and to confiscate their property for the common weal. A John Ball sermon lives again in the pages of

Froissart, and its forthright egalitarianism has come echoing down the ages, as appealing to the serfs of industry as it undoubtedly was to the serfs of feudalism. 'He was regarded as a prophet by the Commons' says one chronicler; and it seems that the Commons were not far wrong.[1] The figure of Tyler is equally real; but whether he was a tiler of Kent or of Essex, whether he was a returned and discontented soldier or a rapscallion cadet of the Kentish family of Culpepper, whether he was a convicted robber or an outraged father is all more than doubtful. What is certain is that, if Ball was the inspiration of the Kentish men, Tyler was their military leader and, at the crisis of the revolt in London, their spokesman and martyr. Even the prejudiced chronicler Walsingham grants Tyler distinguished gifts, though he laments that they were not put to better use, and he also bears grudging witness to the preaching abilities of Ball. The leader of the Essex revolt seems to have been one Jack Strawe – but nothing is known for certain about him and the name itself is in fruitless dispute.[2]

There was, however, enough generalship of a primitive kind to provide a concerted plan at least for the Kent and Essex revolts – it was wisely decided to concentrate on an attack on the capital. The rebels' march on London was both a sound stroke of strategy, and, on the Kentish side, a surprising feat of enthusiasm and endurance – they covered 70 miles in two days, and, on June 12th, from their camp on Blackheath they could look down on London and across the estuary, to burning manors which were signal beacons from the men of Essex. The villeins and common folk of England had risen against a power that had been unquestioned for three hundred years, yet not a blow had been struck against their revolt, and within ten days the capital was at their mercy. Every road out of London was commanded by their piquets; within its walls were the Archbishop-Chancellor, the Treasurer of England, and the other authorities responsible for the hated poll-tax; and there too, by the leave of the men of Kent,[3] was the Queen Mother – the Fair Maid of Kent – and King Richard who was to right all their wrongs. One hated member of the aristocracy was, fortunately for himself, missing – John of Gaunt was in Scotland.

The ease with which undisciplined peasants and artisans had reached such a commanding position, and the failure of those in authority to take any sufficient action to withstand them, amazed contemporary observers, and has puzzled subsequent historians. Walsingham complains bitterly that the ruling classes were asleep to the point of 'snoring',[1] and their inaction was 'great marvel' even to their own historian Froissart. But it is difficult to see what action could have been taken. The only army in existence when the Revolt began was at Plymouth ready to embark for Portugal, where, under the Earl of Cambridge, it was to play its undistinguished part in that Spanish war which was only another phase of the hereditary war against France. It is typical of the lack of responsible national feeling amongst the aristocracy that, so Froissart tells us,[2] this army hastened to put to sea, even against an unfavourable wind, in case it were prevented by a rising of the populace – the ransom-hunting across the Channel was more important than the safety of the kingdom. There was no force for police purposes, the retainers of the Lords were either with the Earl of Cambridge or scattered in hundreds of manors up and down the land, and the greatest Lord of all – John of Gaunt – was an ambassador in Scotland. There was a body of men-at-arms garrisoning the Tower, and the fierce and brutal soldier of fortune Sir Robert Knolles had his own men guarding him at his mansion in the city. There was nothing else for the royal family and their assembled nobles to do but to trust in the strength of the Tower's fortifications, the citizen guard at London Bridge, and the gates of London. Meanwhile, they could calculate that Tyler and Strawe would find the problem of feeding their men impossible – and perhaps revolt would be dissolved by hunger. On their side, the rebels must have been almost equally anxious. Their success so far had been almost too easy, and their leaders must have realized that, if the well-stocked larders of the capital were not at their disposal within twenty-four hours, their adventure was at an end. They needed the city first, and the Tower second: and both must have seemed impregnable. But the men of Essex and Kent had thousands of allies in the poor and suppressed population within the city walls; there were even aldermen who shared their grievances against misgovernment, there were others who were willing to risk a massacre to achieve their own ends in civic politics, and there must have been many nervous burghers who realized that the so-called 'mob' of rebels contained men who knew something of the practice of mediaeval warfare. Sympathy, treachery and fear were to hand over the richest city in England to the mercy of half-armed rebels without a blow struck in its defence.

The rendezvous at Blackheath on the evening of Wednesday, June 12th, 1381 was not merely a plan of concentration by the Kentish rebels. There is evidence that when the march from Essex began, and as soon as Kent was in an uproar, the King (who was at Windsor) exchanged messages with Tyler, promising a meeting near London;[1] and, as the rebels approached Blackheath, the young Richard and many of his court were being escorted to the safety of the Tower by the Mayor of London prior to the promised conference with Tyler. At the camp on Blackheath two large banners of St George and an array of pennants proclaimed the loyalty of the rebels to the King, and the challenge and counter-sign of safety were 'With whom holdes yow?' 'Wyth Kynge Richarde and wyth the trew communes'.[2] Some of the chronicles have handed down a report of a sermon or harangue which John Ball is supposed to have delivered to the assembled crowds on this memorable occasion. Whether or not it was actually spoken at that moment matters little. Its importance is that it was the first unequivocal announcement in English of the creed of social revolt as derived from the miseries of submerged classes, and as inspired by the direct application of simple Christian principles to the structure of society. Here is Froissart's version which he quotes as typical of 'this foolish priest's' wayside pulpit: –

'Ah, ye good people, the matters goeth not well to pass in England, nor shall not do till everything be common, and that there be no villeins nor gentlemen, but that we may be all united together, and that the Lords be no greater masters than we be. What have we deserved, or why should we be kept thus in servage? We be all come from one father and one mother, Adam and Eve; whereby can they say or shew that they be greater Lords than we be, saving by that they cause us to win and labour for that they dispend? They are clothed in velvet and camlet furred with grise, and we be vestured with poor cloth: they have their wines, spices, and good bread, and we have the rye bran and the straw and drink water: they dwell in fair houses, and we have the pain and travail, rain and wind in the fields; and by that that cometh of our labours they keep and maintain their estates: we be called their bondmen, and without we do readily them service, we be beaten; and we have no sovereign to whom we may complain, nor that will hear us nor do us right. Let us go to the King, he is young, and shew him what servage we be in, and shew him how we will have it otherwise, or else we will provide us of some remedy; and if we go together, all manner of people that be now in any bondage will follow us to the intent to be made free; and when the King seeth us, we shall have some remedy, either by fairness or otherwise.' [1]

Here was the simple gospel of social revolt, a sublime ignorance of any 'remedy' save the good will of a young and therefore presumably innocent King, and the dark threat of providing 'some remedy' themselves. On that Wednesday night the camp at Blackheath was expectant, orderly and inspired.

On the following morning, the rebels' hostage – Sir John Newton – was sent to the Tower to invite the King to meet the rebels, and, as surety, his family was detained at Blackheath. He was an officer of the royal household and well known at court. He faithfully translated Tyler's invitation, excusing himself for what he did by force, and assured Richard of his safety. He was sent back to Blackheath with a favourable reply. Richard's barge, with an escort of four smaller barges, was rowed down from the Tower to a spot near the shore between Rotherhithe and Greenwich where the conference was to be held. Accompanying the King were his chief nobles, Archbishop Sudbury and Treasurer Hales. The uproar of the rebels when they saw the barges approaching was sufficiently terrifying to lend weight to those who counselled Richard to prudence. His courtiers prevented him from landing; and the first direct conference between an English King and his people was a difficult bandying of fair promises and stern demands, while the monarch and his court were slowly rowed up and down the Thames out of bowshot from the people on the bank. The rebels demanded the heads of Sudbury, Hales, Sir John Fordame, Clerk of the Privy Seal, Robert Belknap, the Chief Justice, Ranulf Ferrers, Robert Plesington, Chief Baron of the Exchequer, John Legge and Thomas Brampton. Some of the denounced were sitting listening in the barges – no wonder the Earl of Salisbury persuaded the King to retreat. The river-side conference was brought to a summary end, and Richard and his nobles were rowed back to the Tower. The effect on the rebels was explosive – the actual attack on London began forthwith. The suburbs on the south bank of the river were quickly overrun as far west as Lambeth Palace which was soon wrecked and pillaged. The prisons of the Marshalsea and the King's Bench were in Southwark, directly facing the only bridge across the Thames to the city proper. They were both raided and set on fire, and their desperate prisoners were released to add an element of hooliganism to a rebellion which so far had maintained some sense of order and discipline.

The King, his mother and the court were safe but surrounded in the Tower; London was cut off from all communication with the rest of England; but the fortified drawbridge of London Bridge was still up – and the rebels were beginning to be hungry. If the King's advisers had calculated that the drawbridge would save them, they had gravely miscalculated the situation within the city. The Mayor – Walworth – was staunchly for the court and was with Richard in the Tower; but on the side of the rebels there were three aldermen and thousands of the citizens who had twice ejected so great a Lord as John of Gaunt, and who had their own special grievances both against their city masters and the interloping foreign merchants who were in the protection of the King. It is said that, even before Walworth had ordered the drawbridge to be raised, John Horne, the alderman of the fishmongers, had admitted some of his rebel friends within the walls, and that one Thomas Faringdon and certain of the rebel leaders had spent the previous evening drawing up proscription lists. And, fortunately for the rebels, the 'Alderman of Bridge' – Walter Sybyle – was their friend. Faced with overwhelming numbers attacking from the north and threatening over an easily crossed river from the south, now conscious of the growing rebellion of his own citizenry whom he had no force of arms to control, Mayor Walworth had no other alternative than to acquiesce in Sybyle's surrender of the bridge – all he could do was to pretend that he sanctioned the admittance of the rebels on the condition that they remained of good behaviour. At the same time as the hungry and now angry rebels from Blackheath were streaming across London Bridge, another alderman – William Tonge – opened the Aldgate, and the men of Essex rushed through the city to join the men of Kent on St Katherine's Hill at the gates of the Tower. London was at the mercy of what was now an ill-disciplined, angry and crudely armed mob; the King, his ministers and the flower of his court were besieged in the Tower; the more populated half of England had already joined in the Revolt; the only royal army was in Portugal; many of the free Lords were either in Scotland or on their way to Spain; abroad were French enemies who might make the most of such an opportunity and Flemish citizenry who were more likely to send help to the rebels. There has been no crisis of greater magnitude in English domestic history.

The precise sequence of the events of Thursday, June 13th, 1381 will probably always be open to vain dispute, and the confusion of the evidence reflects the confusion of the day itself. The broad facts however are gruesomely clear. It was a day of arson, pillage and massacre. The prison populations of the Fleet, the Westminster and the Newgate gaols were added to the rebel ranks; to the west, the mansion of John of Gaunt at the Savoy, which outrivalled the royal palace of Westminster in splendour and riches, was razed to the ground with the aid of its own store of gunpowder, and all its contents burnt to ashes; to the north, the manor house of the Treasurer at Highbury made another bonfire to be followed speedily by the destruction of his priory at Clerkenwell; just outside the Ludgate, the Inns of the hated lawyers in the Temple were ransacked and every deed and document committed to the flames of its 'great chimney'; and, within the city proper, men settled old quarrels and revenged old grievances at the point of the sword, haled their enemies to the improvised executioner's block in Cheapside, and began a slaughter of Flemings and Lombards which was so brutal that it is the only event of the whole dramatic episode to force its way into the benign pages of Chaucer.[1] Thousands of the invaders could never have seen a city before – and mediaeval London, whose bridge could boast a double row of houses and shops, whose cathedral spire towered 500 feet above the timbered mansions and warehouses of rich burgesses, and whose inns and hospitality with luxuries beyond the rebels' wildest dreams were now open to them, would have turned the heads of seasoned regular troops: its effect on the naive rebels must have been overwhelming. The promise of good behaviour which was well kept at the Savoy – a villein caught pilfering was hurled with his booty into the flames – quickly degenerated into unbridled license under the influence of the London prentices, the released malefactors, and that underworld of poverty-stricken and desperate men who are always the dregs of every great city. Yet there are traces of control even amid the accumulated evidence of riot. The bonfires had a purpose, and, apart from the massacre of foreigners, there was no general massacre of rich burghers. Throughout the day and night, at the camp on St Katherine's Hill, a wary guard kept watch on the royal and noble prisoners in the Tower, and sent messengers far and wide rousing or encouraging revolt in the provinces. The rebels were not burning London – their attacks were in three directions; against John of Gaunt or anyone connected with him, against the record offices of manorial law and therefore against most lawyers, and against any authority, senior or junior, directly or indirectly connected with the imposition and enforcements of the third poll-tax. The siege of the Tower covered all three objectives.

On this Thursday night, Richard of Bordeaux at fourteen years of age began to rule. So far, he had merely been allowed to reign; and his rule was to last for two days over a tiny kingdom bounded by the walls of the Tower of London. As he looked out from its turrets he could survey the fires in the city and beyond in the suburbs, and below him were the camp fires of the rebels and the tumult of their besieging army. His council chamber was rich in wisdom and experience, if not in courage. His mother, his uncle the Earl of Buckingham, his half brothers the Earl of Kent and Sir John Holland, the Earl of Warwick, the Admiral Sir Thomas Percy and the Treasurer Sir Robert Hales, Sudbury, Archbishop of Canterbury, and the Earl of Salisbury who had been one of his father's bravest and shrewdest lieutenants – here were wisdom and experience in plenty; and, if older hearts lacked enterprise in a crisis, Richard could expect to depend on the youth of his cousin the Earl of Derby (son to absent John of Gaunt), his friend the young son of the Earl of Oxford, and the support of Mayor Walworth and some of his chief citizens, who were all in favour of bold courses. But counsel was divided. A sally from the fortress that night, to link up with Sir Robert Knolles and his men-at-arms in the City and attack the rebels when they were exhausted or drunk, was mooted but rejected, chiefly on the advice of

Salisbury. He considered the risk too great – weighing the strength of those in the Tower against the disadvantages of street fighting, and the uncertain loyalty of the mass of the London citizens. There were contemporary critics, and there have been critics who have judged long after the event, who maintained that Salisbury's advice was wrong. They have measured the skill of generalship and the discipline of experienced soldiers against a mob without proper weapons or armour and without professional leadership, and wondered why Salisbury hesitated. They have ignored the fact that in the narrow alleys of mediaeval London men-at-arms would have needed to be armed against attacks from above, from behind and from every side, that the normal tactics of military manœuvre would have been impossible, that they would have been outnumbered a hundred to one, and, above all, that failure might have meant the massacre of the King and the flower of his Chivalry. Sortie was rightly abandoned for plot. It was agreed that something had to be done if the Tower was not to be starved into ignominious submission, and if Sudbury and Hales were to be given a chance of escape. And there was only one person with whom the rebels would treat – the person of the young King himself. It was decided that Richard, with a sufficient retinue, should meet the rebels the next morning at some open place far enough from the Tower to draw off the besiegers, so that, in their absence, Sudbury and Hales might escape by river. There seems to have been some protracted negotiation with the camp on St Katherine's Hill before it was agreed that, on Friday morning, a conference should be held at Mile End – in those days a favourite place for the open-air sports of the citizenry. At this conference, Richard was to agree to all the rebels' demands so that they would rapidly disperse, and at a later date his consent could be invalidated and his promises annulled on the ground that they had been obtained by force. It was a cynical plan. Its success depended on the courage of a boy king who would take his life in his hands and face the mob in the hope that he was saving the lives of his mother, his relatives, his friends and his counsellors, and, by so doing, rescue his throne, and society as he knew it, from what seemed certain disaster. The morality of the plan need not be called in question – no knight needed to have qualms about broken promises to villeins and artisans when the whole Order of Knighthood was in jeopardy. The significant factor in this tragic situation was that all depended on the bravery of Richard – and that Richard's courage stood up to everything that was asked of it. There is a touching phrase in the chronicle which describes Richard climbing to the top of a turret after the conference: he seemed *'pensive et trist'* [1] as he looked over the wild scenes about him and pondered the vicissitudes of the morrow.

Early on Friday morning, the royal party in the Tower was waiting to see if the rebels would withdraw to Mile End. A large body could be seen moving off, but those who remained renewed their wild outcries for the heads of Sudbury, Hales and the lesser refugees. It seemed that the plot might even now miscarry. Richard sent a message to order the remaining rebels to go immediately to Mile End as he himself was about to set out for the conference as he had promised; and he ordered Sudbury and the rest to attempt an escape from the Water Gate. The naive ruse failed: a woman spotted the fugitives and warned the rebel watch. There was just a chance that, when the King and his chief nobles finally left the Tower, a second attempt at escape might be more successful – it was a faint hope and an only hope. Sudbury and Hales at least were not too optimistic, they decided to prepare themselves for what seemed their inevitable end.

Richard is known to every English schoolchild for his bravery before Wat Tyler at Smithfield: his conduct on the day before that famous episode is worthy of equal fame. He rode out of the Tower, taking with him those of his nobles and friends who had any chance of survival when face to face with the rebels, and he left behind him his mother, Sudbury, Hales and the young Henry of Derby. A mere handful of England's Chivalry, led by a mere boy, faced the mercy of thousands of desperate rebels. The plot still held – the granting of every rebel demand might still send enough of the besiegers home to enable the refugees in the Tower to escape. As soon as the royal party was outside the walls, Richard's half brothers, the Earl of Kent and Sir John Holland, either deserted or were despatched to raise help from further afield, but we are told that Sir Aubrey de Vere, the uncle of Richard's greatest friend, was his sword-bearer at the post of greatest danger. At Mile End's 'pleasant fields' a huge crowd was waiting. Their spokesman [2] stepped forward to present the King with a petition that villeinage should be abolished, that all feudal dues and services should be commuted for a rent of 4d. per acre, and that a general amnesty and pardon should be declared. The readiness with which the King and his nobles agreed to the whole of this revolutionary programme is clear evidence that they had no intention of keeping to it once they had weathered the storm. Thirty clerks were employed to produce documents of pardon and freedom duly sealed for every village, manor and shire – a formidable task which was bound to delay the departure of many of the more suspicious rebels. In addition, the representatives of the shires – and Froissart mentions Kent, Essex, Sussex, Bedford, Cambridge, Stafford and Norfolk – were presented with the King's banner as warranty in the meantime. But the concessions failed in their main objective. Some of the rebels began to troop homewards apparently satisfied, but there were many, including all the leaders, who were not so easily tricked. There were probably many of the Londoners who still had old scores to settle within the city walls, and there were certainly many hooligans who would obey no orders which put an end to their spell of license and unopposed pillage.

Either during the Mile End conference or immediately after it, the Tower fell to the rebels. Sudbury and Hales, who had just completed the Mass, were hurried off to immediate execution on Tower Hill, and there too John Legge met his end, together with a friar whose only fault seems to have been that he was in some way connected with John of Gaunt. Even the royal bed was cut up in case it hid fugitives, and the Queen Mother had to submit to some rough handling from the mob – she swooned with fright, and her attendants were permitted to carry her to the comparative safety of the royal office at the Wardrobe in Carter Lane near Baynard Castle. One prize the rebels unaccountably ignored. Young Henry, Earl of Derby, son and heir to John of Gaunt (and future King Henry IV of England), was in the Tower on that fateful Friday. He escaped, thanks to the resourcefulness of one John Ferrour of Southwark – on such slender threads are the puppets of history suspended. Friday ended with another night of revelry and slaughter in London, the King's clerks still busy at their pointless documentation, and the King himself comforting his badly shaken mother at the Wardrobe, and still at the mercy of the rebels.

The conduct of Richard on Friday, June 14th has been

criticized[1] on two grounds: one, that nothing was done to ensure the safety of the Tower; two, that Sudbury and Hales were deliberately sacrificed. The critics have never explained what further precautions for the safety of the Tower Richard could possibly have taken, and they seem to forget that if the ride to Mile End was the act of a traitor to his caste, it was approved in full Council, and they should add to the indictment that Richard was also prepared to sacrifice his mother. This very Lancastrian criticism seems to have overlooked a further charge – perhaps Richard, with uncanny foresight, also intended the murder of Henry of Derby? There is Lancastrian evidence in the Monk of Evesham's contemporary chronicle that Richard rode out from the Tower 'as one in great dread of his life';[2] but that is only evidence that Richard's courage was not foolhardiness – he knew the risk he was taking. Furthermore, the Mile End plot was counselled by so brave a soldier as the Earl of Salisbury in the presence of the Queen Mother, and, judging from the distance of six hundred years and realizing what a forlorn situation was theirs, it is difficult to suggest any wiser course of action. The evidence of the *Anonimalle Chronicle* is that the position of the fugitives in the Tower *was* discussed at Mile End, and that the King agreed that the fugitives should be handed over to justice – but not to the summary mob justice on Tower Hill. We shall probably never know why and how the Tower fell; and the fact that not a blow was struck in its defence is still further evidence that, at this supreme crisis, the aristocracy's only asset was the bravery and popularity of their fourteen-year-old King – they could not even rely on the few troops they had.

The failure of the Mile End conference to save the Tower was compensated by the stimulating effect Richard's sortie had on his counsellors and on all those who, while not daring to oppose such a weight of rebellion at its inception, were anxious to take the first sensible opportunity of crushing it. The 'snoring' aristocrats of England at last seemed to awake from their nightmare, and Saturday saw them ready to dispense with subterfuge, and, now that at last some freedom of movement was possible and that the chief scapegoats no longer impeded them, prepared to hazard all on bolder action. There were many wealthy Londoners still hiding themselves behind strong doors, and able and anxious to fight for their wealth and their privileges. Sir Robert Knolles and his men-at-arms were waiting for a timely signal. Many thousands of the rank and file of the rebels had sated their vengeance, still fondly believed in their charters and royal banners, and were marching back to their villages to enjoy their new paradise. Their leaders must have sensed a feeling of emptiness after so much triumph – they had rooted out and cut to pieces those whom they considered their worst enemies, what more remained to be done? Their King – the King of the Commons – had granted their every wish, and they were still the masters of the capital and the court. It was now that their fundamental weakness was exposed – they had a programme of revenge and a programme of social reform, both of which brought the common folk flocking to their standards, but their only political programme was a crude mixture of nihilism and personal dictatorship, which was certainly beyond the understanding of most of their supporters, and probably far beyond their wishes. To execute traitors and to abolish villeinage with the co-operation of good King Richard was understandable; to establish a realm without nobles or bishops or gentlemen, save the Lord Tyler or the Archbishop Ball and the same good King Richard, was not at that time even a wish-fulfilment dream of the people of England. On this Saturday morning the courtiers in the Tower woke to find they had a leader whose star was in the ascendant, the leaders of the rebels woke to find their forces dwindling and divided, and the rebels themselves woke with that unsatisfactory feeling that perhaps things had gone too far. From the point of view of the established powers and interests it was precisely the right moment to begin an offensive.

The first task of authority was to persuade the rebels to believe in authoritative promises, and go home. The King and his retinue left the Queen Mother at the Wardrobe and rode out by Ludgate and Fleet Street, past the pillaged Inns of Court and the wrecked palace of Gaunt at the Savoy, to the abbey at Westminster. They were met with sad thankfulness by the monks who had just been the horrified witnesses of another Westminster sacrilege. Richard Imworth had been Warden of the Marshalsea prison, and, when it was sacked on the Thursday, he had fled for sanctuary to the abbey. He was hated as a man 'without pity as a torturer',[1] and even the sacred shrine of Edward the Confessor could not save him from the vengeance of the released prisoners. They broke into the sanctuary, tore him from the marble pillar he

71

was clutching and hurried him to the block in Cheapside. As Richard heard the news, he must have realized that he and his friends were still far from safety. They invoked the help of their ancestors, their saints, and their God, as they knelt in confession and prayer, and thence rode out for a final effort to persuade the remaining rebels to go home. The fact that action was preceded by this solemn ceremony is evidence that the King and his court were prepared for desperate measures, and we learn from a later comment that they had taken the precaution of wearing shirts of mail beneath their clothes. Presumably they could have ridden away to find help – they decided on the more dangerous but wiser course of securing London first. A meeting with Wat Tyler and the rebels was arranged to take place at Smithfield, then as now a market just beyond the New Gate of the City. The King and his retinue drew rein with their backs to the church of St Bartholomew the Great, and the rebels were ranged under their King's banners opposite. Mayor Walworth was ordered by Richard to summon Tyler to the presence. Tyler rode over on a small horse, and, far from being abashed, he seems to have conducted himself with a lack of ceremony and a degree of familiarity which probably surprised his followers as much as it offended the royal retinue. 'Brother,' he began, in a greeting which links Tyler with sixteenth-century saints and twentieth-century 'comrades', 'be of good cheer, for you now have 40,000 men at your back, and we shall all be good friends.' But Richard was not to be put off with camaraderie. He asked bluntly why the rebels refused to go home; and Tyler immediately changed his tune, swore loudly that he had no intention of going home until his every demand had been met, and threatened a drastic answer to anything less. When the King asked for his demands, Tyler claimed no law but the law of Winchester,[1] no lordship but the King's, the disestablishment of the Church, only one bishop, confiscation of church property for the good of the people, no serfage, no villeinage, and freedom and equality for all. To this extravagant catalogue Richard calmly replied that he would grant everything he could, saving his own *regaltée*, and that therefore Tyler and his men should go home. The anonymous chronicler makes a point of the fact that the handling of the whole tense situation so far was Richard's alone – without help or counsel from any of his retinue.

At this point, the witness of the chronicles is at variance in

72

detail, but it is agreed on the fact that Tyler seems to have gone out of his way to neglect the ordinary rules of courtesy in the presence of the King – rudely rinsing his mouth because of his thirst is one example. But at last Richard's retinue seemed to have found enough courage to take a hand – one of them denounced Tyler as the greatest thief in Kent. Tyler ordered his men to dispose of his accuser, and the King ordered Mayor Walworth to arrest him for contempt. Tyler resisted, and struck with his dagger at Walworth, who was only saved from death by his shirt of mail. Walworth drew his sword and wounded Tyler, and one of the household servants rushed to his aid to finish the deed. The wounded Tyler spurred his horse away, and shouted to his men for help. They were probably unable to see clearly what was happening in the scuffle, and hesitated – some thought they were making Tyler a knight – but when Tyler's horse dragged him half-dead across the market place they realized that their leader was being murdered. It was then that Richard – a boy of fourteen – wrote his name in every romantic book of hero-worship: as the thousands of rebels drew their bows he spurred across and faced them alone. 'Let me be your leader,' he shouted; and bows were lowered in admiration for the bravery of a youth. He rode back to his retinue, and it was agreed that he should lead the rebels out into the country, while his friends roused all the aid they could. The impulse of a moment was capped by the sustained courage which enabled Richard to ride alone at the head of the mob, and guide them to the meadows known as Clerkenwell Fields.

As soon as the rebels had followed their King out of the market place, Mayor Walworth rode post-haste through the city summoning all the loyal ward watches (who had been prevented by the scale of the rioting from any other action than keeping safe indoors) to assemble with all speed to save Richard. Aldermen Sybyle and Horne, who had opened London to the rebels, failed in a desperate attempt to persuade the citizens that the King was already dead, and Sir Robert Knolles and his men-at-arms at last led the loyal citizenry to the rescue. Tyler's rebels were surrounded.[1]

Meanwhile Walworth rode back to Smithfield to see what had become of Tyler himself. He found him dying in the ancient hospital for the poor opposite the church of St Bartholomew the Great, but there was just time to drag him from his palette and

73

execute him in the market place outside. His head was mounted on a lance, and Walworth rode off with it to Clerkenwell. When the rebels saw that Tyler was actually dead, and that they were surrounded, parleying changed to abject surrender. Some of the King's retinue seemed anxious to display their new found courage by indulging in a general massacre, but the wiser influences of the old Salisbury and the young King prevailed. The rebels were pardoned and dismissed to their homes – the men of Kent being safeguarded across London to the bridge by two knights specially detached for this service. And, as the rebels dispersed, Tyler's head was sent in grim warning to replace Archbishop Sudbury's head above London's drawbridge on the Thames. Richard and his victorious retinue rode gladly back to the city, and there is a homely touch in the chronicler's description of the immediate knighting of Walworth and three other loyal London citizens. Richard commanded the Mayor to don a bascinet before he received the accolade, and Walworth pleaded that as a mere tradesman he had no claim to the noble Order of Knighthood. The King insisted, and then, taking a sword in both hands, he knighted him *'fortement et od bone volunté'* with the excusable exuberance of a youth who knew that he himself had every cause for celebration.[1] The Queen Mother, who must have been terrified by the lying rumours of Sybyle and Horne, was now ready to welcome her son at the Wardrobe. It was a moment as memorable as when she had welcomed her husband as the victor of Poitiers. The Black Prince had brought her a captive King as token of chivalrous victory, her son brought her deliverance from hitherto unimaginable horrors, and the triumph of society as she knew it over dark forces normally beneath her notice.

The caution of Salisbury's advice throughout the three days of crisis in London was in large measure justified by the situation in the shires outside – London had to be recaptured first before the various risings elsewhere could be dealt with safely. News travelled slowly,[2] and, although the Revolt was hopeless once the capital had been regained for authority, the rebellion in the country flickered on through July and August, was rekindled in the south in September, and it was not until November that it finally petered out. All over the country we find the same temporary paralysis of the gentry and their same powerlessness so long as the rebels held together; but the causes of the several outbreaks varied according to local grievances. From Scarborough and Chester in the north down to Somerset, Devon and Cornwall in the south-west, the 'Great Society' had enough organization to stimulate revolt, but it was incapable of co-ordinating either aims or strategy, and at no time did it produce a national leader. It is unnecessary to relate the details of these separated risings. In all of them the gentry were either compelled to change places with the outlaws, and to taste that precarious way of life which in the legends of Robin Hood sounds so attractive but which, judged by the description of the poet Gower in his *Vox Clamantis*, must have been both grim and wretched, or to become hostages or even forced leaders of the rebels. When they rejected both roles, they paid the prompt penalty of execution.

Meanwhile, the forces of law, order and privilege were being mobilized in London. Even as early as June 15th, immediately after Richard's return from Mile End, a writ had been issued against the guilty, who were to be proceeded against according to the ordinary law of the land. On June 18th, the Chancery sent letters to all the royal officials in the rebel shires urging the firm but legal restoration of order. By June 20th, the King and his nobles had assembled the loyal gentry and their retainers in a formidable army on Blackheath, where, a week before, Tyler had ruled the rebels of Kent. From there, the final crushing of the Revolt was planned. Special powers were given to the Earl of Kent and the sheriffs in Kent and Hampshire; the Earl of Buckingham, Robert Tresilian the new Chief Justice, and the King himself were to tour the shires north of the Thames, and, later, the old Earl of Salisbury was to undertake a similar mission in the west country. The rebels of the south and the capital had been tricked into surrender – and the excuse for broken promises was frankly stated in the King's letter revoking his grant of liberties: –

'seeing that perforce we have granted freedom to the bondmen and that they shall be free to buy and sell wheresoever they like and that no acre of land in the said counties, which is held in bondage or servitude, shall be held at more than 4d. and if less shall not in future be raised, now, as we did this perforce and in haste we annul it . . .' [1]

75

The gallant young knight who had heard the common folk of England greet him as *their* King, who had put himself at their head when the rest of the nobility were trembling for their lives and property, who had given them the pledges of his personal standards and his most solemn sealed charters and pardons, was after all the true representative of his caste. It is tempting to the romanticist to imagine that Richard must have had some qualm of conscience; but there is no historical evidence for it. The more likely picture is that for the first time we see Richard revealed as a personality – a young King who kept his wits and his courage in the most desperate crisis of his time, when almost every one of his peers seemed to have lost both. For that unhappy contrast the nobility made Richard pay in full. The dying embers of the Revolt were stamped out without that savagery which had characterized the suppression of the French 'Jacquerie' twenty-three years before – that may have been due to a wholesome fear of the forces which had been roused to rebellion or to a shrewd judgment of the wisdom of mercy – but nevertheless the hero of Mile End and Smithfield was to be displayed to his people as the tool of a Bloody Assize; Richard was to be the scapegoat for the baronage – after so glorious and so brief a freedom, he was again in the power of his elders.

Richard, accompanied by the Earl of Buckingham and Chief Justice Tresilian, marched out of London towards the end of June. The men of Essex had been the first to rebel, and they were the first to suffer punishment. At Billericay, the flourishing of Mile End charters was no protection against Buckingham's men-at-arms. At Waltham, a deputation asking whether their newly won liberties were valid was met by the uncompromising sentence of the King himself: 'Serfs you have been and are; in bondage you shall remain – not as heretofore but incomparably worse'.[1] At Colchester, as the Chronicler says '*sive juste sive ex odio*',[2] nineteen rebels were strung up to a single beam.[3] From Essex, the Royal Assize turned back to Hertfordshire, as the fighting Bishop Despenser had already disposed of the East Anglian rebels. At St Albans, Tresilian staged a terrible miscarriage of justice.[4] The townsfolk and the abbey had reached a reasonable compromise, neither were willing to surrender the ringleaders of the local revolt to Tresilian, and no jury could be found to legalize the indictments. Juries were forced to endorse Tresilian's black-lists, and

76

fifteen leaders, including John Ball, were hung, drawn and quartered, and eighty more imprisoned.

From these savage scenes, Richard proceeded by way of King's Langley and Henley to Reading, where John of Gaunt at last arrived from Scotland to congratulate his nephew on their joint survival. During August, the Assize moved into Kent. Meanwhile, in London, a Commission, which included Mayor Walworth and Sir Robert Knolles, had acted with comparative leniency – only Jack Strawe and a few villeins who had refused to quit the city were executed, and even the aldermen who had betrayed the gates in the 'Hurling Time'[1] were not condemned. The other towns and cities where the rebels had had brief successes were all severely fined,[2] but there was no general proscription. At the end of September, there was a last flicker of revolt in Maidstone where the men of Kent rose once again, but this time – and it is not to be wondered at – they demanded the head of Richard who had deceived them, and heralded John of Gaunt as their king! By November, resistance and punishment were both at an end, and the Parliament which was summoned to Westminster in that month declared for a general amnesty with a comparatively short list of exceptions. It has been calculated[3] that the casualties on both sides probably totalled no more than 700, and we have records of no more than about 110 executions. Such figures, coupled with the silence of Froissart, who had been sickened by the brutal atrocities of a peasants' revolt in his own country, are testimony to the comparative wisdom of the final settlement. The Lords of England had annulled every concession – and once more they were in the saddle; they could ride beaten horses but not dead ones.

Apparently, the Peasants' Revolt of 1381 was a failure. Its immediate success was much too catastrophic to be permanent. Its leaders were now dead and their supporters exactly where they had been before it began. The landed aristocracy with its superstructure of landed nobility was as powerful and secure as ever. Historians of the calibre of Rogers and Stubbs have been proved[4] by subsequent research to have erred when they claimed that the Revolt resulted in the extinction of villeinage. The break-up of the 'manorial system', and the commutation of feudal dues for money rents, the change from serf-labour to wage-labour had begun half a century before, and the progress of this economic development was neither retarded nor very much accelerated in 1381 – it was continued. On the other hand, the experiment of a poll-tax was not tried again for over a century.[1]

But a purely material assessment of results is not enough. The landed aristocracy had received a terrifying warning of new forces at work in the lower strata of society. The traditions of John Ball were soon married to the anti-clericalism of Wyclif's Lollards, and the Peasants' Revolt foreshadowed both the era of religious intolerance and the final triumph of the Reformation. In a sense, the rising was the first emergence of 'the people' in English political life, and it is in this sense that it was undoubtedly premature. Both the people and their leaders were aware of their grievances, but they were undecided and divided about their objectives. Their hopes were centred on the leadership of a King; and it needed the Tudor despotism (both benevolent and bloody), the Cromwellian revolution (both democratic and despotic), and the long era of limited monarchy (both aristocratic and middle class) before, in the Parliaments of the twentieth century, 'the people' have at last emerged. The use and implications of parliamentary sovereignty are not even yet fully worked out, but its first English inspiration and its first martyrs come from those men of southern England who for three fateful days ruled King, Court and capital.

The effect of the Revolt on Richard himself is difficult to judge. There were rumours at the time that he sympathized with the rebels.[2] But this may have been merely judicious propaganda deliberately engineered by the leaders of the Revolt, or it may be an obvious gloss on the fact that the rebels hated their Lords but were anxious to love their King. His courage at Greenwich, at Mile End, at Smithfield and at Clerkenwell Fields had a threefold effect: it showed up a decadent baronage in a very unflattering light, and therefore warned it to watch with special care any attempt of monarchy to supersede oligarchy; it was followed by a most cold-blooded breach of faith, and therefore in the long run taught the people to put their faith in their own representatives; and it revealed to the young King that where his relatives and guardians had failed he 'of his own *regalitée*' might yet succeed.

PART II

Early Manhood, Rebellion and the Seven Quiet Years

IV

EARLY MANHOOD

THE SOCIAL REVOLT of the common folk of England had been an explosion rather than a movement. Although there are traces of fitful outbreaks for some years after 1381,[1] the severity of the special Assizes, and the hopeless position of the villeins and submerged townsmen (once the owners of land, labour and privilege had exerted their authority), rendered further full-scale rebellion impossible. The 'Field of Folk' was for the most part restored compulsorily to its previous quiet; there was no sign as yet that seeds had been sewn to be cultivated by Lollard preachers, fertilized by succeeding grievances, and finally brought to fruition and harvest when Europe awoke to its re-birth. Richard, on the other hand, had for the first time proved himself a King. He had heard the vulgar herd cheer him as their leader, he had seen nobles cower when he himself had dared the bold approach, he had noted the devastations of license and had tasted the thrill of leadership; above all, he had acted of his own free will, and, where counsel had been negative and timorous, his own inspiration had brought success. An aftermath, which had re-chained him to the Lords of the realm and compelled him, in the interests of the contemporary conception of sovereignty and of the class of which he was titular head, to break his word and deny his charters, was a bitter and undeserved sequel. With a populace stamped back into the soil, and an adolescent King forced back into a position which allowed him the pomp but not the substance of power, the history of the next five years is, not surprisingly, the story of youth kicking against the pricks, while the great baronage play for position and struggle for supreme authority. And one baron throughout these five years played a major part – 'time-honour'd Lancaster' held the stage until he departed for his final Peninsular War . . .

When the Peasants' Revolt began, Gaunt had been negotiating

81

a treaty with the Scots.[1] With all the skill of an experienced diplomatist he seems to have kept the dangerous news of the fall of London away from the hereditary enemy north of the Border, and it was not until a further truce had been arranged that the Scots realized that they had been deprived of a magnificent opportunity for a major raid into England which might have upset a dynasty. Their eventual reaction to the news of the Revolt is an illustration of that horizontal stratification of feudal society which was only slowly being split vertically into national blocks. The Scottish Lords offered their armed support to a fellow leader of Chivalry who was only incidentally their national enemy. Gaunt's reply was as nationalist as the offer was feudal – he informed them that any Scot crossing the Border in arms would find fighting enough before he reached York. Gaunt then prepared to return south, but fresh news made him pause – apparently the rebels had demanded his head, Richard had outlawed him, his palace and castles were in ruins, and, near at hand, Henry Percy, Earl of Northumberland, had ordered the gates of Bamborough Castle to be shut against him for usurping Northumberland's own rights to Lordship on the Border. Gaunt turned north, took the Scots at their word, asked for their protection, and was feasted in the abbey of Holyrood for a critical month as the honoured guest of the Scottish nobility. When authentic news at last arrived that the King, far from having outlawed his uncle, was anxious for his help and counsel in settling affairs now that the Revolt was over, Gaunt again set out for England with a noble Scottish retinue. At the Border, an escort from the jealous Northumberland was now under royal orders to greet him. Gaunt dismissed it, and a quarrel began which was the first major baronial quarrel of the reign, typical of many to follow, and symptomatic of the general decadence of a Chivalry which allowed the ideals of crusade and knighthood to degenerate into the selfishness of personal ambition and faction fight.

Henry Percy, Earl of Northumberland, owed much to John of Gaunt, but he had a keen sense of his own rights on the northern marches, and had been only too ready to believe the rumours that the most powerful baron in England was in disgrace – his jealousy had outrun his discretion. Gaunt, on the other hand, had all the force of injured innocence to add to injured pride – he was not the man to ignore an insult which touched his personal honour. At Berkhamsted a Council was held where the disputants exchanged angry charges in the presence of the King. When called to order, Gaunt had the wisdom to obey, but Northumberland lost all control of himself and flung down his gage of battle in the traditional fashion of Chivalry. Richard seems to have acted with a wisdom beyond his years. Northumberland had committed a technical offence against the current code – he had issued his challenge in the royal presence. His arrest was immediately ordered, and on securities being offered by other barons, the dispute was referred to the decision of a full Parliament to be held at Westminster. The preparations for this November session of the Parliament of 1381 were typical of the coming epoch. Percy marched his armed borderers into the city of London, and actually secured his own enrolment as a London citizen in order to win the support of the capital against its old enemy Gaunt. But, if armed force was to be the disguised arbitrament, Northumberland had acted foolishly. Gaunt had far the greater force at his personal command, and twice Northumberland's sense: he gave the City of London to Percy and encamped five hundred Lancastrian men-at-arms at Fulham within easy reach of the royal palace of Westminster. Civil war seemed imminent, and Richard saw himself not for the first or last time powerless in the face of the armed rivalry of his greater baronage; as subsequent events proved, he was not slow to learn a lesson and follow an example.

When Parliament met, its proper business – the governance of the realm – was held up until the baronial dispute was settled. It was clear that Gaunt was wholly in the right – he had held the King's commission when shut out of Bamborough Castle, and he had behaved correctly at Berkhamsted. It even became clear to Northumberland himself that he had struck in the wrong cause at the wrong time, and had affronted not only Gaunt but the King. Civil war was averted by a grovelling apology from Northumberland to both Richard and Gaunt – an apology omitted from the Rolls of Parliament but carefully recorded in Gaunt's private records.[1] Gaunt had survived yet another personal crisis with some distinction.

Parliament then proceeded to approve of the cancellation of the royal charters of manumission given under duress during the 'Hurling Time', to attribute the Revolt itself to general misgovernment, to criticize court extravagance, and to make arrangements for the royal guardianship. Richard was provided with two new guardians – the Earl of Arundel and Sir Michael de la Pole. Arundel represented no one but himself – he was an arrogant and unpleasant specimen of mediaeval baronage at its worst, and the only possible explanation of his appointment is that he was to act as an effective baronial counterweight to de la Pole, who had been a faithful servant to Gaunt whose influence also secured the important post of Chancellor in the person of the Lancastrian Richard le Scrope of Bolton. Sir Michael de la Pole,[1] when appointed guardian to Richard, was fifty years old. He had been made a baron as far back as 1366, and was the son of Sir William de la Pole, a wealthy Hull merchant. He had served with distinction under both the Black Prince and John of Gaunt. In the Good Parliament he had supported Gaunt and the royal prerogative. He had married wealth in the person of a Suffolk heiress, and, when two years later he was appointed Chancellor, he brought to his office an experience and a heritage not merely military and moneyed, but *bourgeois* and efficient, loyal and non-clerical. De la Pole was a Lancastrian, but he was also perhaps the first of that type of great lay public servant[2] on whom the Tudor monarchy was later to rely for devotion, advice and the efficient conduct of affairs. Richard found him as useful and as loyal as Elizabeth I was to find Walsingham.

It is at this period of Richard's reign that various rival 'parties' began to crystallize; but the word 'party' is misleading unless its subsequent connotations are ignored. 'Faction' is a truer description. Still more misleading is the myth (so magnificently built up in the sonorous prose of Bishop Stubbs) that Lancastrian meant 'constitutional'. Under Richard II, 'Lancastrian' meant the personal following of John of Gaunt, which might at certain points be anti-royal and at other points pro-royal, which finally became identified with a change of dynasty in the person of Gaunt's son Henry IV, but which never thought so much out of its period as to imagine itself as an experiment in constitutional or parliamentary government. There were other factions – the Mortimers, the Fitzalans, the Courtenays, the Beauchamps, and soon the faction of the King's uncle Buckingham and the faction of the King himself. And, although appointed in the Lancastrian interest, the semi-permanent officials of the court were also beginning to form a separate group with its own loyalties. Of the purely court officials, Sir Simon Burley[1] still remained the most powerful. His influence had begun when Richard was a child, and it was soon to have a second channel of approach to the King – the first was through the Queen Mother, the widow of his former leader; the second was to be through Anne of Bohemia shortly to come to England as Richard's Queen thanks to Burley's diplomacy. He was ably assisted by a less well-known court servant – Sir Baldwin Raddington,[2] who remained Controller of the Wardrobe throughout every future crisis until his retirement on pension in 1397 – a pension which was even continued by Henry IV. Raddington, like Burley, had served under the Black Prince, and he applied his military experience to the building up of a royal bodyguard. Of lesser officials, the names of John Bacon and Richard Medford have come down to us – their secretaryships in the office of the royal signet (the most personal of the seals) cover the next seven years of the reign, and during the whole of that time they were an important part of a new and significant mechanism for the exercise of royal authority.

But who were Richard's closest friends and boon companions? De la Pole and Burley were his very elderly and respected instructors, but a youth of sixteen needed more companionship than was obtainable from men thrice his years. At this time, he found a friendship in Thomas Mowbray, soon to be made Earl of Nottingham and later Duke of Norfolk. He was only a year older than Richard, but unfortunately he was a great baron in his own right, and, when a few years later he married a daughter of Richard's well-hated guardian the Earl of Arundel, he gradually drifted into alliance with the baronial factions opposed to the court. Richard never forgave him for this desertion, although at one period it suited his purpose to appear to have forgiven him. Richard found a closer and more loyal friend in Robert de Vere, ninth Earl of Oxford, connected by blood and marriage with the throne, and only four years older than himself. Contemporary chroniclers refer to him with all the prejudice of writers who were being read under the succeeding Lancastrian dynasty, and subsequent historians have usually followed their lead and branded him with that tendentious label 'favourite'. There is no evidence that he was brilliant in anything other than his dress and deportment, and there is also no evidence that he was idle and frivolous. He was no upstart like Piers Gaveston, and his later change of marital partner[1] was perhaps a sign of progress in an age when marriage was usually based more on calculation than on romance. Very little is definitely known either for or against him: his reputation has suffered because of the inglorious story of his defeat at the battle of Radcot Bridge, but he has never been given the credit that is due to a friendship which earned the first marquisate in English history, and which was strong enough to lend a pattern to the puzzling final years of his royal friend's reign.

Richard was approaching manhood faced with the over-awing might of the Lancastrian faction, threatened with the lesser rivalries of other baronial groups, but buttressed by the stout weight of Burley and his officials, and comforted with the close companionship of de Vere. To this tense situation a new personality was now added. Richard's marriage was no exception to the mediaeval rule – it was an affair of state. Its only singularity was that it soon became an affair of the heart, and therefore had its subtle influence on the politics of the reign. In addition, it was a link with Bohemia, and therefore had its effect on both the Wyclifite and Hussite movements for religious reform. The negotiators of the marriage were de la Pole and Burley, and, in the complicated plotting of mediaeval diplomacy, they scored a signal success. The traditional foreign policy of Bohemia was alliance with France – her blind King John had met defeat and a brave death fighting the English at Crécy. But France was now Clementist, and Urbanist diplomacy aimed at a European league against the French anti-Christ at Avignon. France too courted the Bohemian alliance, but Urban won it; and the young Princess Anne, sister of King Wenceslas of Bohemia, was to forge another link in the ring round France by a marriage to Richard of England. It was a grave reflection on English sea-power at this period that Anne's journey across the Channel required a safe-conduct from France. On January 14th, 1382, Richard and Anne were married in the chapel of Westminster Palace – Richard was just fifteen and Anne just sixteen years of age.

The comments of the chroniclers on the marriage were bitter.

Walsingham grumbled that, although the daughter of the Duke of Milan had been offered to Richard with a huge dowry, Anne had to be taken without a dowry, and at the cost of some £15,000. Adam of Usk bluntly states that she was 'bought for a great price', and Higden uses the same phrase.[1] The chroniclers were strangers to continental diplomacy, and they reflected the current and intelligible grumbles of the tax-payers. In its ultimate results it was a tragic marriage, but not because it was expensive. Anne brought with her a train of needy Bohemian nobles and ladies, and taunts against foreign spongers were added to taunts against the needless cost of the marriage itself. The hope that Bohemia would join in the war against France was never realized, and, to add to popular disapproval, Anne failed to produce an heir to the throne. On the other hand, the marriage developed into mutual devotion so far as Richard and Anne were concerned. As with Richard's friendship with de Vere, there is little certain evidence to illustrate the effects of this devotion; but by the structure of contemporary life Richard was born to be a lonely King – to choose baronial friends was bound to be dangerous – and he found in Anne a Queen of whom later even the Lancastrian chroniclers spoke well, and after her death he showed the depths of his grief in the passionate order to destroy the palace of Sheen in which she died. A recent historian has dared to argue from the evidence of her effigy in Westminster Abbey that Anne was no beauty. Beauty in women is difficult to judge without prejudice, and by what standards is it measured? In gazing upon the first authentic portrait of an English Queen it should be sufficient to state that, if classical beauty is not there, at least there is the kindliest of expressions, and, perhaps, a confirmation in effigy of the term used of her by those who knew her well – she was 'good' Queen Anne. The most enduring monument to her influence is that, whether she herself was sympathetic or not, it was through the channel of her followers that the pamphleteering of John Wyclif affected the Hussite movement in Bohemia, and that the Roman Church was first assailed by the batteries of Ziska. Meanwhile, Queen Anne was but sixteen, with an excellent education – she could read and write both Latin and German[2] – and an affectionate husband as young as herself. Doubtless both the royal adolescents leaned largely on that other feminine influence – the experienced Queen Mother – and who can blame them if in their leisure hours they found happiness with a de Vere, while, when serious business was to be done, they had the advice of a Burley and a de la Pole? To state that Richard was merely the victim of 'favourites' is to ignore the human factors which are behind all the facts of history.

The diplomacy of this period is complicated, and was of course carried on without reference to Richard. But it provided a practical school of foreign affairs in which he could learn easily, because his old tutor, one of his new guardians, and his formidable uncle Gaunt were all three intimately concerned. It was largely the diplomacy of the Lancastrian faction, and, though it ended with Gaunt as the father to two dynasties, it also saw him cease to be King of Castile, and cease to function as anything more in domestic politics than an elder statesman of acknowledged fame and influence. The diplomacy of 1382 to 1386 was to result in the disappearance of an old brigade and the emergence of new factions – including Richard's own – which continued to the tragic end.

Pope Urban's 'Grand Design' for a European coalition which would encircle Clementist France never resulted in effective action, but its conception affected English diplomacy, and there was always the hope that the two alternative policies of the so-called 'Way of Flanders' and the 'Way of Portugal' might not be mutually exclusive. Both Flanders and Portugal provided excellent bases for flank attacks on France, and the Lancastrian preference for the Portuguese flank was only emphasized because of Gaunt's obstinacy in attempting *en route* to win a Spanish throne in fact which he already held in title. A second session of Parliament met after the royal wedding and its chief concern was with this new diplomacy. There was an English volunteer army already in Portugal under the command of the Earl of Cambridge, but it had been sent largely at Gaunt's instigation as a mere token force for a following main body which he hoped to lead in person. He asked for a grant of £60,000 towards an expedition by the 'Way of Portugal' against the Clementist Franco-Castilian alliance. At first the grant was refused, but in the autumn Parliament of the same year, 1382, the eloquence of the Lancastrian Bishop of Hereford at last persuaded the assembly to agree to Gaunt's projected expedition. By the time the expedition was sanctioned it was too late. Portugal, grown weary of expecting Gaunt's promised reinforcements, had made terms with Castile, and Cambridge's men also had lost heart and were on the verge of open mutiny. The expedition was a dismal fiasco, and Gaunt's personal disappointment became almost a national disgrace – Cambridge and his men were compelled to return to England in ships hired to Portugal by the Castilians!

The same Parliament which had so feebly attempted the Way of Portugal also sanctioned with perhaps more enthusiasm, but with an even worse sense of timing, the Way of Flanders. In May, Philip van Artevelde, the son of James van Artevelde, had led the burghers of Ghent in a successful revolt against the Count of Flanders, whose power was centred on Bruges, and whose diplomatic attachments were wholly French and Clementist. It was a brilliant and brief triumph. Froissart, the faithful chronicler of the international nobility, tells us that the cry went up that in the face of the burghers' revolt 'all noblesse would perish',[1] and there is more than a suspicion that English barons, so recently delivered from the perils of their own Peasants' Revolt, were in no hurry to aid any popular movement elsewhere, even though for the moment it happened to be on the same diplomatic side. The hopes of van Artevelde were crushed on the fatal field of Roosebeke before the English had agreed to send him aid in the form of the ill-fated Flemish expedition known as the 'Norwich Crusade'. Henry Despenser was a fighting baron who had fought for Pope Urban as a young man and as a reward had been 'provided' with the bishopric of Norwich – he was therefore one of those Caesarean clergy against whom Wyclif fulminated, and by his family attachments he was no friend to Wyclif's patron Gaunt. His easy success during the crushing of the Peasants' Revolt in East Anglia seems to have convinced him that he was a general of genius, and his vanity and enthusiasm won the ears of Parliament and the favour of Richard himself. In spite of the criticism of Wyclif and the opposition of the Lancastrians, he preached his crusade successfully, and all the spiritual bribery of the Church was enlisted to swell his funds. He landed in Flanders an optimistic crusader against Clementist France, he wasted men and funds (which might have helped Gaunt) in ravaging a Flanders more faithfully Urbanist than himself, and his incompetence as a general might have resulted in an even worse disaster if it had not been partially counteracted by the presence of so proved and skilful a soldier as Sir Hugh Calverley. The 'Norwich Crusade' ended abruptly with Despenser encircled by overwhelming French forces in Gravelines, and his relief thanks to the intervention of the Duke of Brittany. He returned to England in disgrace, and was deprived of all his temporalities as punishment. The Way of Flanders had proved as much of a fiasco as the Way of Portugal.

Meanwhile, at home, the Lancastrian party had re-established itself even more firmly in power – Michael de la Pole had become Chancellor, and for three years he was at the head of affairs. In spite of his long attachment to Gaunt, he was no mere puppet. Under his efficient control, the expenses of the royal household were less than they had ever been,[1] and every charge of peculation and misappropriation subsequently trumped up against him was easily though fruitlessly rebutted. His chancellorship was still coupled with his guardianship of Richard, and his enthusiastic support for the overwhelming powers of the royal prerogative as proclaimed by Gaunt to the Good Parliament, as so carefully reaffirmed at Richard's coronation and as supported by Burley, may have had a considerable share in building a similar exaggeration in the mind of the young King. Gaunt had not given up his Spanish ambitions, but the recent double fiasco rendered immediate progress impossible, and Gaunt did useful work in helping de la Pole to compensate for England's dangerous isolation, and obvious impotence, by the safety of truces. In the summer of 1383 he made a short truce with the Scots, and in the following January he achieved a similar truce with the French – both gave England breathing space when she badly needed it. Meanwhile, the situation in Portugal had changed dramatically. The treaty which had sent Cambridge packing had included a marriage between King John of Castile and the heiress to the King of Portugal which might have involved the immediate merging of the two Peninsular monarchies. The sudden death of the Portuguese King raised this succession question immediately, and the emergence of a strong Portuguese nationalism led by the late King's half-brother, famous in the history of Portuguese independence as 'John of Good Memory', again renewed Gaunt's ambitions. Portugal sent to her old ally for help. In the then state of England's domestic affairs there was no hope of an immediate and official readoption of the 'Way of Portugal', but the Lancastrian influence, and the boredom of unemployed knights and men-at-arms, sent a welcome stream of volunteers who were to play a distinguished part in the war for Portugal's independence. A few volunteers were not what Portugal or Gaunt needed, and it took two more years of persistent scheming before Gaunt himself was to lead an English army on his final campaign in the Peninsular. England's truce with the Scots ran out early in 1384, and immediately Archibald Douglas, Lord of Galloway, crossed the Border in a major raid. Gaunt was the only soldier available to avenge the insult, and he had the distasteful task of leading a short expedition to harry the Lowlands in the spring. He had owed his safety to the Chivalry of Scotland during the 'Hurling Time', and his strict conceptions of knighthood therefore again protected Edinburgh from fire and sword – his expedition was merely a polite demonstration in force undertaken with reluctance and carried out with discretion. The fulfilment of Gaunt's Spanish ambitions was still postponed.

On April 29th, 1384 Parliament was summoned to Salisbury where the court was also in residence, and, with a passion for parcelling history, tying it up, and labelling it, most modern historians have dated from this Parliament the beginning of Richard's 'First Tyranny'. It is a more misleading label than most. Richard at seventeen was understandably anxious to assume real kingship, but he was firmly prevented from doing so by the baronial factions. Suppressed ambition found its only vent in explosions of adolescent temper, and culminated in a pitiful attempt at forcing the issue by arms. The proceedings of the Parliament opened with the reference of the question of foreign affairs to the Commons.[1] They seem to have been both surprised and flattered, and, while confirming that diplomacy was really beyond their province, they readily approved Gaunt's efforts for peace with both Scotland and France. If they had known how intently Gaunt was planning intervention in Spain they might not have been so amenable. But a pleasant atmosphere was suddenly vitiated by a violent speech from the Earl of Arundel. In no uncertain terms, he blamed the parlous state of the kingdom onto an extravagant court and bad advisers. It was an attack on the young King and his young friends, thinly veiled as an attack on de la Pole and the other court officials. Richard reacted violently, and we have his youthful outburst recorded in the chronicles. White with anger, and looking straight at Arundel, he shouted, 'If you charge me with the responsibility for bad governance, you lie in your throat: go to the Devil.'[1] It was the anger of the ward at last exploding against the hated guardian. If he had kept his temper he would have had an excellent opportunity of pointing out the invidiousness of his position. As it was, Parliament was shocked into uneasy silence, and only the skill and tact of Gaunt at last eased the tension, and gracefully explained away Arundel's attack. Richard appeared satisfied, but no doubt noted that Gaunt was ready to excuse Arundel if not to support him. It was the first of several similar displays of Richard's ungovernable temper.

During this same Salisbury Parliament a much more serious and mysterious affair exposed the unhealthy state of public affairs. The King was in the quarters of his friend de Vere when a Carmelite friar named John Latemar was ushered in to reveal an alleged conspiracy of the citizens of London and other cities, led by the Duke of Lancaster. Richard again temporarily lost control of himself, and ordered the instant arrest and execution of Gaunt.[2] A few minutes later, he was calm again, and ordered the friar to put his information into writing and name his witnesses. Meanwhile, the Lords and Commons had been impatiently awaiting the royal presence at High Mass in Salisbury Cathedral, and Gaunt was sent to enquire into the reason for the King's absence. The moment Richard saw Gaunt his temper broke loose again, and he shouted to the guards to arrest him. Gaunt's astonishment was apparently genuine. When he had heard what his crime was, Gaunt offered to prove his innocence with his life, and his pro-testations seem to have been so convincing that Richard vented his wrath on the friar and ordered *his* immediate execution. Gaunt urged a wiser course – let the friar be compelled to reveal the instigators of this plot against his own honour and the King's justice. Latemar named Lord la Zouche as a witness, and, on being questioned, la Zouche was as emphatic in declaring his innocence as Gaunt had been, and a second witness did the same. The friar was then committed to the prison of Salisbury Castle in the custody of Sir John Montague (the King's Seneschal) to await a judicial enquiry into the whole affair. On its way to the prison, the party was met by Sir John Holland and four knights, all of whom were friends of Richard and one of whom was definitely an opponent of Gaunt. On Holland's initiative and in the presence of Montague, the unfortunate friar was seized and subjected to various indecent tortures (the least of which was slow roasting) but still without eliciting any confession or information. The victim of these atrocities found kindlier treatment from the governor of the prison, but his mutilations and injuries left him a dying man. He lingered a few days, and, after an authorized second interview with la Zouche before witnesses, only had the strength to pay tribute to la Zouche's knighthood before his agonies ended in death. Even his corpse was not left in peace – it was dragged through Salisbury before being handed over to the friars for decent burial. In due course the usual signs and wonders appeared over the tomb of a martyr.

It is an inconsistent, baffling and yet instructive story vouched for in general by all the contemporary chroniclers, and in detail by Malverne, who had it from a Sir John Clanvowe, whom he claims as an eye witness of the scene in de Vere's lodgings.[1] The inconsistency of a plot which allied Gaunt with the Londoners is obvious, the fortitude of a friar who could suffer such extremities of pain and yet keep silent suggests the courage of the insane,[2] and the sadism of knightly torturers, who included some of the highest in the land, is a revelation of that fact which romances of Chivalry have so glossed over – mediaeval Europe was still close to barbarism.[3] Although there is no real evidence to prove it, it is probable that there was an attempt to attack Gaunt by implicating him in a plot against Richard, and it is possible that, as the plot was revealed in de Vere's chambers, when de Vere and Richard were due at an important ceremony elsewhere, de Vere was the clumsy inventor. The reactions to the mystery are more significant than the mystery itself. Gaunt was supplanted by de Vere in general unpopularity, and the wilful and high-tempered vacillations of the King were signs of worse storms ahead. Neither Gaunt nor Richard had had anything to do with the torture scenes, and even the Lancastrian chroniclers tell us that Richard 'wept for pity' when he heard of them. The supposed plot had one significant result – it left Richard still suspicious of Gaunt, and it caused

93

his first quarrel with Gaunt's younger brother Thomas of Woodstock, Earl of Buckingham. Buckingham, on hearing of the imputa-
tions against his brother, stormed into the royal presence, drew
his sword, and challenged any man to call Gaunt traitor. It was a
public affront to Richard which he was for the moment powerless
to answer.

The 'factions' now emerged more sharply defined. Gaunt and
his associates withdrew to weave diplomacy in favour of the King
of Castile. De Vere headed the intimate circle of Richard's young
men and women.[1] The Earls of Buckingham, Arundel and Warwick
joined in an anti-Lancastrian and anti-court alliance. Michael de
la Pole, though a friend and retainer of Gaunt, headed the lay
civil service which tried to keep the ship of state on an even keel.
One great baron remained unattached – Gaunt's son, Henry,
Earl of Derby. He was about two years older than Richard, and
had incurred the enmity of his uncle Buckingham by an astute
marriage arranged by that most astute marriage-maker, his
father. Henry of Derby was at this period not so much of a
Lancastrian as a powerful independent – waiting his opportunity
and adding to his possessions. Amid so much self-seeking, and such
a primitive struggle for power, what little pattern is visible suggests that insensate suspicion of Gaunt prevented de Vere's faction
allying with de la Pole and the powerful Lancastrian interest, and
so left to the King and his court the almost impossible task of
withstanding the Buckingham faction unaided.

There were two other powers in young Richard's England
which were worth courting – the Church and the city of London.
But the Archbishop of Canterbury was a Courtenay and a friend
of Buckingham, most of the bishops had closer baronial than
royal connections, and one of them – the Bishop of Ely – was an
Arundel (far abler than his secular brother) and a powerful link
between Church and baronage. The Church was a difficult ally.
Richard's only remaining source of strength lay in London, and
there he attempted to find the political and financial support
he needed.[2] During the desperate days of June 1381, Walworth,
the Mayor of London, had been at Richard's side both in the
Tower and during the critical moments at Smithfield, and
Richard had not forgotten. Walworth was of the fishmongers'
guild – one of the victuallers who also included the King's

friends John Philpot and Nicolas Brembre. The victuallers were opposed by the rival aldermen of the drapers' guilds, who looked to Gaunt as their patron and protector, and whose leader was an interesting personality named John of Northampton. Civic politics are difficult to follow even today – they reflect the politics of the state and yet have a curious texture all their own. The victuallers were King's men by personal favour, and also because of their service as financiers – some of them were the capitalist middlemen who reaped handsome fortunes through the wool staple – and they were also the aristocratic party opposed to the new powers of the populace so crudely expressed during the recent Revolt. One of the terms of the alliance with the burgher's revolt in Flanders had been that the wool staple should be permanently in Flanders, and when Bruges had become untenable, owing to the disaster at Roosebeke,[1] it was fixed at Middleburgh in Zeeland where it remained until 1389. The London victuallers preferred a staple abroad – as international financiers it was to their personal advantage, and royal favour had thus partly satisfied their ambitions. The policy of John of Northampton and the drapers is not so easy to follow. Their protection by Gaunt offset the protection of the victuallers by Richard, but their popularity with the lower orders of the city is difficult to reconcile with the mob's hatred of Gaunt. John of Northampton himself seems to have had what would in a later period be termed democratic leanings: at least he was prepared to court the poor by ruining the victuallers in a consistent 'cheap food' policy. In November 1381 he had achieved the mayoralty, and, until he was driven from office by the victualler Brembre in October 1383, he carried through reductions in the prices not only of fish but of all foodstuffs. To the delight of the lower orders, he secured the acquittal of the aldermen Carlyll and Sybyle, who had been brought to trial for their surrender of the city's gates to the peasants of Kent and Essex. And the sympathy of the ordinary Londoners for Wyclif's attacks on clerical privilege and morality gave John of Northampton yet another opportunity of hitting at the victuallers. Walworth owned much property in Southwark where the stews of London were, and, although public morals were properly the business of the Church, John of Northampton staged a raid on this disreputable quarter, pilloried some of its prostitutes, and took pains to expose the fact that not only victualler

Walworth but the Bishop of Winchester were drawing handsome rentals from this tarnished source. But the drapers finally over-- played their hand, and, in November of 1383, the court took drastic action. The election to the mayoralty of the grocer Nicolas Brembre was carried by force, and many of John of Northampton's supporters were either slain outright or harried to prison or exile. The drapers replied by complaining of the illegality of the proceedings, calling for a new poll, and, a foolish move, asking for the help of Gaunt. The city was in a tumult, and John of Northampton was himself arrested on returning from a meeting of protest. In August 1384 he was tried by the Council sitting at Reading under the presidency of Richard himself. Unfortunately for the ex-mayor, Gaunt was away in the north, and John of Northampton had the temerity to demand a postponement of the trial until his patron could be present! It was so flagrant an appeal to 'maintenance' that Richard's outburst was justified – 'I will teach you that I am your judge, whether my uncle is absent or not.' [1] In that petulant phrase is a key to these confused years of quarrel and counter-quarrel. Richard was being curbed to the point of exasperation. Once again Richard ordered immediate execution, and once again recovered himself quickly and revoked the sentence. A second trial was ordered before Chief Justice Tresilian in the Tower. Tresilian, nervous of a case within such close reach of the city, attempted to avoid the responsibility; but the King's insistence ensured John of Northampton's condemnation and committal to prison in Tintagel Castle. There he remained until the revolution of 1388 released him. At the next mayoral election, another draper, Twyford, opposed Brembre, and again Brembre was elected by force – armed men were concealed behind the arras of Guildhall, and drove out Twyford's supporters when they had reckoned on an easy victory. Brembre remained Mayor and the King's friend until his trial and execution in 1388. Richard had scored a rather cheap victory against his uncle Gaunt, but in doing so he had alienated the majority of the citizens of his capital city.

Richard's suspicions and de Vere's open hatred of Gaunt were not yet satisfied. There was to be a second 'plot' against Gaunt. It was preceded by a dispute on foreign affairs – Gaunt had pressed for an expedition against France, Richard and the court circle favoured a preliminary expedition against the Scots, and Gaunt refused to co-operate. The details of the plot are so obscure, and the accounts of it so contradictory, that all that can be said with safety is that the court contemplated violent and drastic action against Gaunt and used the Christmas festivities of 1384 to plan his downfall. Mowbray and de Vere seem to have been the plotters, and there is no evidence that Richard was directly involved. The 'plotting', if there was any, must have been sadly bungled, because Gaunt was forewarned. He avoided a Council at Waltham in February 1385, where he was to be seized, and instead with a powerful escort marched to the palace of Sheen to face Richard himself. Taking all the precautions of an old campaigner, he marched into the presence wearing chain mail under his clothes, warned Richard against the dangerous course he and his misguided advisers were pursuing, and refused all further co-operation with his nephew until there were signs of reform. Richard seems to have listened with surprising calmness, and a few weeks later the good offices of the Queen Mother effected at least an outward reconciliation. Gaunt for a time discreetly retired to his castle at Pontefract.[1]

The futility of the court party's actions was so exposed that even so bold an enemy of Gaunt as Courtenay, Archbishop of Canterbury, was impelled to speak for him at an interview with Richard, and he did not mince his words. Immediately afterwards, Richard dined with his London friend Brembre, and later took the air on his barge on the Thames. Off Westminster, they chanced to meet the barge of the Archbishop and Buckingham, and the so-called 'Water Conference'[2] took place. Courtenay seems to have repeated his fatherly advice, and once again Richard failed to control his anger – he even drew his sword, and only the intervention of Buckingham prevented what might have been a disastrous tragedy. Richard's temper had added the power of the baronial churchmen to the strength of his other opponents.

Meanwhile Charles VI of France was planning an attack on the grand scale against an England very clearly in poor condition. It was to be a combined invasion – one army attacking from the Flemish base of Sluys, another in alliance with the Scots from the north. A large fleet was assembled at Sluys, and a body of French lancers under the famous Jean de Vienne was actually landed in

Scotland. The invasion from the Low Countries never started – the French troops were too occupied with rebellious burghers, and England decided on an immediate attack on Scotland. It was to be Richard's first practical lesson in warfare, and the whole strength of the feudal levies of England was summoned to Newcastle on July 14th, 1385.

En route for the Border, the royal army had reached Beverley Minster in Yorkshire when another baronial quarrel broke out which reveals the general lawlessness of feudalism. A favourite squire of Sir John Holland had been killed in a brawl with the retainers of the young son of the Earl of Stafford. The murderers had found sanctuary, and Richard refused to allow Holland to break it. Holland's reply was typical of the man and his period – cheated of revenge on the murderers, he sought out the young Stafford instead, and slew him with one blow. A disgraceful brawl now developed into high politics – the Earl of Stafford claimed the King's justice against Holland, or else he and his retainers would take justice into their own hands. Holland himself had taken sanctuary in Beverley Minster. Richard decided to banish Holland and order the confiscation of his goods, and the fact that the young Stafford was one of his Queen's retinue and of his own age outweighed the prayers of the Queen Mother who pleaded in vain for her elder son. It is difficult to see what other course Richard could have taken – Holland had behaved as a common murderer and deserved even greater punishment, and it was Richard's prime duty to ensure that the expedition was not ruined by so disreputable a cause of delay. The continuing evils of 'maintenance' and private justice were glaringly exposed, and the feudal array lumbered on to the Border outwardly united but with surcoats hiding the cankers of baronial feuds and jealousies.

At Durham, the indispensable veteran leader of the day – John of Gaunt – joined the royal forces with his own levies, and in the 'Ordinances of War made at Durham' [1] the power of Lancaster is revealed in the convincing light of figures. Of 4,590 men-at-arms, 1,000 were Gaunt's. Of 9,144 archers, 3,000 were Gaunt's. Gaunt's men were half as many as the King's, three times as many as Buckingham's, and five times as many as Northumberland's. The tragedy of these early years of Richard, and last years of Gaunt, is that Richard's suspicions were too strong even for the conciliatory influence and wisdom of the Queen Mother. The immense power of Lancaster could have been put behind the throne – it was thought wisdom to allow it to be squandered on the 'Way of Portugal'. And it was now that the Queen Mother left the scene for ever – it was said that she died of a broken heart at the news of Holland's wild deed and subsequent exile. The widow of the Black Prince had seen the glorious prospects of Crécy, Poitiers and Nájera fade into the horrors of the Peasants' Revolt, light up for a brief moment when her royal son returned triumphant from Mile End and Smithfield, and dim again to the dreariness of the succeeding years which had just ended in the squalor of the brawl at Beverley. Her part as mediator and kindly conciliator to a King whose temper was so highly strung was left to Queen Anne – a not unworthy successor.

On August 6th, 1385 the invasion of Scotland began, and the event was signalized by the creation of two new dukes and an earl. Hitherto there had been only one duke – the Duke of Lancaster. Now Gaunt's younger brother, the Earl of Cambridge, became Duke of York; his youngest brother, the Earl of Buckingham, became Duke of Gloucester; while Michael de la Pole was made Earl of Suffolk. The Scots, in traditional fashion and encouraged by Jean de Vienne, adopted du Guesclin tactics and retreated to the north and west to avoid any danger of a pitched battle which they might lose. The abbeys of Melrose and Newbattle were ravaged, and Edinburgh and the abbey of Holyrood were sacked and burnt in spite of Gaunt's protest. A dispute on major strategy now arose. Gaunt was in favour of pushing on across the Forth – or, as Froissart insists, into the west Lowlands, where they could cut off the retreat of Scots who had countered the eastern invasion by a raid on Carlisle and Penrith.[1] Richard was against it – he quite rightly pointed out the risks in an invasion of a terrain bare of supplies and largely unknown, especially when all English stores had to come by the eastern coastal route. But once again his ill-temper spoilt a good case. 'You and your Lords may live upon your private stores, but the common soldier perishes by the way. I will not push into these wilds to destroy my army,' was a justifiable policy; but he could not forbear to taunt Gaunt with a reminder of the futility of his march across France in the face of the enemy's similar strategy in 1373, and de Vere even suggested that Gaunt was hoping that Richard might lose his life in the bogs

and moors of the Highlands. Finally, the King decided upon withdrawal through Berwick, and announced that he himself would do
so whatever Gaunt might decide. Gaunt calmly answered that the
King was his leader, and that he would follow wherever he was
led. Another mockery of reconciliation was staged, and Richard's
first experiment in warfare ended. The expedition had brought no
glory or spectacular success, but it had sufficient effect to keep
France from using Scotland as a base for three-quarters of a
century.

While the feudal levies had been harrying the Scottish Lowlands, English volunteers had played a great part in the crushing
victory of John of Good Memory over the Castilians at Aljubar-
rota – a victory which is known in Portuguese history as 'The
Battle' because it assured Portuguese national independence.
When the news arrived in England, it seemed that at last the time
had come when Richard might be rid of the never-ending quarrels
with Gaunt by encouraging him to take the 'Way of Portugal'.
But, before Gaunt's life-long ambitions could be realized, the
Council had to face Parliament for funds, and, in the autumn
session of 1385, the Commons were only prepared to provide
supplies on their own terms. They were ready to finance an
expedition to Portugal as well as an expedition to relieve the men
of Ghent – the news that Ghent had already fallen to the French
had not yet arrived – provided that the clergy made a corresponding grant. Archbishop Courtenay immediately objected to an
attempt of the laity to make 'the Church of England to become
the hand-maiden of Parliament', and certain knights of the Lollard
way of thinking countered him with a bold proposal for dis-
endowment. Richard ignored the Lollard petition, and the clergy
tactfully voted the grant. But the Commons now went further, and
touched the sacred royal prerogative – they petitioned that not
only should the King 'live of his own' but that he should make no
further gifts for a year, submit his private accounts to the scrutiny
of a parliamentary Commission, and publish the names of his
ministers and officials for the coming year. This was too much;
and Richard angrily answered that he would do exactly as he
pleased with regard to his personal gifts and his ministers, and
that he would submit his accounts to no one.[1] To emphasize the
snub, on the last day of the session, Richard raised his friend de

Vere to the first marquisate in English history, and supported the title of Marquis of Dublin with Palatine rights over the Irish Pale, and an annual income of 5,000 marks from Irish revenues backed by the English Exchequer. Such generosity to his greatest friend was admirable, but the nature and timing of the gift were inexcusable – the Commons were added to the Lords as embittered opponents of the King's friends.

With the Commons dismissed and disgusted, preparations for the final Way of Portugal went on apace. For nearly two years, the Portuguese ambassadors had waited for this moment at their lodgings in the Falcon Inn in Gracechurch Street; at last their patience was to be rewarded. A mood of grandiose optimism swept over England. Pope Urban revived his dreams of a grand European alliance against Clement, issued four Bulls in Gaunt's favour, and a last crusade was preached from St Paul's. The Carmelites – always loyal to Gaunt – preached the crusade throughout the churchyards of the land, and the sale of indulgences was brisk and popular. The London and Lombard financiers paved the road to the Peninsula with their usury, and Richard's personal loans were added to the Duke's coffers. An army of between 5,000 and 10,000 was assembled, and Gaunt and his family were honoured with a regal farewell – he and his Duchess were presented with gold crowns by Richard and Anne. On July 7th, 1386 John of Gaunt at last sailed for the Peninsula from Plymouth taking with him many of his faction and the King's turbulent half-brother Holland, who had been pardoned on condition that he joined the expedition, and who had recently married a daughter of Gaunt's after a rough wooing which had anticipated the actual ceremony. For three years, the Lancastrian faction proper was to be out of Richard's way – only Henry of Derby was left behind to safeguard Gaunt's English interests.

After Richard had shown such promise in the crisis of the Peasants' Revolt, his years of discretion had exhibited indiscretion after indiscretion. It is easy and proper to make excuses for the headstrong follies of youth, but Richard's subsequent history never displayed him as a weak fool. His temper at this period was ungovernable and tactless, but those who accused him of being in the power of worthless favourites were themselves unscrupulous self-seekers and were insulting men of the calibre of de la Pole and Burley. Gaunt was misjudged not only by Richard but by the other baronial factions, and by the new class of city financiers – Gaunt's ambition was consistent, but it aimed at a throne in Castile and not at Westminster. Richard's inner councils had to depend on the inexperienced advice of his greatest personal friend, de Vere, and the growing comfort of a beloved but still a foreign Queen;[1] his potentialities as a wise and strong monarch were being vitiated in an evil atmosphere which saw nothing wrong in a Gaunt placing private dynastic claims before national needs, and no danger in factions which put personal jealousies and ambitions before a proper regard for a youth who needed support, and a light rein if he were not to kick over the traces to early disaster.

V

REBELLION

IF THE EXUBERANCE of Richard's send-off to his uncle Gaunt was partly due to the hope that at last he himself might be allowed to rule, his reaction to the realities of a new situation must have been proportionately bitter. Gaunt, the leaders of the Lancastrian faction proper, and a clutter of turbulent baronage might seem well out of the way, but Gloucester's faction immediately took their place, and that was a change very much for the worse. Furthermore, the moderates of the Lancastrian persuasion – the able men like Burley and de la Pole, now Earl of Suffolk, who carried on the day-to-day government of the realm, and whom only the most partisan have ever characterized as mere 'favourites' – had lost their oldest friend in Gaunt. Although they could rely on the support of Richard they could not be equally sure of his more intimate friends – the de Vere circle. The fair breezes that took Gaunt to Portugal left Suffolk and Burley dangerously exposed to the bitter winds which now swept round court and throne in England. Gaunt, from the magnitude of his power and the nature of his position, might have been open to suspicion; but Gloucester, from his lack of power and his own ambitious nature, was infinitely more dangerous.

Thomas of Woodstock, Earl of Buckingham and now Duke of Gloucester, was the seventh and youngest son of Edward III; he had inherited neither wealth nor great estates and therefore had to depend on the strength of his own right arm, and his own ingenuity, to carve his way to substantial fortune and power. His military career so far had been neither glorious nor inglorious. A fiasco in Brittany in 1380 was probably not his fault, and had been offset by his successful defence of Dover against the French and Spaniards, and the capture of eight Castilian vessels off Brest shortly afterwards. During the 'Hurling Time' he had been with the King in the Tower,[1] and Richard's hour of glory may have sown the seeds of hatred and jealousy in the guilty conscience of an uncle who at the moment of crisis had lost his nerve. He had attempted to purge that guilt by the savagery with which he had quelled the Essex peasants at Billericay. Since then, he had made himself consistently offensive to Richard, and had even drawn his sword against him in defence of the honour of his brother Gaunt. His ingenuity, on the other hand, had planned power through marriage, and when he successfully won the hand of Eleanor, co-heiress of the Bohun inheritance (including the Earldoms of Hereford, Essex and Northampton), he had expected to be the sole beneficiary and to inherit all the Bohun estates. It was Gaunt who had thwarted this grand marital design by taking Eleanor's sister Mary de Bohun from her cloister and marrying her to his heir Henry, who thereby took half the expected Bohun inheritance from Gloucester. Thus far, therefore, his career had scarcely been crowned with the success he coveted: the departure of Gaunt gave him new opportunity.

He had already grouped round him the nucleus of a formidable faction including Richard Fitzalan, Earl of Arundel (as un-scrupulous and as self-seeking as himself, and even more con-temptuous of King and Court), Thomas Beauchamp, Earl of Warwick, Thomas Arundel, Bishop of Ely, Archbishop Courtenay, and the Earl of Arundel's son-in-law the Earl of Nottingham, who, as Thomas Mowbray, had been very close to Richard. No one has ever pretended that these great barons and baronial clergy represented any principle except that of greed – they were perfect examples of that decadence of the mediaeval baronage which Bishop Stubbs has so eloquently exposed; they would stop at nothing to achieve power and to relegate the King and their political enemies to impotence.

In October 1386 the miscalled 'Wonderful Parliament'[2] met. It met in uneasy mood. Throughout August and September the whole country had been dreading for the second time a full-scale French invasion from the Low Countries. The preparations for defence had involved the usual compulsory quartering of soldiery on citizens with its resultant grievances. Although once again the French plans miscarried, the danger was real enough for Gloucester and his faction to pose as the defenders of the realm and to disguise their own ambitions under the banner of national emergency. The Commons were apprehensive and surly; the city of London was equally apprehensive, and still split between victualler and draper factions; the King and his court circle were without popular support. The Parliament did not of course attack the court directly – it attacked the chief ministers, and demanded the dismissal and impeachment of the Treasurer, John Fordham, and the Chancellor, Michael de la Pole, Earl of Suffolk. Richard took immediate umbrage, and in his haughtiest mood sent his famous message from Eltham Palace, that he would refuse to dismiss even one of his scullions at Parliament's command[1] – neither did he propose to attend Parliament until it came to its senses. On the other hand, he was willing to grant an interview to a deputation of forty knights at Eltham. The tactlessness of Richard's message is as censurable as its frankness is admirable – his nineteen years had not yet taught him that indignation which might be righteous might also be tactically in error – especially when real power belonged to the opposition. His invitation to the knights was construed as a plot to dispose of the best of the Commons by foul means, but it is more likely that this was only the story put about by Richard Exton, then Mayor of London. He was an enemy of the King's friend Brembre, and is named by Walsingham[2] as the 'exposer' of the plot, where 'exploiter' would have been a better word. Richard, in a mood of wilful rashness, chose this moment of all others to elevate de Vere by royal charter to the Dukedom of Ireland. It was an almost childish challenge which Gloucester and his friends could not ignore. Instead of forty knights, Parliament sent Gloucester himself and Thomas Arundel, Bishop of Ely, to Eltham. There is no authentic documentary evidence of what took place at this fateful interview, but there is no reason to doubt that angry and exaggerated statements were made on both sides. The continuator of Knighton's chronicle[3] tells us that Gloucester quoted the authority of an ancient Statute for at least annual Parliaments, and for the statement that, if the King did not attend, Parliament could disperse after forty days' grace. Richard's reply was that, if this was their attitude, he would seek help from the French King; to which Gloucester's riposte was as apt as it was treasonable – he reminded Richard II of the fate of Edward II. Whether, in so many words, Gloucester went so far as to threaten the King with deposition is not proven, but at least it is clear that his threats were violent enough to make Richard think again. There was of course no 'ancient Statute', and the deposition of Edward II was not covered by any general Statute and was obviously a revolutionary process, but at this stage Richard's only friends were his almost powerless personal following, and Suffolk and Burley, who were already the scapegoats for all the national disgraces of the time. The fact that Richard did finally give way is a sign of grace, or at least of burgeoning wisdom – only a few years before he had ordered instant executions and reprieves with the same hastiness as Alice's Queen of Hearts; now he was restrained enough to surrender and to postpone a reckoning with Gloucester.

On October 23rd the King appeared in Parliament, and Gloucester whetted his appetite by securing the immediate dismissal of Suffolk and Fordham. In place of a friend, who was also one of the most efficient administrators the Middle Ages produced, Richard had to suffer as Chancellor his enemy Arundel, Bishop of Ely, as Treasurer John Gilbert, Bishop of Hereford, and as Keeper of the Privy Seal, John Waltham – all of the Gloucester faction – and he also had to promise that he would replace his Steward of the Household with one of Gloucester's nominees. The humbling of the King had begun. It was followed by the impeachment of Suffolk in seven articles,[1] most of which alleged peculation rather than treason. They were clumsily framed, and Suffolk had no difficulty in pointing out that, if he were guilty, so was the Council. The King spared no efforts to save his fallen Chancellor, but they were as useless against such prejudiced judges as the Duke of Gloucester and the Earl of Arundel as the able speech of Scrope, who made the most of Suffolk's thirty years' distinguished service to the State. Suffolk was pronounced worthy of death, but his sentence was reduced to imprisonment in Windsor Castle and the forfeiture of his properties. So unconvincing were the charges under which he was condemned that he was not stripped of his title. Richard did not hesitate to show that he still stood by an old friend and servant – loyalty was one of his most consistent virtues – and at the Christmas festivities at Windsor, which followed the 'Wonderful Parliament', he boldly remitted Suffolk's forfeitures and invited him to share in the royal feasting.

But the 'Wonderful Parliament' not only attacked the King through his distinguished Chancellor, it again saddled him with a

Commission of Government.[1] It was a Commission of fourteen, including of course Gloucester and the two Arundels, and it was granted very exceptional powers 'to amend the administration'. It was given complete control of the governmental machinery of the day – including the Exchequer and the Great and Privy Seals – and Richard was compelled to swear that he would obey its majority decisions. There was only one window in Richard's prison, but it was to be exceedingly useful. The Commission had such exceptional powers that they were granted for twelve months only: Richard might hope to escape from his political fetters on November 19th, 1387. His forced agreement to the Commission was signified in a phrase which acquires added significance from later events – he personally protested that he sanctioned nothing that had been done in the foregoing Parliament which affected '*sa Prerogatif et les Libertées de sa dite Corone*'.[2] When it is remembered that the Commission not only had control of the State but even the custody 'of all his jewels and goods' with 'full power and authority general and special to enter his said house and all the offices of the same and all his other courts and places as often as them please',[3] the full measure of Richard's degradation can be gauged, and the full measure of Richard's resentment – half dissembled for the time being but very much alive beneath the cloak of that mystical conception named his prerogative. He permitted himself two small gestures of immediate defiance – the open fraternization with de la Pole, and the appointment of his friend Sir John Beauchamp of Holt as Steward of the Household without permission of the Council.

The Commission could afford to ignore Richard's reservations and petty protests – they were sure of ultimate victory, and their responsibility for the realm was popularized by immediate gifts of good fortune. In the minor naval battle of Cadzand (off Margate) Arundel captured a hundred vessels laden with wine for the French forces at Sluys, and the free distribution of such welcome booty bought the easy favour of the thirsty London populace. The vast French preparations at Sluys had been planned too late – the autumn gales in the Channel were too much for the primitive, single-masted, castled tubs of the day, and Gloucester's party could claim that their temporary command of the Narrow Seas had saved England from a major invasion. Brest was relieved and the country round Sluys was plundered. That the projected invasion was a serious threat is proved both by the feverish preparations made by the Londoners – 'as though maddened by wine' they repaired the city walls, and destroyed the slum property which had been allowed to cluster along them and impair their military efficiency – and by the interesting story of the wooden wall prepared in Flanders to protect the French invaders when they landed. This early attempt at prefabricated invasion planned a wall three miles long and twenty feet high with a fortified tower for ten men every two hundred yards. A daring raid captured a part of this wall together with its constructor (an exiled Englishman), and, as a trophy, the captured part was re-erected at Sandwich.[1] The Commission commanded early and easy success[2] – their subsequent deeds displayed their real character.

Richard's Christmas at Windsor with Suffolk and the Duke of Ireland combined very serious consultations with the traditional festivities. The Crown, the court, and the elder household advisers and government officials had lost all power at the centre of affairs – whither could they turn for help against those who were so thorough in their vindictiveness that they even dismissed from minor offices such non-political royal friends as Geoffrey Chaucer?[3] The answer seems to have been that the only hope was to plan as secretly as possible for armed help from the provinces, and legal justification from the judges. If the final issue meant civil war, Richard had every mediaeval right, but very little might, on his side. He was now in his twentieth year and was reduced to the position of a mere figurehead. We do not know exactly what counsel was given to the King, but, if the Duke of Ireland urged standing and fighting for his inheritance, this was probably balanced by the shrewder advice of a Suffolk who advised the exploitation of an unassailable legal position. The folly of de Vere's advice lay in the lack of a royal army and of the means to hire one, but throughout the spring and early summer of 1387 Richard's progresses to York, Lancashire, Cheshire and North Wales had more military than ceremonial significance,[4] and there is a record that one of Richard's personal recruiting officers was at work with silver and gilded crowns in East Anglia, where he was later arrested.[5] It is at this time that the chronicles first make mention of the King's bodyguard of Cheshire archers and Welsh pikemen, and indeed, Burley and Raddington, who had accompanied the royal tour, were both competent military purveyors.

The difficulty was that Richard without his Seals had no proper authority to levy great forces, and, without the Exchequer to provide money, he was also without the means for hiring them. Nevertheless, a military force of sorts was under de Vere's command by the end of the year.

But Richard had also taken steps to make sure of his legal position. On August 21st, 1387 he presented ten very pointed questions to the Chief Justices of the realm, specially summoned to his court then at Shrewsbury. It was a confidential taking of legal opinion. Tresilian, Chief Justice of the King's Bench, Belknap, Chief Justice, with Holt and Burgh, Justices all of the Common Bench, and Cary, Chief Baron of the Exchequer, were faced with ten questions specially drawn up by one of Richard's serjeants-at-law. They were so framed[1] that the law lords of England had no escape from saying that the Commission of Government was contrary to the royal prerogative, that those who had procured it, and had enforced the King's consent to it, were worthy of the extreme penalty of the law, that Parliament must first discuss matters submitted to it by the King before it proceeded to raise matters on its own initiative, that the King could dissolve Parliament at his pleasure, that the person who had urged Parliament to consult the records relating to the deposition of Edward II was a traitor, and finally that the condemnation of the Earl of Suffolk was in error and revocable. A year later, when these lawyers, with the exception of Tresilian, were on trial for their lives, they pleaded that their answers had been given under duress, but it is difficult to see what other answers they could have given consistent with their integrity as good lawyers. The duress story is understandable when they were faced later with the ruthlessness of a Merciless Parliament which had already executed Tresilian with barbaric illegality. There is no hint of duress at the time the questions were put, and Richard seems to have been anxious that the judges should not come to any hasty decisions – he gave them a week to think over their answers, and then repeated the same questionnaire at a meeting in Nottingham. At this second meeting, Cary was replaced by Fulthorp but what significance this may have had it is impossible to determine, and the answer of the lawyers was again unanimous, and precisely the same as at Shrewsbury. Richard had made doubly sure of his legal rights, and only those who have accepted the Lancastrian version of these events, and who mistake the early origins of the English constitution for evidence of precocious notions of constitutionalism, can condemn Richard's acts as 'unconstitutional'. There was no 'constitution' that he could break; the royal prerogative was no legal fiction but a legal if mystical fact. On the other hand, to consult the justices at all was a significant but unwitting step in that march from precedent to precedent which centuries later finally subjected the English crown to the majesty of the law as defined by Statute.

According to the chronicler Walsingham,[1] Richard took a further step in the attempt to build up enough strength to withstand the Gloucester faction – he sounded the opinion of some of the sheriffs as to whether they would summon the shire levies to his armed assistance. The answer was disappointing. A third desperate appeal for help was made to the Pope – but again the answer, if more diplomatic, was equally disappointing and negative.[2] The results of all the royal efforts were concentrated in the small force, under the red and white banner of Richard, which de Vere had assembled at Chester, buttressed by the paper sanction of proved legality – a poor answer to the determination of a Gloucester who controlled the capital, all the sovereignty of the Seals, and the combined feudal levies of the majority of the great barons.

Were the questions to the justices a political mistake? They were certainly a political innovation; and they raised a new issue which touched the baronage in a very tender spot – they applied the fateful word 'treason' to acts other than the very narrow definitions of the Treason Statute of 1352.[3] To be adjudged a traitor in the fourteenth century involved even more than an ignominious and painful death[4] – it meant the forfeiture of property and possessions, and that 'tainted blood' which disinherited heirs. Many noble families had suffered in the reign of Edward II, and the statute of 1352 had been an attempt to confine the dreaded word 'treason' within the smallest possible limits. Private war, for example, if construed as treason, meant that the land and goods of the traitor were forfeit to the King for ever, but, if construed as merely a felony (as the 1352 Statute determined) only for a year and a day. Again, 'accroaching on the King's prerogative' before 1352 was treason with all that that verdict involved, and in 1387 Richard, by his questions to the judges, was preparing to go behind the 1352 Statute and thus arm himself with a legal weapon of deadly consequence if wielded against his present political enemies. It was so deadly that, when Richard was defeated, even Gloucester hesitated to use it, and preferred to claim for Parliament full supremacy, and to ignore both the legal opinion of the King's judges and the Statute of 1352. He was determined to punish but was chary of attempting definitions of treason which might, with a new turn of the wheel of Fortune, involve himself and his friends in the worst fate a mediaeval baron could possibly imagine. Apparently Richard had made every effort to keep his dealings with the lawyers a secret – if he had succeeded, his plan might have been justified by success; it has been too readily condemned as a mistake simply because it failed. It failed because the secret was betrayed to Gloucester[1] by one of the witnesses – Robert Wickford, Archbishop of Dublin – and, although the judges' answers were only in the nature of a grand jury's true bill, they were sufficient warning that trial and condemnation were more than likely. Gloucester and his friends immediately prepared for drastic action.

From September to November 1387 de Vere was busy establishing his power in Chester – he was first made Justice of Chester and then Justice of North Wales, and, judging from an inventory which still survives,[2] he set up a household of some consequence. A personal affair now helped to precipitate the major crisis. De Vere had been first married to a niece of Gloucester, but, since the arrival of Queen Anne and her attendant ladies from Bohemia, he had fallen in violent love with a certain Agnes Launcekron. A complaisant Church enabled him to repudiate Gloucester's niece and to marry the beloved foreigner.[3] It was an affront to Gloucester, an affront to that growing nationalism which was beginning to resent foreigners as mere parasites or robbers, and an interesting example of how great events can be affected by personal loves and hates.

In November, Richard left de Vere at Chester, returned to Westminster with his other friends, and summoned Gloucester, Arundel and Warwick to his counsel. It has been suggested – but on the slimmest evidence[4] – that this was simply a plot to capture them. Whether this was true or not, the leaders of the Commission refused the invitation, took their private armies to Waltham Cross in open defiance, and on November 14th published an 'appeal of treason' against the King's friends Archbishop Neville, de Vere, Suffolk, Tresilian and Brembre. This first 'appeal' was not subscribed to by Nottingham and Derby – they were warily seeing which way the wind would blow – and its form is interesting. Gloucester, as Constable of England, was the head of that military court which settled disputes of Chivalry according to the Roman Civil Law and by trial by combat. He has left to posterity a serious treatise on its rules of procedure, and his library certainly included 'two large books of Civil Law in Latin'.[1] The normal method of charging a person before this court of Chivalry was by appeal, and it seems that it was Gloucester's intention to summon his enemies to the bar of his own court, and so avoid the unpleasant possibilities of either disregarding or obeying the 1352 Treason Statute. The 'Lords Appellant' have frequently been extolled as the champions of the constitution and the law, as Richard has been condemned for tampering with both and setting himself above the law. In this instance, neither the praise nor the blame is justified. In a period when even precedents were awkward to handle, when even the perpetuity of Statutes was not established, and when a group of unscrupulous magnates had determined on action while action was in their power, the constitutional historian may see the first glimmer of future lights, but he is not entitled to canonize men of the stamp of Gloucester with haloes borrowed from subsequent progress. The sordid truth was that the Appellants were prepared to rid themselves of their opponents without any reference to Parliament at all, and at the bar of their own biased judgments.

Richard seems to have been dumbfounded by the news of the rebellion at Waltham Cross – '*vero stupefactus*' [2] says the chronicler. But, if he had underrated the desperation of Gloucester, he quickly recovered, and acted with circumspection and skill in referring the appeal to Parliament. It was a clever gain of time – enabling de Vere to prepare from his Chester base the rescue of the King, and enabling Neville and Suffolk to escape abroad. Tresilian concealed himself in Westminster, but the faithful Brembre bravely remained in London openly campaigning for his young master. The writs for a new Parliament demanded that the members sent to Westminister should be '*in debatis modernis magis indifferentes*'; a fruitless proviso as it happened, but proof that Richard still hoped to find some friends in the Commons.[3] The appeal of Waltham Cross was repeated by the three leading barons before the King at Westminster on November 17th, and they took the precaution of taking strong bodyguards and wearing chain mail. Immediately afterwards, the news arrived that de Vere's army was marching from Chester towards the Severn valley – civil war was about to begin.

There are varying stories of Gloucester's reaction to the news that he would have to fight as well as threaten to fight. One version is that he planned the immediate deposition of Richard,[1] another that Warwick argued that de Vere should be disposed of first. The agreed fact is that Derby and Nottingham now burned their boats and took sides against the King, and any argument against immediate dethronement would find weighty support in a Derby whose father was a Gaunt who would never have allowed his younger brother Gloucester to usurp the throne. While Richard took refuge in the fortress of the Tower, Derby was appointed to the command of the Appellants' armies, and he immediately moved to the north-west, until news of de Vere's march down the Severn prompted a wheel to the south to intercept him as he reached the upper Thames valley. The battle of Radcot Bridge (near Eynsham on the Thames) was the inglorious end to de Vere's heroics.[2] De Vere had about 4,000 men, and was supported by Sir Thomas Molyneux, Constable of Chester, Sir Ralph Vernon and Sir Ralph Ratcliffe. It is doubtful if the Appellants' forces greatly outnumbered him. But de Vere marched straight into Derby's trap as he came down from the Cotswolds to the river, and his men scarcely stopped to give battle. It was a foggy December 20th, and a flank attack magnified the strength of the Appellants, and turned a battle into an immediate and overwhelming rout. There was little bloodshed; de Vere, by swimming his horse across the Thames, escaped to reach France, and the Appellants' easy victory was only besmirched by the murder after surrender (or, as another version has it, during a parley) of Molyneux. The news of the defeat was a humiliating and bitter Christmas greeting to Richard as he waited in the Tower, while the victorious Appellants led their forces in triumph through Oxford – we have the description of one of the chroniclers who watched them from his tutorial windows[3] – to encamp at the gates of London. The King's first bid for the power which should have been his by right had failed; a group of rebellious barons had the laurels of a cheap victory to disguise the crudity of their policy of ambition and self interest.

From November 19th, 1387 the powers of the Commission of

Government, appointed a year before, had legally expired – the Appellants' actions since that date had clearly been revolutionary. On the other hand, by sanctioning de Vere's march and intriguing with the Londoners, Richard had broken an oath of protection which he had given to the Appellants on November 18th, following the reference to Parliament of their appeal. There were wrongs and rights on both sides; and as, from the end of the year, all acts of government were authorized *'per Concilium'*, the Appellants could make out a doubtful case that their continued government was legal. They were equally determined that their victory should be exploited to the full. While the King was virtually a prisoner in the Tower, the Appellants made sure of the allegiance of London,[1] where Brembre's efforts had roused some support for Richard. Brembre was promptly arrested, and all the power of the London guilds, other than the victuallers, was recruited to the side of the Appellants. The next step was to come to terms with the King.

Once before Richard had been a prisoner in the Tower – surrounded by armed peasants and citizenry. This time he was an even lonelier figure. His closest friends were in exile, in prison, or in fear of their lives. His uncle Gaunt was in Spain. His remaining nobles were now his gaolers, their men-at-arms at the gates, their private armies surging round the walls and fraternizing with the Londoners. Against such a force Richard's only weapon was his mystical *'regalitée'*, and his own wits. His twenty-first birthday saw him beaten almost to his knees, and the depth of his degradation is a measure for the astonishing and dramatic story of his subsequent recovery, his calculated revenge, and the final folly and tragedy of his end.

There were now five Appellants. But, although Derby and Nottingham had openly ranked themselves with the Gloucester trio, they must not be identified with them – they were the remaining and very powerful rump of that Lancastrian faction who, by filial affection and personal interest, preferred a Gaunt to a Gloucester, and were uneasily aware that the presumptive heir to Richard was neither but Roger Mortimer, fourth Earl of March.[2] All five Appellants, having taken precautions to blockade Richard both by land and water, arranged a parley through the mediation of Archbishop Courtenay and the Earl of Northumberland. They entered the Tower carefully guarded, and left 500 of their retinue to secure the gates. There is an intriguing dispute of evidence as to exactly what took place inside. The simple story is that Richard immediately conceded everything that was demanded of him. The more dramatic story is that only after Derby had taken him to a window, and shown him the threatening besiegers outside, did Richard consent. The darkest and perhaps the true story is that a reckless Gloucester actually proclaimed Richard deposed 'for two dayes or thre', and that so crude a usurpation was only circumvented because of the opposition of Derby, Nottingham, and possibly of Warwick, and hushed up so that posterity might be unaware both of Richard's degradation and of Gloucester's treason.[1] That there were definitely two parties in the Appellants' camp is indicated by the fact that the King asked Derby and Nottingham to supper with him after the interview, and that both joined the King and Queen in pleading later for the life of old Burley. At all events, by fair means and foul, Richard was compelled to agree to the third appeal, and to the arrest of a long list of men whose only crime had been their loyalty to the throne; he also had to agree to the cancellation of the writs which had attempted to ensure an impartial Commons, and the substitution of new writs issued on January 1st, 1388 in the ordinary way, for a full Parliament which was to meet on February 3rd. Four of the five prospective victims of the Appellants had escaped – only Brembre had stood his ground, and he was now in prison. The proscription list was extended to include Sir Simon Burley, Sir John Beauchamp, the Steward, the Justices who had given Richard such dangerous answers at Shrewsbury and Nottingham, knights of the household such as Salisbury and Berners, some of the King's personal clerks, his confessor, and some of his chaplains. All was ready for the 'Merciless Parliament' of 1388.

It is fortunate for the modern historian that the doubtful legality of so much of the work of this Merciless Parliament was recognized even by contemporaries, and, in addition to the Rolls of Parliament, there is the contemporary pamphlet of Favent (which was propaganda on behalf of the Appellants) and the contemporary collection of an unknown royalist Monk of Westminster (who may have been an eye witness of most of the proceedings) to provide a balanced picture of the famous – and infamous – 'Parliamentum sine Misericordia'.[2]

The proceedings opened in the White Hall of the palace of Westminster. The King was on his throne, with the Chancellor, Bishop Arundel, on the woolsack immediately in front and below. On the King's right hand sat the higher clergy, and on his left all the great barons, with the exception of the five Appellants, and a great assembly of knights and burgesses packed the hall tightly to the corners. The five Appellants then dramatically made their entry – arm in arm and clad in cloth of gold – made their obeisance, and took their seats. When the whole assembly was seated, the Chancellor rose, and, facing the audience, declared the proceedings open. Sir Robert Pleasington, who had been a Chief Baron of the Exchequer, then made the fourth and last appeal on behalf of the five Appellants and declared them free of all intent of treason. The Commons next stated in general terms the necessity for redress of grievances before they could consent to supplies, and, significantly, requested another Commission of Government to carry out reforms and govern the country efficiently. Then came the real business of the day. Geoffrey Martin – one of the new class of non-political, non-clerical, and able civil servants – read out the very long document (written in French) of thirty-nine articles which constituted the Appellants' case. It took two hours to read, and, according to Favent, moved its audience to anger and tears. It reads today as a well presented brief to prove that any move or act in opposition to Gloucester was treason; it was careful not to accuse Richard himself, and laid all the blame on his incompetent advisers, the Archbishop of York, Suffolk, de Vere, Tresilian and Brembre; it cleverly picked on such points of debatable legality and wisdom as the consultations with the judges and the attempt to influence the sheriffs, and made the most of them; it coupled a great deal of abuse with an attack on every act and every appointment of the Duke of Ireland, and it made a shrewd bid for Lancastrian support by reviving the charge that the King's advisers had plotted Gaunt's death in 1384–5. But the appeal was not to have a smooth passage. There were several uneasy queries to be dealt with before the power of Gloucester threw over even the pretence of legality, and proceeded to a series of judicial murders. Who first resorted to arms, and who was encroaching the royal prerogative? De Vere, who was attempting to rescue it, or Gloucester, who had virtually usurped it? Was incompetence proved against a man of Suffolk's record, and

REBELLION

since when was incompetence high treason? Was the new procedure of parliamentary 'appeal for treason' justified by precedent
or law? The last query summed up the others, and actually
caused a crisis. 'The judges and sergeants, and other sages of
the law of the realm, and also the sages of the Civil Law' were
asked by Parliament to give their considered opinion as to the
legality of the appeal.[1] They promptly replied that it was illegal
by every standard known to them – a reply which must have
infuriated Gloucester in that it was made by his own recently
appointed judges, and not by the men who were condemned
as fawning supporters of Richard for their equally correct replies
to the King's questions of Shrewsbury and Nottingham. The
lawyers of this period seem to have been worthy upholders of
a brave tradition of independence. The Appellants, however,
brushed aside these difficulties, and persuaded the Lords to declare
that the appeal was within the purview of 'the Law and Court of
Parliament', that the Lords, with the King's assent, were the
correct judges in such a case, that England could never be ruled
or governed by the Civil Law, and that, in view of the foregoing
and of the fact that the appeal was 'bone et effectuel solone les Leys et
Cours de Parlement', they proposed to proceed to judgment. Some
historians[2] have seen in this quite revolutionary procedure the
first appearance of the sovereignty of Parliament, and the
supremacy of the House of Lords as the highest law-court in the
realm. It is true that the language used by the Appellants would
have been good constitutional law centuries later, but their 'constitutionalism' in the fourteenth century was the necessity and
expediency of desperate men confronted by the obstinacy of their
own lawyers, and handicapped by the weakness of their own case.
They were quite prepared at first to bring all the proceedings
before the court of Chivalry. When the King made this easy way
out impossible, they were equally prepared to agree that the code
of Chivalry – the Civil Law – was inapplicable. When the law of
the land was declared to be against them, they did not hesitate to
declare that the law of Parliament – as defined by themselves and
their peers – was superior not only to the Civil Law but the Common Law. On the other hand, the Appellants had to find some
way out of the impasse, and their 'parliamentary appeal of
treason' was at least less savage than that process of attainder
which in the next century was to declare so many noble families

guilty of treason by the simple injustice of an Act of Parliament. The trials of Richard's friends proceeded before judges who were judges in their own case, whose legal basis had been shattered by their own lawyers, and whose purpose was the perpetuation of their own power, the subduing of a King who had refused to co-operate with them, and the savage punishment of every opponent on whom they could lay their hands. If Bishop Stubbs' theory of a Lancastrian 'constitutional experiment' is a brilliant myth, Professor Tout's blessing on this Merciless Parliament is a profanation – Gloucester has no shadow of claim to be regarded as a pillar of any constitution.[1]

The Lords' deliberations on the appeal lasted well over a week – there was quite a strong body prepared to thwart Gloucester, or at least more than doubtful about the whole proceedings. In spite of the doubters, and without the consent of either King or Commons, the four absentee respondents were sentenced to death as traitors by a mere declaration without legislative or judicial sanction, and the Lords proceeded to deal with the one respondent whose person they held – Brembre, the ex-Mayor of London. The legal difficulties were now multiplied, because Brembre was a man of experience and courage. He promptly asked for counsel – a request which would have been granted under the common law, but which was denied to him under Gloucester's new-fashioned 'Law of Parliament'. He then asked for a copy of the indictment and time to prepare his defence – which in the fourteenth century were not obvious rights – and those too were denied him by 'Law of Parliament'. The articles of the appeal were then read out to him seriatim, and he was compelled to answer to each charge. He answered 'not guilty' in every instance, and claimed 'ordeal by battle'. On the next day, Richard himself made a bold speech in defence of his friend, and a shower of gloves, including all five Appellants', rained down at the King's feet.[2] One chronicler estimated that 305 challenges had reinforced the Appellants' case – but 'ordeal by battle' was refused, on the grounds that it was only admissible where there were no witnesses. The King withdrew amid the uproar, and twelve of the Lords were appointed to investigate the truth of the charges. To the consternation and anger of the Appellants, this committee reported on the following day that they could not find Brembre guilty of any capital crime.

An awkward situation was interrupted by the dramatic dis-

covery of Tresilian. He had been in hiding near Westminster, and
the stories of his arrest vary – Favent says that he had been hidden
in the house of a *'tremescens paterfamilias'*, while the Monk of Westminster reports[1] that he had found sanctuary in the Abbey, and
that Gloucester in person dragged him from the protection of the
Church to his fate. He had already been condemned to death in
his absence, and, in spite of his protests against both the legality of
the appeal and the violation of sanctuary, he was forthwith drawn
on a hurdle and hanged on Tyburn gallows. The Chief Justice of
England, who had harried the peasants in his bloody assize after
the Peasants' Revolt, and who had subsequently become one of
the King's staunchest friends in the legal profession, was granted
short shrift and an ignominious death sanctioned by a 'Law of
Parliament' which was unknown to any lawyer and which the
chronicler describes as the *factum sive judicium parliamenti*[2] – he was
clearly not sure whether it was a crime or a judgment.

The Appellants, having claimed their first victim, returned to
the awkward problem of Brembre. In their lust for another victim
at any cost they were now reduced to the expedient of using
against him the evidence of his enemies in the city. Two representatives from each of the greater guilds in London were asked
whether it was true that Brembre had planned to be 'Duke of
Petty Troy',[3] and had not only drawn up proscription lists of his
civic opponents but had even prepared a special block and axe
for their execution. The answer was inconclusive because it was
given on strictly party lines – the victualler guilds for and the
draper guilds against Brembre. It was a move which shows not
only the desperation of the Appellants but their ignorance of civic
politics. They tried again, and thought they had made sure of
the result by consulting the ruling mayor, recorder and aldermen
only – in other words their own supporters. But once again city
loyalty gave no unconditional surrender – they answered warily
that, if Brembre were proved guilty of these charges, he was indeed
worthy of death. The Appellants' patience was by now exhausted,
and, after a trial of four days, Nicolas Brembre was sentenced as a
traitor and executed – according to one version on the block and
with the axe he had prepared for his enemies.

The so-called 'Law of Parliament' had involved the Lords in
real legal difficulties, and, in spite of the fact that a majority of
the Parliament (to the number of 305 challenging gloves) was

against the King's friends, it was now promptly jettisoned in favour of the process of impeachment, which associated the Commons with the accusers and allowed the prisoners to speak in their own defence. John Blake, the serjeant-at-law who had drafted the questions to the justices, and Thomas Usk, a former clerk to John of Northampton who had betrayed him to the court faction in 1384, were speedily charged, condemned and executed. Then followed the trials of the King's confessor the Bishop of Chichester, and the King's justices; but, by the intervention of the other bishops, their condemnation did not involve a traitor's death – they were all exiled to various parts of the Irish 'pale'. If the Commons had had their way, they would have been executed; but the Appellants in this one instance exercised a restraining influence. On the other hand, when the four knights of the household came up for trial, both the Commons and the chief Appellants showed as little respect for mercy as for justice. The trial of Burley, Beauchamp, Berners, and Salisbury again revealed the opposition of a considerable party in the Lords, and a split within the ranks of the Appellants themselves – and it was well over a month before they were condemned and executed. Richard fought with every device of delay, and every effort of persuasion, to rescue Burley – he was crudely told by Gloucester that he thereby risked his throne. Richard even permitted his Queen to kneel to his hated uncle and beg for the life of her husband's oldest friend and tutor – and Gloucester rudely told her to pray both for herself and her husband. Burley's nephew Baldwin Raddington – a known royalist – risked his own life to beg for Burley's; Derby and Nottingham were against Gloucester; the Duke of York quarrelled with his younger brother in open Parliament, and, accompanied by Lord Cobham, pleaded with the Commons for mercy – but all to little purpose. The old comrade-in-arms of the Black Prince was merely granted the privilege of the block rather than the ignominy of the gallows, and was executed on May 5th for the alleged treason of plotting the deaths of the Commission Council in 1386. He was followed to execution on the same block by Beauchamp and Berners, whose alleged treason was that they had suborned the youth of the King to conspire against and hate such loyal subjects as the Appellants. Salisbury, who had been accused of conspiring with France, was hung and drawn.

The bloody work of the Merciless Parliament had now involved in death or exile every one of the King's closest friends, and its only spark of mercy was to release the remaining lesser chamber knights and royal clerks under surety of good behaviour. In spite of the opposition of lawyers, of moderate Lords, and of saner counsels within their own ranks, the three chief Appellants had reduced the King to a cipher – all that remained was to provide, as far as they possibly could, against the consequences of their own obvious illegalities, to reward themselves for their prodigious efforts in the cause of Richard's good name and fame, and to prove that they were better governors than the men they had murdered, and the King they had humbled.

That the Appellants' declaration of the supremacy of the 'Law of Parliament' was merely a temporary expedient, and was never intended as a contribution to constitutional progress, is demonstrated by the fact that, once it had served their purpose, they were at pains to make sure that no Parliament could ever again claim to be a law unto itself. By yet another twist in their interpretation of the law of treason it was declared high treason for anyone to attempt to reverse the judgments of their Parliament, and yet that its enactments were not to be taken as a precedent.[1] It was a muddled attempt to deny the supremacy of future Parliaments while ensuring the perpetuation of its own usurped supremacy, and they were so fully conscious of their own bad case that they specifically enacted that, in spite of their own interpretations of treason law, the Treason Statute of 1352 was to be revived for the future. Every one of their sentences had gone beyond that statute – they had sentenced their victims to a forfeiture even of their entailed estates, and, although it was prohibited by *'de donis conditionalibus'*,[2] this savage decree was strictly enforced, with a proviso that it should never be used again! The Lords Appellant at the height of their merciless triumph were uneasily aware that, in spite of all their efforts to the contrary, they had forged deadly weapons which one day might be turned against themselves.

Meanwhile, to the conquerors the spoils. The huge sum of £20,000 was voted to the Appellants 'for their great expenses',[3] in spite of the fact that they had claimed to be eager for state economies. With Gloucester and his friends financially satisfied, there was one other bribe to pay – Sir John Holland, Lancaster's Constable and Richard's half brother, had returned from Spain in April to report progress, and he had therefore been in time to witness the worst illegalities of the Appellants; he was a dangerous witness, who might however be bought. His price seems to have been the Earldom of Huntingdon and an allowance of 2,000 marks a year – a sum 500 marks greater than the allowances granted to Gloucester and York when they had been created Dukes. It is also likely that, as Holland reported that Gaunt was abandoning his claim to Castile and might soon be back in England, the appointment of Gaunt as the King's Lieutenant in Aquitaine was both an attempted bribe and an attempted delaying action – Gloucester would not have welcomed the return of his elder brother at this juncture.

Two final acts completed the work of the Merciless Parliament. First, the King was compelled to submit his personal affairs to a governing Committee consisting of William of Wykeham, Bishop of Winchester, the Bishop of London, the Earl of Warwick, John Lord Cobham, and the Lancastrian Richard le Scrope of Bolton; while affairs of state – the actual government of England – were still entrusted to the Appellants, although their Commission's legal title had not been renewed. Second, as frequently happened, there were many petitions and bills left unanswered at the end of the session, and, in order to release the members after such a long and arduous Parliament, a special committee of the Lords was given full parliamentary authority to deal with them even though Parliament had adjourned. It was a precedent ten years later for a similar committee for which Richard has been condemned by most constitutional historians. In fact, it was the least reprehensible and most sensible of any of the acts of the Merciless Parliament, and not the malicious invention of a despot.

How did the Appellants use their power, once their enemies were out of the way? Gloucester himself led the war party, but the war against France was carried on in very half-hearted fashion, and the majority of the Appellants, once they were in power, seem to have seen the wisdom of the peace policy of their predecessors. The truth was that England was in no condition to wage war with France and was even incapable of dealing effectively with raiding Scots. In the summer of 1388, England was threatened by a two pronged attack – the main Scottish army harried Cumberland, while a force of some 3,000 mounted men and 2,000 infantry under the Earl of Douglas reached the gates of Newcastle. The Earl of Northumberland sought the safety of his castle at Alnwick, and left the fighting to his sons Henry (Harry Hotspur) and Ralph. Hotspur attacked too soon, lost his personal banner and swore to recover it immediately. On August 15th, 1388, although his forces now outnumbered the Scots, Hotspur lost the famous battle of Otterburn, known to the ballad writers as the 'hontyng off the Cheviot' or the battle of Chevy Chase.[1] He slew the Douglas in single combat, but both he and his brother were captured and taken prisoner to Edinburgh. A major invasion of England had been met with mere local levies owing to the incompetence of the Council. The captured knights cost the country heavy ransoms. The Border was unsettled for years. It was scarcely what was expected of a war party which never ceased to taunt Richard with his lack of military prowess.

In civil affairs, the Appellants' record was equally undistinguished. In September 1388 Parliament was summoned for the first and last time in English history to Cambridge, where it met in the priory of Barnwell. The rolls of this Parliament have been lost, but there is ample evidence in the chronicle of the Monk of Westminster,[2] and on the statute book, to prove it one of the most interesting Parliaments of the Middle Ages – not for what it achieved but for what it discussed. It dealt chiefly with three great mediaeval social problems – the practice of livery and maintenance, the wages and mobility of labour and the responsibility for the poor, and the sanitation of towns.

The Commons complained against both royal and baronial 'livery', and the consequent evil of justice overridden or perverted by the armed force or threats of baronial retainers. It was an evil which touched the Commons very closely – especially the knights of the shire who were not sufficiently wealthy to support retinues of their own, but who were wealthy enough to have considerable property worth protecting in the shire and hundred courts. In the following century, the letters of the Pastons of Norfolk give an authentic picture of the ruthlessness and success with which the 'private companies' applied the habits so profitably practised in the French wars to an English countryside nominally at peace and theoretically protected by all the majesty of the law. The fourteenth century was not quite so lawless as the fifteenth, but it was lawless enough. The root cause of the abuse was that the livery and maintenance of the crown – the King's uniform and the King's justice – had not yet obtained a monopoly of that force which is one sanction of justice, and Richard anticipated the Tudors by suggesting to the Cambridge Parliament an all-round disarmament – his own white hart would disappear with the bear and the ragged staff, and all the other symbols of private power, while the royal standard of England would remain supreme. To his enemies, and especially to Gloucester and his friends, this proposal must have seemed as malevolent and cunning as it seems rational and beneficent to modern eyes. Both views are probably correct – Richard's intelligence was of a high standard, and his proposal was clever politics and sound statesmanship. Although well aware that the royal revenues could not yet afford to keep a standing army which could also be a permanent police force, he doubtless enjoyed suggesting baronial weapons for restraining baronial misbehaviour. A compromise was arranged. As from the next Parliament, all wearing of cognizances more recent in origin than the accession of Edward III would cease – a compromise which ensured that nothing whatsoever would be done, but which satisfied the Commons for the time being. Richard, without a standing army and with an overburdened Exchequer, was compelled to build up, under the famous insignia of the white hart, that armed support which every greater baron already had, and which had shown at Radcot Bridge how formidable it could be, and at Otterburn how irresponsible. Livery and maintenance continued to make a mockery of mediaeval law, until the Tudors could afford royal artillery to make a nonsense of mediaeval armour.

The Statutes of Labourers next occupied the attention of Parliament, and resulted in a series of savage regulations[1] which demonstrates how shocked the ruling classes of England had been by the Revolt of 1381, and how utterly without representation the masses of the population were – knights and burgesses were as bitterly against the poor as barons and prelates, and Richard was sufficiently of his period to share their bitterness. Labourers were forbidden to move from one place of work to another without a licence from the Justices of the Peace under pain of forty days' imprisonment. Sturdy beggars and begging pilgrims were to be treated as runaway labourers. Children of labourers were not to be taught a trade if their labour was required on the land. Labourers were expected to carry bows but were forbidden to carry cutting or thrusting weapons. While the Justices of the Peace were to receive 4/- a day, and 2/- a day for their clerks, from the fines they imposed, maximum wages for labourers were fixed between 6/- and 10/- a *year* 'or less in districts where they are accustomed to get less'. Fortunately for the common folk of England there was greater strength in the forces of economics than in the reactionary repression of the Lords, and the periodical renewals of Statutes of Labourers were quite impotent to halt the process of economic emancipation, although they made that process as slow and as bitter as possible.

The almost total lack of sanitation in mediaeval towns had undoubtedly increased the casualties of the Black Death and its subsequent lesser visitations, and, in this Cambridge Parliament, the so-called Statute of Barnwell was the first urban sanitary act in our history. Its preamble is a revealing document:–

'For that so much dung and filth of the garbage and entrails, as well of beasts killed as of other corruptions, be cast and put in ditches, rivers, and other waters, and also within many other places, within, about and nigh unto divers cities, boroughs and towns of the realm and the suburbs of them, that the air there is greatly corrupt and infect, and many maladies and other intolerable diseases do daily happen, as well to the inhabitants, and those that are conversant in the said cities etc. as to others repairing and travelling thither to the great annoyance damage and peril of the inhabitants dwellers repairers and travellers aforesaid . . .'[1]

Certain primitive regulations were made for the removal of dung and refuse, and the proper cleansing of streets and lanes. In a reactionary Parliament it was the one sign of progress.

In January 1389 a Great Council was held at Westminster. The grim lesson of Otterburn had been learnt, and the Border defences were strengthened by making Nottingham (the Earl Marshal) Warden of the East March, and Northumberland Warden of the West March, with a force of 600 lances and 2,000 archers at their disposal. The Council then seems to have been concerned about the possibility of Gaunt's arrival home – they conferred on him the actual Duchy of Aquitaine in the hope that it would keep him out of the way still longer; and to balance this profitable honour they named Gloucester the King's Lieutenant in Ireland, in spite of the fact that de Vere's Irish Dukedom had been criticized as an illegal alienation of the 'regalia'. But, apart from the reactionary labour legislation of the Cambridge Parliament, and these minor manœuvres at Westminster, the government of the Lords Appellant was singularly sterile. Rendered impotent by the consciousness of its own illegality it remained satisfied in the satiation of its hatreds and the enjoyment of its spoils.[1]

The effect of the Merciless Parliament on Richard was profound. Apart from the comfort of his wife he now had no one to whom he could turn for help, and it is not surprising that, after the Cambridge Parliament, he found distraction in a more prolonged indulgence than usual in the pleasure of the autumn hunting – a fact easily distorted by the antipathetic chroniclers into a disgraceful callousness and an immoral levity. But Richard found wisdom in his adversity, his future plans are in sober contrast to the temperamental outbursts of his adolescence. The son of the Black Prince had been brought up from his earliest years in the over-emphasized consciousness of his mystical 'regalitée': yet he had suffered at the hands of his own relatives a degradation which had deprived him of every personal friend and counsellor; he had even seen his Queen grossly insulted. For the future, he would walk warily; but every step he took would take him closer to his revenge, and nearer to the full realization of that 'dominium' in which he believed with all the sincerity of a man whose religion was a real part of his daily life. As he pondered the future, he could see one way out of his difficulties. The most powerful Lord in England, his uncle John of Gaunt, whose sense of 'regalitée' had been so often preached to him in public and in private, was due back from Spain, and if there was any man that Gloucester feared it was Gaunt.

Gaunt's expedition to Spain[2] in July 1386 had scarcely brought spectacular glory to English arms, but it had had brilliant successes of a different kind – it had denied Gaunt the throne of Castile, but it had made him the father of two dynasties, and was sending him home vastly richer, and at last satisfied. His armies had overrun

Galicia, and, in alliance with the Portuguese, had reduced Castile to terms – and Gaunt had been as brilliant in diplomacy as he was undistinguished in war. His daughter Philippa had been married to King John of Portugal, and his daughter Katherine to Henry of Castile. My Lord of Spain had divested himself of his own royal title but only to present two of his children with royal escutcheons, and the price of his condescension was the enormous sum of 600,000 gold francs (which were actually paid in three instalments) and an annuity of 40,000 gold francs in addition (which was paid almost up to the end of his life). Two monarchies – of Portugal and of Castile – would now trace their ancestry to John of Gaunt; it was no deed of Gaunt's which was soon to add the royal arms of England to his family tree.

It was in the full knowledge of the possibilities of turning the tables on Gloucester by the return of Gaunt that Richard took his next carefully calculated and dramatic step. On May 3rd, 1389 Richard entered the council chamber at Westminster – it was most probably a meeting of the Great Council and not merely of the Gloucester Commission: Richard could still count on some support from the former but none from the latter. To the astonishment of the Lords he asked them his age. They replied that he was turned twenty – an underestimate because he was now turned twenty-two. Richard followed up with the dramatic conclusion:

> 'Therefore I am of full age to govern myself, my household, and my realm, for it seems wrong to me that I should be treated with less consideration than the meanest of my subjects. For what heir in my realm, when he has passed his twentieth year and his parent is dead, is prevented from freely conducting his own affairs? Why therefore deny me what is conceded to others of lesser rank?' [1]

No wonder that the assembled Lords were '*attoniti*'; but their astonishment must have been equalled by their chagrin – Richard had surprised them with an unanswerable case, because every indictment of the Merciless Parliament had blamed royal advisers but in no instance had dared directly to blame the King. They were compelled by their own logic to reply that Richard was entitled to everything that was rightly his. Of Richard's speech in reply there are two versions – the version of his critic Walsingham and the version of the friendly Monk of Westminster, and

Professor Tout has ingeniously combined the two in the following version: –

'You know well that for the twelve years of my reign, I and my realm have been ruled by others, and my people oppressed year by year with grievous taxes. Henceforth, with God's help, I shall labour assiduously to bring my realm to greater peace and prosperity. Up to now, I have been allowed to do nothing without my protectors. Now I will remove all these men from my Council, summon to advise me whomsoever I will, and transact my own business myself. I, therefore, order as a first step that the Chancellor shall surrender to me the seal.' [1]

The Appellants and the assembled Lords had no other course than to obey.

It is a dramatic story. The young King, apparently stripped of all power and cut off from every friend and all friendly advice, had acted on his own unaided initiative [2] with so sure a sense of political realities and political contingencies – Gaunt was on his way – that Gloucester and the Appellants were beaten without a word of protest. They had shown a ruthless efficiency in seizing power, they had shown a savage relentlessness in using power, they had been too reckless to ensure that at least that power was put on a legal basis, and their year of illegal government had shown no improvement on the record of the able men they had so cruelly put out of their way. Gloucester never had more than the makings of a *condottiere* in him, and, if his ambition ever soared as high as a throne, its truer level was the saddle of his charger, and the panoply of his own outmoded Court of Chivalry. And, throughout this fascinating episode of the Lords Appellant, it is interesting to see how Gloucester's apparent all-powerfulness was always at the mercy of a Gaunt, whose son held a deadly watching brief within the Appellants' own innermost councils. The Lords Appellant taught Richard some bitter lessons – he was wise enough to profit by them, and slowly and surely to prepare a final settling of accounts.

VI

THE SEVEN QUIET YEARS

THE SEVEN YEARS which intervene between the bloody drama of the Appellants and the tragic climax to Richard's reign have seemed a veritable doldrums to chronicler and historian alike. The chroniclers have made up for lack of incident by picturesqueness of imagination – signs and wonders, prodigies and earthquakes colour their dull material; the historians have carelessly hurried over a chapter which in time covers a third of the reign and which, although complicated in detail, is revealing in implication. The English chroniclers, writing or revising when a touchy usurping Lancastrian was only too ready to take offence, magnified any incident which could add to the discredit of the deposed, and were unable to appreciate that the years 1389 to 1396 were in some ways the most brilliant years of mediaeval England; more recent historians have not troubled to counterbalance the Lancastrian chroniclers with friendly English or unbiassed French, or to disentangle threads which make the tapestry of the final curtain an understandable pattern.

For most of the people of England these seven years were indeed 'quiet' – there was no war with France, and the political executioners were unemployed. But, at court and in Council, there was ceaseless and significant activity. In the County Palatine there was a civil war; in the capital a royal quarrel of hitherto unimaginable dimensions; in Ireland an overseas expedition on the French scale, but in a better cause. In spiritual affairs, there was the surprising emergence of the Lollards, and two famous acts of state. There was the arbitrary hand of death to mould events to an unplanned shape, to uncover the soul of a King, and to expose 'quietness' for the illusion it is usually found to be when history seeks the roots of events and considers culture as important as politics. Finally, in foreign affairs there was a long truce with France to be sealed with the pomp of a second royal marriage.

Richard, at twenty-two years of age, was at last King. Throughout the twelve years he had already sat on the throne he had been either in tutelage to older relatives and friends of his father or humiliated and thwarted by a baronial caucus. As a youth he had proved his personal courage; on too many occasions since he had displayed a temper which he had not yet learned to control. His first serious effort at statecraft had failed but had taught him much. His overthrow of Gloucester and the Appellants had displayed a touch of political genius – their usurpation of sovereignty had been undone by the simple and peaceful process of calling their bluff. But Richard's quiet assumption of full powers left him dangerously alone during the critical few months before his uncle Gaunt could return from building dynasties in Spain to spend his remaining years in England loyally propping the dynasty which he had so often been suspected of plotting to upset. Richard had to walk warily, and his first steps proved that he realized it. That Archbishop Arundel should be deprived of the Great Seal was the necessary corollary to Richard's new powers, but the appointment of William of Wykeham in his place gives the lie to historians who would like Richard's *coup* to appear as a first *coup d'état*. William of Wykeham, revered founder of both Winchester College and New College, Oxford, pillar of all the conservative proprieties and model of time-serving orthodoxy, was the perfect choice to reassure all three estates of the realm – his very mediocrity was excellent propaganda. The Treasury was forced on Brantingham, Bishop of Exeter, another elder civil servant as politically colourless as Wykeham. It was only to be expected that both Gloucester and Warwick would be omitted from the Council – but even this was only a temporary exclusion. The replacement of the Earl of Arundel as Admiral and Captain of Brest by the King's half-brother John Holland, now Earl of Huntingdon, was almost justifiable in a settlement clearly designed to appease rather than revolutionize. In the sphere of justice, the Appellants' choices were confirmed, although five new judges were appointed. In the Exchequer, the Chief Baron was the only Appellant nomination to be disapproved. The only really sweeping changes were made in the appointments for Ireland, where Richard thus early showed his interest in those Irish affairs which were neglected by every other mediaeval English King except Henry II and John. Gloucester's Lieutenancy of Ireland was not even mentioned, and

Sir John Stanley, who had been the beloved Duke of Ireland's deputy, was made Justice; it is in smaller matters of this nature that Richard reveals to history what he disguised from contemporaries – a purposeful policy of ultimate vengeance. In finance, Richard's first acts were unexpectedly generous. The wealthier Commons were mollified by a postponement of a portion of the last subsidy voted, and even the Appellants were surprisingly appeased – the balance of the £20,000 they had persuaded the Merciless Parliament to vote to them for their meritorious services was actually paid. By proclamation to the sheriffs, the graces and pardons of the Merciless Parliament were confirmed, and impeachment for anything done by it was specifically ruled out. Most striking of all, there is no evidence that Richard made any persistent attempts to recall his surviving friends from exile. De Vere was in Louvain, and Suffolk in Paris, and it would have been folly for Richard to do what friendship prompted – both had been condemned to death as traitors in their absence. A few months later Suffolk died,[1] and neither Archbishop Neville (who was also in Louvain) nor de Vere ever saw England again.

One new appointment made by Richard is worthy of special attention. Edmund de Stafford was made Keeper of the Privy Seal. He was a lesser lord, and his career had begun in the Church where he specialized in the study of the Civil Law. He had been Chancellor of Oxford University (where he later became the second founder of Exeter College)[2] and since 1385 he had been Dean of York. When appointed Keeper he was a distinguished scholar and administrator, without attachments to any faction, and already elderly by mediaeval standards – he was forty-five. He was to remain in Richard's service to the end, and in 1396 he became his Chancellor. The interesting fact is that he was reappointed Chancellor by Henry IV in 1403, and remained honoured and revered until his death at the very ripe age of seventy-five. Richard, in his own day and since, has been frequently accused of misjudgment in the choice of friends and advisers; yet if to Burley and de la Pole is added the name of de Stafford the record goes far to disprove the accusation. Stafford was a wise and far-seeing choice for an office which was the focal point of royal government, and neither Richard nor his peers had at this time any awareness of any other form of government.

Richard's sureness of touch in handling so delicate a situation may have owed much to the knowledge that his uncle Gaunt was on his way home, but he nevertheless deserves more credit than he has hitherto received for a political settlement worthy of the astutest of statesmen. On August 11th, 1389 Richard's anxiety to see Gaunt found expression – he sent him an urgent letter asking him to return 'with every possible haste'.[1] The ex-King of Castile, still reluctant to tear himself away from the Continent, and somewhat worried by the difficulties of his new responsibilities in Bordeaux, asked for a delay until the following February. It was refused, and, on October 30th, Richard sent him a summons to return forthwith. On November 19th Gaunt landed at Plymouth[2] and made ready to attend the King's Council at Reading on December 10th. Richard took the trouble to meet him in state.[3] Three years before, Richard had been only too glad to speed his departure; now he was overjoyed to welcome him back as an elder statesman above suspicion, and quite without implication in the butchery of the First Rebellion. Here indeed was a prop to majesty if the records of the Good Parliament spoke truth, and here was an appropriate answer to the reckless and bloodstained Gloucester. The kisses of peace at Reading were followed by a triumphal ride to Westminster – where Gaunt was greeted by mayor, sheriffs, abbot and monks, and conducted to a special service of thanksgiving first in the Abbey and later in St Paul's. For the rest of his life Gaunt was to be the peacemaker – at home as well as abroad.

The first Parliament of the new dispensation met at Westminster in January 1390. Its first act was another example of clever political stage-craft.[4] The great officers of state – the Chancellor, the Treasurer, and the Lords of the Council – were persuaded to resign their seals voluntarily and to submit themselves to a scrutiny of their stewardship. It was an elaborate and somewhat theatrical way of asking for a vote of confidence in the days before that phrase had any constitutional significance. On the following day, Gaunt, speaking for the King, even asked the Commons for their opinion of the Council, and all its officers received their approval. Richard therefore reappointed them all, and, again with general approval, added both Gaunt and Gloucester to their number. But the touch of showmanship was well balanced by the care with which Richard pointed out that such consideration for Parliament was not to be taken as a precedent, and that he at all times reserved his right to appoint and remove his ministers without question – a piece of constitutional realism which no one was prepared to dispute.

Within a few months of Richard's assumption of full power, his enemies were all reinstated, but with the powerful counterweight of Gaunt superimposed. The restoration of the Appellants was not forced upon Richard. It was an astute way of building up support for himself behind a screen which gave the Appellants shelter for the time being, and no cause to grumble. Even Gloucester, Arundel and Warwick had been restored to the Council. The aged and neutral Brantingham had quickly retired in favour of the Appellant Bishop Gilbert, and, although the second dummy of the appeasement scene – Wykeham – clung to office for another two years, he was then replaced by the Appellant Thomas Arundel. Nottingham and Derby were back in the Council, and Gloucester was even given the office of Justice of Chester and North Wales – a quarter supposed to be peculiarly royalist. Only in minor appointments did new names appear – John Waltham became Bishop of Salisbury, Huntingdon was made Chamberlain of the Household, Sir Thomas Percy, brother of Northumberland, became Vice-Chamberlain, and Edward, son of the Duke of York and cousin to Richard, was created Earl of Rutland. Richard's first group of friends were dead or in exile – he was now beginning to build up a new group, but he was acting quietly and avoiding advertisement or suspicion. In return for the support of Gaunt, Richard paid handsomely, and, as events turned out, unwisely – the County Palatine of Lancaster, and its Dukedom, were made the hereditary property of Gaunt and his male heirs in tail, and a month later 'Monseigneur d'Espaigne' became 'Monseigneur de Guyenne' in virtue of his new Dukedom of Aquitaine.[1] The colossal Palatinate powers of Lancaster were now hereditary; but Gaunt was the King's friend, and his heir was not yet a threat to the throne.

But these interchanges of office and marks of royal favour only affected the court circle and the baronage – the policy of continuity with the Cambridge Parliament of the Appellants went still further. Its Statute against Provisors was confirmed, its attempt to restrict the abuse of liveries was repeated with as little effect, because, as one chronicler put it, 'the nobles were unwilling',[1] and its savage Statutes of Labourers were repeated with the amendment that wages should be based on a sliding scale assessed by the local Justices of the Peace – the wealthy Commons too received their share of appeasement. As for the people of England – the 'Field of Folk' – there was no one to speak for them, and their only means of expression was still the futile method of open revolt. A curt entry in the chronicle of Walsingham reveals how little the so-called three estates were concerned with the condition of the people, and how the embers of 1381 still smouldered – 'in the same Parliament certain new insurgents from Kent were taken, drawn and hung'.[2] The state of general lawlessness is confirmed in a Statute which restricted pardons for criminal offences – in future strict enquiry was to be obligatory and pardons only granted under the Privy Seal – and in various restrictions placed on such prerogative justice as obtained in the unpopular courts of the Constable and the Marshal:[3] the former had been an instrument of Gloucester, the latter an instrument of the Crown under its officer the Steward of the Household, and both were to be used again before the reign closed.

One picturesque incident of this period is fortunately preserved. In the middle of the critical rearrangement and resettlement of a disturbed kingdom, Richard sent a pair of red velvet shoes, jewelled in a pattern of flowers, to the Abbey of Westminster to replace the pair spoilt when, overtired by the lengthy coronation ceremony, he had dropped one shoe as he was being carried by Sir Simon Burley through the surging crowd.[4] While his every public act proclaimed his zeal for continuity and his apparent willingness to forgive, a charming private gesture reveals that Richard could not forget. Neither his own requests nor the prayers of his Queen had saved Burley from the man whom it was now expedient to include in his Council. Did Gloucester appreciate the true significance of so seemingly pretty a gesture?

In July, Gaunt returned recent compliments by entertaining the royal court at Leicester. In the chronicler's phrase 'rejoicings were heaped on rejoicings', and the atmosphere was so congenial that Gaunt took the opportunity to refer to his old London *protégé* John of Northampton, who was still a prisoner. Richard pointed out to his 'sweetest uncle' that it was beyond his power to act; to which Gaunt protested in no measured terms that at least the King had the power of mercy. Richard did what he could – he allowed the man he had once hastily condemned to death to return to London and enjoy at least partial rights of citizenship, but, if the chronicler's verbatim report of the conversation is correct, he did so gracefully only in the hope that one day he might extend the prerogative of mercy to cover his own exiled friends overseas.[1]

The junketings at Leicester were followed in October by a magnificent tournament at Smithfield. Jousts were the fourteenth-century equivalents of the twentieth-century diplomatic banquets – they were international events when much secret diplomacy was transacted under cover of a gorgeous ceremonial which flattered foreign visitors and gave the populace something to cheer. The Smithfield jousts were the English return match for the celebrated jousts of St Inglevert of the previous year.[2] In Normandy, the name and fame of English Chivalry had been worthily upheld by Richard's half-brother Huntingdon and Gaunt's son the Earl of Derby. At Smithfield, Richard himself won, or was tactfully awarded, the honours of the first day, the Count of St Pol was the gallant representative of France, and the Earl of Ostrenantz of Germany. These were the first moves in a diplomatic *démarche* which at last recognized the futility of the perpetual war with France. Gaunt's peacemaking in England, and his outstanding prestige at home and abroad, marked him out as the obvious English ambassador in the approaching negotiations with the enemy across the Channel. There was still a war party in England, but its chief – Gloucester – realized that for the moment he could not swim against the tide. He decided to follow Derby on a crusade in Prussia against the King of Lithuania, but, whereas Derby ultimately returned with considerable laurels, Gloucester was quickly defeated by a storm which sent him back to England by way of Norway and Scotland before the end of the year.

The continental scene at this period was overshadowed by a grave threat from the east. The Ottoman Turks were at the gates of Hungary, following on their victory over the Serbs at Kossovo (1389). The accession of the famous Sultan Bajazet threatened Constantinople with a fate only postponed with difficulty until its final catastrophic fall in 1453. Facing the Turks was a Christendom still divided by the Great Schism, and the chances of a united

crusade were wrecked on the rocks of Rome and Avignon. Nevertheless, there was every possibility, in view of the threat from the
east, of at least a peace between England and France. Froissart
tells us that, while the gentry fought, the fishermen on both sides
of the Channel found the brotherhood of the sea more compelling
than a war which had long since lost its meaning for them, and
both Froissart and the English chroniclers were at pains to
emphasize the current friendships of the English and French
upper classes.[1] The force of economics was a pressure in the same
direction. The ransoms of a Crécy or a Poitiers were large, but
they benefited only a few – they were occasional windfalls and no
substitute for a regular income – and helped the royal treasury
least of all. Neither in France nor in England had anyone yet
solved the formidable problem of supporting a national monarchy
by the economic mechanisms of the feudal class structure. Similarly,
the Great Schism compelled each rival Pope to maintain the show
of complete power on the means of half the normal papal revenue.
Wiser minds, if they could have seen the European picture simpli-
fied as the telescope of history sees it, would have found ample
justification for an end to the Schism, for peace between England
and France (and therefore Scotland), and for a joint crusade to
save western Europe from its eastern invaders. There was,
fortunately, enough of wisdom to see at least the need for peace.

In the Parliament of 1391, with Gloucester temporarily out of
the way, serious peace negotiations were at last authorized. The
Commons asked that 'Monseigneur de Guyenne' should be
Richard's chief ambassador, 'he being the most sufficient person
of the realm', and gave Richard the confidence of a special
petition that he 'should be as free in his royal dignity as any of
his predecessors, despite any statute to the contrary, notably those
in the days of Edward II, and that if any such statute had that
effect under Edward II it should be annulled'.[2] The Commons'
appraisal of Gaunt was justified. He was the most important feudal
dignitary in Europe – he was personally known to kings, counts
and dukes, his two sons-in-law were Kings of Portugal and Castile,
he was richer than the King of England, his Palatinate was now
hereditary, he was old in experience both military and diplomatic,
and it was in his personal interests, as Duke of Aquitaine and as
father-in-law to the monarchies of the Peninsula, that the war
with France should finish. He proceeded to do his utmost to that

end to the satisfaction of his King, but not to the satisfaction of professional soldiers like Gloucester, or monkish chroniclers who complained bitterly[1] of the colossal expenses which his grand manner involved.

Gaunt landed at Calais in March 1392 with a peace-seeking embassy which included his brother the Duke of York (but omitted his bellicose brother the Duke of Gloucester) and also such comparatively reasonable younger men as Huntingdon, Sir Thomas Percy, and his own son the Earl of Derby. Their welcome was truly regal.[2] Their progress to Amiens, where Charles VI was to meet them, was graced with all the pomp and colour of Chivalry, and in the city itself every knight of Gaunt's retinue found his lodging emblazoned with his appropriate arms. Four thousand watchmen kept the peace, and even a fire-brigade was in readiness. Hospitality was lavish and free, and at the great banquet in the Archbishop's palace England's chief representative sat at the French King's right hand, and was served by the Dukes of Orleans and Bourbon. The mission was not successful in negotiating a treaty of peace, but at least it brought back a truce which could be extended. The chief difficulty was the request of France that England should surrender Calais and raze its fortifications – a request that stimulated a French friend of Chaucer to compose a popular ballade of the time which has survived – it has the refrain *'paix n'arez ja s'ilz ne rendent Calays'*.[3] In fairness to the French negotiators it must be stated that Gaunt also put forward an absurd claim – he demanded the unpaid balance of King John's ransom and the status quo of the Treaty of Bretigny. Both claims were the high prices of good bargainers hoping eventually to come to terms. In the following year, similar lavish ceremonial was staged at Lelinghen, and again only a truce resulted, chiefly because of the madness which from time to time incapacitated the King of France. Negotiations were again interrupted in 1393 by Gaunt's preoccupation with a rising in Cheshire, and handicapped by the unwise addition of Gloucester to the negotiators, but, by 1394, in spite of complications arising from the pressure of the rival Popes, peace was possible, and on May 24th, 1394 Gaunt at last accepted the Truce of Lelinghen which was to continue for at least four years – long enough for the truce to be reinforced by a royal marriage. Gaunt, supported throughout by Richard and the ablest counsellors of his realm, had actually secured peace with France for at least a generation. It was popular with everyone except the Gloucester faction and their liveried retainers, whose only fortune was in the fortunes of war, and those clergy who, on instructions from Rome, disliked any compromise with the supporters of Avignon. Some of the great outstanding points of dispute were still left unsettled, but the main objective of peace had been secured.

An incident behind the scenes illustrates the difficulties Richard and Gaunt had to face. The fortress of Cherbourg, owned by the King of Navarre, had been pawned to England in 1378, but it was a condition of the transaction that it could be redeemed after three years at the price of the loan. In early 1394, the French lent the King of Navarre the redemption money, and Richard did not hesitate to honour his bond – the money was acknowledged and the fortress was handed back. An act so creditable to Richard was taken as a mortal affront by the war-party of Gloucester and his friends, and three years later it was even made into a charge against Richard. And an incident of another kind illustrates the development of a new spirit amongst those Lords who throughout the feudal era had been nearer to their social equals across the Channel than to their social inferiors at home. During the negotiations at Lelinghen great difficulty was experienced because the English version of the French language – the Norman French – was not understood by the French ambassadors, and the English could not follow the discussions which took place in official French. The difficulty was resolved by the presentation of all proposals in pure written French: it marks the beginning of that supremacy which French still enjoys as common diplomatic language, and the beginning of the end of that horizontal stratification of the nobility of both countries which had delayed the rise of nationalism so long.

If in the immediate governmental settlement, and in subsequent foreign affairs, the Quiet Years of Richard's reign proceeded smoothly; at home and outside court circles there was rougher weather. In 1392, Richard's skill faltered – he again quarrelled violently with his capital city. London was his main source of ready cash – a necessity which placed all the mediaeval kings at the mercy of moneylenders. The expenses of diplomacy were no less than the expenses of war, and, even if the malevolence of

monkish chroniclers be correctly discounted, there is no doubt
that Richard's court was both expensive and luxurious. It was
not unusual for the city to be asked to make an advance to the
Exchequer, but on this famous occasion the Londoners not only
refused a request for £1,000 but went so far as to assault a Lombard merchant who provided the sum in their stead. Both King
and Council were outraged, and even the chronicler inveighs
against the Londoners as 'greedy, arrogant and turbulent folks,
these supporters of Lollardy and contemners of God and the
ancient traditions'.[1] But Richard's reaction, intelligible in a high
tempered man, was inexcusable in a King who now needed every
friend he could possibly find. The ancient liberties of the City of
London were sequestrated. The Mayor was deposed and the city
governed by a Warden who was the King's nominee – Sir Edward
Dalingridge. The royal courts were removed from London to
York, and the Mayor, sheriffs, aldermen and other prominent
citizens[2] summoned under penalty to hear Richard's sentence at
Nottingham. The Mayor and sheriffs were imprisoned and all
London's liberties cancelled. For five months the ban remained,
and it was only owing to the intervention of their old enemy
Gaunt, and the conciliatory influence of Richard's Queen, that
in September the quarrel was patched up – at a price. It cost the
Londoners £10,000 for their pardon and a fine of £3,000 for their
contumacy, but, in spite of a spectacular reconciliation scene at
Christmas (when the King was presented with a camel amongst
other gifts), it cost Richard every friend he had in the city – the
'Londoner's King' of the coronation year had finally lost London.
From the point of view of Richard's self interest it was an act of
folly, but Richard cannot be understood unless it is appreciated
that at all controversial moments he was a consistently mediaeval
king. In the poll-tax scale of 1379 the Mayor of London had been
rated the equal of an earl or a bishop, but these were money scales;
in the scale of social prestige, king, earls, barons and bishops were
of a quality which scorned the tally of cash. If the effortless
superiority of the well-born and the well-educated over the less
fortunate born to a life of 'trade', as exhibited in the novels of
Thackeray, Trollope and Meredith, is borne in mind, it will be
realized why Richard's treatment of the Londoners 400 years
before met with such general approval from his Lords and even
from some of the chroniclers. Richard was never a democrat, and

his keen sense of his own inalienable *regalitée* had been affronted in no uncertain fashion; the spectacular nature of the punishment he meted out is the authentic stamp of the mediaeval autocrat. The point which has been so often missed about Richard's quarrel with London is that, by the feudal standards of his own day and in the judgment of his peers, Richard was wholly in the right.

In the following year, 1393, occurred the mysterious Cheshire Rising – important enough to interrupt Gaunt's peace-making in France, and, even though its details are obscure,[1] a revelation of the unquiet state of England during these so-called Quiet Years. If Kent during Richard's reign was the county of organized popular discontent, the north was the area of unorganized lawlessness. Gaunt's Palatinate of Lancaster, the royal Palatinate of Chester, and the harried border territories further north were accustomed to a life of foray and counter-foray. When Welsh or Scots left them in comparative peace there were always the lesser local Lords who, at such a distance from royal justice, could take the law into their own hands, and, when the King's writ did reach out to them, those who refused it could happily become outlaws and, from the security of forest, fell and moor, rob and rape as they willed. The Rolls of successive Parliaments had been drawing the attention of the Council especially to the anarchy prevailing in the north – tenants were being dispossessed by force of arms, wives and heirs kidnapped and put to ransom, heiresses forced to marry their captors – and, when the justices did sit, they were threatened with the interference of bands of armed and unbridled baronial retainers. Peace with France had put men-at-arms out of work and left fighting Lords without a battle field – the professional soldiery of the Hundred Years War was a constant menace to a system of English justice based primarily on the goodwill of neighbours rather than on the sanction of armed force.

Disturbances had occurred in Chester five years before when Gloucester had first been made its Justice, and in the following year Justice for life. The citizens may have had a sound political grievance in the sense that they resented any sign of the alienation of Chester from direct touch with the crown, but their methods of expressing it did not please Richard, and, in confirming their liberties, he imposed a fine of 3,000 marks. Only 1,000 marks were actually collected, and the balance was resisted by force. Open revolt broke out in 1393 under the leadership of a local lord – Sir

Thomas Talbot – and was quickly linked with a similar revolt in Yorkshire, where a certain William Beckwith had taken to the greenwood after slaying Sir Robert Rokeby in a local feud. So much is fact – there is much more which is supposition, and the suppositions are connected with the greatest names in the land. Was it possible that Arundel and Gloucester had fomented the disorder? It was rumoured that the insurgents planned to kill both Gaunt and Derby, and neither Gloucester, as Justice of Chester, nor Arundel, who throughout was sitting with considerable forces in his castle at Holt-on-Dee (a mere fifteen miles from Chester), made the slightest effort to quell the rising. Was it a misfired attempt of the war-party to thwart the peace-making policy of Richard and Gaunt? Every church door in the disturbed areas advertised inflammatory libels against Gaunt. Was Richard himself a party to the rising? On May 6th, in a proclamation to Gaunt, Gloucester and the sheriffs of Shropshire, Staffordshire, Derbyshire, Leicestershire and Warwickshire, Richard expressly protested his innocence of any attempt 'to destroy the magnates of the realm' – a proclamation which reveals how widespread were the disorders, and how wild were the rumours noised abroad. Did Richard protest too much? Such questions are best answered by the actions of Gaunt. In the summer, he was urgently summoned from France by Richard to head a special commission of royal Justices to the disaffected counties, where one chronicler maintains that 20,000 men were under arms. Gaunt acted with speed and moderation. Travelling first to Yorkshire, then to his own Palatinate, and finally to Chester, he seems to have realized that the roots of the disorder were not political but economic – revolt had been led by the unemployed and unemployable returned soldiery. Gaunt's was no Bloody Assize: on the contrary, he had the wit to enrol the malcontents for service in his new Duchy of Aquitaine, and even the ringleaders were granted mercy. It was the policy of a mediaeval Pitt faced with the militarism of the clans.

The sequel to the Cheshire Rising is better documented. In the following year, 1394, Gloucester was removed from his life appointment as Justice of Cheshire and North Wales in favour of Mowbray, Earl of Nottingham – it should have been another sign to Gloucester that the King had forgotten nothing.[1] But, if the tide was flowing against Gloucester, his chief partner in the crimes of the Merciless Parliament – Arundel – also refused to recognize it.

In the spring Parliament of 1394 he seems to have decided to fore-stall any charges which his enemy Gaunt might be prepared to make against him by a reckless attack which in implication even involved the King.[1] In full Parliament he indicted Gaunt on six charges. The Duke of Guienne had been seen walking arm-in-arm with the King; the King was wearing the collar of the Lancastrian livery;[2] the King's retainers were doing likewise; the Duke was in the habit of using such 'rough and bitter' words that other members of the Council were overborne before they could say their say; the grant of the Duchy of Aquitaine was derogatory to the King; the Duke had squandered public money on a private war against Castile. It was a clumsy attempt to revive Richard's old suspicions of Gaunt, to play on his newly won pride in throwing off his tutelage, and to enlist the support of all Gaunt's enemies. Arundel was acting as though he were living in the days of the Good Parliament, and ignoring the fact that Gaunt was now a popular elder statesman with the King as his best friend. Richard answered Arundel's charges seriatim. If he walked arm-in-arm with Gaunt, it was no more significant than walking arm-in-arm with his other uncles. He had himself taken the collar from Gaunt's neck on his return from Spain, and was proud to wear it 'en signe de bon amour d'entier cor entre eux'. If his retainers did likewise, it was he who had given them the lead. He was un-aware of any time when any earl had been refused the opportunity to speak as he wished without fear. The grant of Aquitaine had been agreed in full Parliament. The final point – a shrewd one – was nicely answered: half the cost of the Spanish army had been freely voted by the Commons, the balance had been acknowledged as a personal debt by Gaunt but remitted by the consent of Parliament in return for Gaunt's services en route to Spain at the relief of Brest and elsewhere. Parliament examined charges and answers, and unanimously exculpated Gaunt. The King, there-fore, with the assent of all present, demanded a public apology from Arundel, and the Rolls of Parliament give us its exact words: 'Sire, sith that hit semeth to the Kyng and to the other Lordes, and eke that yhe ben so mychel greved and displeisid be my wordes, hit forthynketh me, and bysech yowe of your gode lord-ship to remyt me your mautalent'.[3] Arundel's attack had sadly miscarried, and he retired from the Council to nurse a grievance which was to burst out afresh a few months later in the year.

Richard II, from the effigy by Nicolas Broke
and Godfrey Prest in Westminster Abbey, 1395

Richard II as the young King, a contemporary portrait on wood
by an unknown artist, now in the nave of Westminster Abbey

Anne of Bohemia, Richard's first queen, from the effigy by
Nicolas Broke and Godfrey Prest in Westminster Abbey

Edward, Prince of Wales (the Black Prince),
from the effigy in Canterbury Cathedral, c. 1376

John of Gaunt, from a window
in the chapel of All Souls, Oxford

Edward III in old age from the effigy by John Orchard
in Westminster Abbey, c. 1390

Henry IV, from the alabaster effigy
in Canterbury Cathedral, c. 1420

(*above*) Richard's shield from the roof of Westminster Hall, 1394-5

(*left*) His White Hart badge — one of over eighty variants in Westminster Hall

Richard for his part was still anxious to maintain a *façade* of goodwill even to such avowed and open enemies as Arundel, and on April 30th he granted Arundel a special pardon for all past misdeeds – it was another four years before Richard was ready to remove the *façade*, to revoke a pardon freely given, and at last to pay back so many insults.

In court circles, the year 1394 was a year of deaths which profoundly affected English history. In March, Gaunt's second wife Costanza of Castile died.[1] Chaucer had immortalized his first duchess, Blanche; but he had no lament for a duchess whose marriage had been a convenience, who had always remained a Spaniard, and whose virtuous and devout life had been so colourless that Gaunt had been excused for preferring the company of the brilliant Lady Catherine Swynford. Gaunt's liaison had been openly acknowledged for years – Lady Swynford did the honours of his household, and was welcomed and honoured at court. But Gaunt was still a stickler for some of the proprieties. On Costanza's funeral at St Mary's Leicester he lavished the extravagant sum of £550, and in his will he was careful to provide a chantry and an obit for her soul. Costanza's death made possible the future legitimization of Gaunt's children by Lady Swynford. It is possible that Gaunt's true heir Derby did not take kindly to these marks of royal favour to the illegitimate, and that from this time dates a further estrangement of the Appellant Derby from the King which finally grew to proportions which would have horrified the loyalty of Gaunt, even if it would have gratified his vanity and sated his wildest secret ambitions.

In July, Derby's wife died, that Mary who shared with her sister Eleanor the rich Bohun inheritance and who was therefore sister-in-law to Gloucester. It has been suggested that this may account for the fact that Derby now seemed also to draw apart from the Gloucester faction, and he certainly had no part in the beginning of the final crisis of the reign. He is a shadowy figure throughout the Quiet Years, never whole-heartedly an Appellant, always rather aloof from faction labels of any kind, and preferring to bide his time in the crusade of the Teutonic Knights against the Letts, and later in a pilgrimage to Jerusalem.[2] It was perhaps typical of his caution that he did not marry again until he was firmly seated on the throne.

In June, Richard himself had also become a widower. His

beloved Queen Anne had lived down her first unpopularity. She was no longer blamed for the expenses of a wedding others had arranged, or for the extravagances of her compatriots. When she appears at all in the chronicles, she appears as peace-lover and peace-maker, failing to soften the heart of a Gloucester but bringing her husband to see reason when his temper got the better of his judgment. Her effigy displays a benignity which still gives us an inkling of the power of a sweet nature in a brutal age, and goes some way to explain the depths of Richard's grief. Adam of Usk tells us that '*illa benignissima domina*' died at the manor of Sheen, which, 'though a royal one and very fair', did King Richard, by reason 'that that lady's death happened therein, command and cause to be utterly destroyed',[1] and in all the chronicles there is a unanimity of affection in phrasing which goes far beyond what either loyalty or good manners would explain,[2] especially when it is remembered that she was the wife of the villain of the piece as played to subsequent Lancastrian audiences. It has frequently been suggested that Richard 'went to pieces' after her death, and a recent historian has stated as fact what even a modern psychologist would hesitate to put forward as an absolute diagnosis. 'The course of Richard's mental disease', he writes, 'was certainly accelerated from 1394 . . .' although '. . . it cannot be said that it took an active or dangerous form before the early months of 1397'.[3] That Richard displayed what appears to phlegmatic moderns a somewhat excessive grief is in keeping both with the evidence of his fiery nature and with the customs of a period when men were not ashamed to weep in public – but to be emotional is not necessarily to be a neurotic or a victim of schizophrenia. Throughout Richard's life, his rage could be unbridled – but he had demonstrated it on many occasions when Anne was at his side. He was to demonstrate it again when she lay in state in Westminster Abbey. But, as he grew to full stature as King, there is also a shrewdness of political judgment and an almost Monte Cristo purposefulness in working towards the fulfilment of his *regalitée* and the satisfaction of his vengeance. And it is equally idle to speculate on the might-have-been. If Anne had given Richard an heir, what would have been Derby's chances in 1399? If Anne had been at Richard's side through the final crisis, how would history have been changed? Let novelists but not historians devise what answer they will. A lonely King whose only friends had either died on the block or in exile had now lost the Queen he had loved – his grief was bitter; there are no grounds for saying it was diseased.

At the funeral of Anne, the Earl of Arundel went out of his way to insult Richard's grief.[1] The Queen's body first lay in state at St Paul's and was then carried in procession to the burial service in Westminster Abbey. Arundel failed to arrive at St Paul's and was even late at Westminster. When, heaping insult upon insult, he asked to be excused 'for certain urgent private reasons' before the obsequies were over, it was too much for Richard's patience – he snatched a wand from one of the vergers, and struck the earl with such force that he drew blood and felled him to the ground. If the solemnity of the place and the occasion condemns Richard, it also condemns Arundel; and, where Richard may be pardoned for excess of grief, there can be no excuse for the conduct of Arundel. The incident again displays Richard's temper, but it also illustrates the type of baron who could pose as the saviour of his country at the same time as he denied in his conduct even to his peers every tenet of Chivalry and good manners. Arundel was arrested, but released after a week – Richard was not yet ready for the final reckoning.

In the late autumn of the year of Anne's death Richard's first expedition to Ireland set sail. For nearly 200 years no English monarch had set foot in Ireland; why did Richard of all our mediaeval kings take such an interest in Ireland that he made two expeditions thither? The theory that the first was a distraction to cure the grief of a widower has had to be abandoned in the light of the evidence that Richard was preparing to visit Ireland before Anne's fatal illness.[2] Activity is always an antidote to grief, but there were more rational reasons too.

Richard owed his title of 'Seigneur d'Ireland' to Henry II, and if Henry II's plans for conquest on ruthless Norman-Plantagenet lines had been carried out – they were interrupted by the reactions to the murder of Archbishop Thomas à Becket – it might have been less of an empty title. After the days of the first invasion under Strongbow, and the misguided viceroyalty of Prince John, the occupying Norman-English barons had either withdrawn inside the ever narrowing circle of the Dublin 'Pale' or married into the semi-barbarous Irish nobility, and had lost touch with the life, manners and customs of England. In theory, Ireland in Richard's time was a Lordship merged in the regality of the English crown,[1] and, again in theory, it was administered in very similar fashion to the Counties Palatine. Within the jurisdiction of the Dublin Pale there was a replica of the English Exchequer, Law Courts, Chancery, and even a poor imitation of an English Parliament. One chronicler[2] gives as the main reason for Richard's interest the perhaps exaggerated fact that, whereas in his grandfather's day the annual revenue of the Irish Exchequer was £30,000, it now showed no income but a cost of administration amounting to £20,000 a year. The neglect of previous kings had been due to their preoccupations elsewhere, and not to any lack of appreciation of Ireland's potential usefulness. In the pages of Froissart we have a well-painted picture of a very gloomy Celtic twilight, but there is also evidence that Ireland had made some economic progress. In the eleventh century its traders in frieze had reached Ely, and, after its Danish invaders had been finally defeated at the battle of Clontarf, a flourishing trade chiefly in hides and cloth had sprung up with Scandinavia. Its culture was limited to the cloister, but, if the arts of manuscript and illumination[3] are a guide, it was comparable to the best that England could show. Politically there was already an Irish Question. The clan system, which reached back into the dim regions of Celtic mythology with a national folklore which had its patron saint in the English slave who became St Patrick, had never been welded into a unity by the harsh process of a superimposed feudalism and a centralized monarchy, and, if Ireland had been left a little longer to its own devices, it would have been interesting to see what constitution undiluted celticism might have contributed to the political welfare of mankind. The curse of mediaeval Ireland was that when her overlords bothered about her they did not bother enough, and, by the beginning of the fourteenth century, the Englishry were rapidly adopting the Irish language, dress and customs. In 1367 the Statute of Kilkenny had attempted to stop this infection by savage penalties – it merely emphasized the infection's strength and the English weakness. In 1374 England's Viceroy attempted to compel the English colonists in Dublin to send representatives to England with full powers to assent to taxation – the attempt failed: four centuries later a similar situation cost England the American empire. In

1394 Richard had no war on his hands, his own throne was secure, his Council was efficient and for the time being contented under the authority of Gaunt, his Parliament might grumble, as it always did, about his household expenses but it represented a section of the population which was prospering. The Scottish Border was comparatively quiet and Scotland itself was included with France in the prospects of a long peace, yet across the Irish Sea was Richard's own Lordship in a state of anarchy and a growing liability on an Exchequer always overdrawn. Richard's Irish expedition was no hasty distraction[1] – it was carefully and ably planned, its motives were both economic and political, and its prospects of benefits to his Exchequer and glory to his *regalitée* seemed bright. Even the Church could give him approval – Ireland was Clementist – but the theory[2] that Richard was a Roman crusader attacking Avignon by way of the Leinster mountains is indeed far-fetched, and has no more evidence to support it than the story that Henry II needed a papal Bull before he took the first steps on the long and tragic road which links Strongbow with Michael Collins and De Valera.

Richard's first move[3] was to order absentee Irish living in England to return to Ireland; but many exemptions were permitted. Preparations on a really large scale were then begun. In August 1394, while his own household began its progress towards Haverfordwest, writs were despatched to all sheriffs calling up reservists, yeomen and archers were enlisted by the royal Exchequer, and ships and sailors were impressed from the Cinque Ports and mobilized first at Bristol and then at Milford Haven. An advance guard of squires and archers had been despatched in July under Sir John Stanley, Baldwin Raddington and the Bishop of Meath, and had already landed in Ireland. The main body was, as in the days of Crécy and Poitiers, an expansion of the household plus the large retinues of great Lords – for the most part under the command of the younger representatives of each house but all paid as King's soldiers from the Exchequer. Only one of Richard's uncles accompanied him – the one he could trust least, Gloucester. York was left behind as keeper of England, while his heir Rutland, the friend and contemporary of Richard, took the Yorkist levies overseas. Gaunt meanwhile obtained special permission to depart for his Duchy of Aquitaine, where the Gascons were bridling at his new title, and resenting what they regarded as a loosening of their ancient direct ties with the English crown. Of the younger generation, in addition to Rutland who was now made Earl of Cork, there went the young Earl of March (the presumptive heir to Richard, his future Lieutenant, the son of a Viceroy, and a great Irish landowner in his own right), Thomas Mowbray, Earl of Nottingham (also an Irish landowner), Thomas Holland the younger – nephew to the King, Sir Thomas Despenser, and a number of clerics and royal officials who included the Westminster monk Thomas Merke who was later to become Bishop of Carlisle and Richard's last friend. Derby was absent on his pilgrimage to the Holy Land.

This impressive expeditionary force sailed from Haverfordwest, landed at Waterford on October 2nd, 1394 and remained in Ireland for eight months. Not a single pitched battle was fought; but it is doubtful if Richard expected one. He was well-informed about the special circumstances of Irish warfare as there were plenty of Anglo-Irish in the Pale who knew its methods only too well. The centre of resistance was in the mountains of Leinster – Strongbow's original conquest – where Art Oge MacMurrough, King of Leinster, had his headquarters in the Hy Kinsella. He was a skilful practitioner in every device of guerrilla tactics and was fighting on a terrain admirably suited to them. The English army's progress from Waterford to Dublin was a running fight with wily and almost invisible foes, and it seems to have been conducted with as much skill as was possible.

Froissart is an admirable guide for this demonstration in force.[1] He was not present in person, but in the following year he came to England and met a squire named Henry Christead who had taken an active part, and whose life story illustrates well the relationships between Irish and English at the time. When serving with the Earl of Ormond in the previous reign, Christead's horse had bolted when his party had been ambushed by the Irish, and he had been neatly captured and held in 'a strong house among the woods, waters and mires' of one Brien Costerec, whom he terms a gentleman and a 'goodly man'. There he remained for seven years without complaint, and even felt himself complimented by the gift of one of Brien's daughters in marriage. In a subsequent action between the Irish and Lionel Duke of Clarence, Brien was taken prisoner when riding the same courser on which Henry Christead had been captured – it was apparently a distinguished and famous horse to the Irish. Brien reported to Clarence that Christead was still his prisoner and an exchange was arranged. But the interesting aspect of this romantic story is that Christead was by no means overjoyed at his release, and Brien was grieved that he could think of no other way of obtaining his ransom. Christead's eldest daughter remained with her Irish grandfather, and he and the rest of his family settled down in Bristol. Christead was enlisted in Richard's expedition because he knew English, French and Irish perfectly. He described to Froissart the habits of a fighting and independent race who knew how to make the most of difficult country: 'They be hard people and of rude engine and wit . . . they set nothing by jollity nor fresh apparel, nor by nobleness' and he confirms that the expedition was well thought of both in intent and results by 'the merchants, cities and good towns of the realm' who had financed it.

The English army reached Dublin in November after an exhausting month, and there Richard ceased to be the soldier and became the diplomatist with the sanction of overwhelming force at his back. He made great use of the Earl of Ormond, 'who could right well speak the language', and of Christead, and a general submission was in due course arranged. Eighty Irish chiefs, speaking in Irish, paid homage to Richard as Lord of Ireland, and the submissions were enrolled in Latin with Ormond and other Anglo-Irish acting as interpreters. Froissart tells Christead's picturesque story of how four of the Irish Kings were entertained by Richard, and of Richard's anxiety to teach them the civilized manners of his court. Christead was appointed their tutor – to wean them from their friendly communal manners to the distinctions of high-table in hall, to individual drinking vessels and dishes, to the use of breeches rather than kilt and plaid, to the use of saddle and stirrups on horseback, and to the elaborate ritual of the chivalrous Order of Knighthood. It was, however, the 'sweet communication' of the Earl of Ormond which finally persuaded the Kings of Meath, Thomond, Connor and even the undefeated Art Mac-Murrough, King of Leinster, to accept at Richard's hands their accolades after a night of vigil in the cathedral church of Dublin. Froissart was puzzled to know how so overwhelming a victory was obtained at so little military cost. Christead's answer was that it was due to 'the great puissance that the King had over with him, with every man well paid' which 'abashed the Irishmen',

149

and adds two points which others have missed: apparently 'the sea was closed from them on all parts, whereby their livenges and merchandises might not enter into their countries', and Richard's standard was altered from 'the libbards and flower-de-luces quarterly' to the arms of St Edward, 'that is a cross potent gold and gules with four white martinets in the field'. To the harshness of blockade Richard added the blandishments of heraldry – St Edward (the Confessor) as a subduer of the Danes was a hero to the Irish. It is not therefore surprising that when, in the following January, Gloucester was sent back to England to ask Parliament for more funds for the expedition, they were granted with enthusiastic approval, and Richard set seriously about the organization of his Irish lordship. In a letter to the English Council which has survived,[1] Richard explains his Irish policy in some detail. He had to deal with three groups – the 'wild Irish our enemies', the Irish rebels (i.e. Anglo-Irish), and the obedient English, and he explains that in his opinion a policy of leniency was justified. He proposed to combine appeasement with the definite creation of 'English land' – in other words, the reorganization of the Pale – by means of a further infiltration of English colonists. But in February he received a letter which, while approving of all that was done or proposed to be done, asked for his return to England. The Council were worried by negotiations with Scots and French, and by the sudden emergence of Lollards. Richard, with more money and general approval from England, seems to have been naturally unwilling to interrupt a task so well begun, and it was not until Archbishop Arundel and Bishop Braybrook of London had gone over to interview him in person that he decided he must return. A second Irish Parliament was held, the Earl of March was appointed as the King's Lieutenant in residence, and it was not until May 1st that Richard sailed in the good ship *Trinity* from Waterford, his plans for his Irish lordship far from complete. His first Irish expedition was wholly to his credit. Where Henry II had tried nothing but brute force, where his son John had spoilt good plans by unseemly levity and snobbery, where succeeding Kings had been content with mere instructions to Viceroys, Richard went in person, and, to the satisfaction of all concerned, succeeded by methods of intelligent understanding and chivalrous diplomacy. It was the first and last time that England ever used such methods in Ireland.

In the year 1523, on the eve of the English Reformation, Bishop Tunstall was writing to Erasmus of the effect of Lutheranism in England: 'It is no question', he says, 'of pernicious novelty, it is only that new arms are being added to the great band of Wyclifite heretics.' In the Statutes of the Realm for the fifth year of Richard's reign, 1381–2, it is stated that

> 'there be divers evil persons within the realm, going from county to county, and from town to town, in certain habits under dissimulation of great holiness and without the license of the ordinaries of the places or other sufficient authority, preaching daily, not only in churches and churchyards but also in markets, fairs, and other open places, where a great congregation of people is, divers sermons containing heresies and notorious errors'.[1]

The emergence, therefore, of the Lollards as a movement of consequence enough to bring the King back from an enterprise on which he had set heart and mind, and which had been successfully initiated but only half completed, was an event both of immediate and future importance. Though the origin of the name Lollard is obscure there is no doubt as to the origin of the sect – they were the followers of John Wyclif, and their other name describes their function, they were his 'Poor Preachers'. Since the days of St Francis, the mediaeval Church had had to choose between two policies – the way of evangelical poverty and asceticism, and the way of a political hierarchy wedded to the pomp and power of this world. St Francis, Ockham and Wyclif had found themselves defeated by the Hildebrandine conception of the papacy, but they were not therefore revolutionary protestants aiming to set up a rival Church – they were reformers within the Church in grave danger of final excommunication. Wyclif had given this general movement two great metaphysical and theological principles. His theory of *Dominium*, translated into everyday speech, involved the right of every man to call his soul his own, and his theory of *consubstantiation* was a subtle criticism of current catholic theory. In the crude language of Wyclif's less intellectual followers, the Lollards protested against the miracle of 'transubstantiation', and objected to 'eating a god' every time they partook of the wafer of the mass.[1] After Wyclif was banned from teaching his beliefs at Oxford he was well content to retire to his rectory at Lutterworth, and from there he occupied his time in his voluminous pamphleteering, his translation of the Latin Bible into English, and his organization of the Poor Preachers. When he died on the last day of the year 1384, his disciples were equipped to carry on his work. From then until the time of the English Reformation there is a continuous record of Lollardism. It began with many missionaries, and only later attained the glory of not a few martyrdoms; it became the 'proximate cause' of a religious revolution long prepared and deeply rooted. Wyclif's three great disciples – Nicolas Hereford, John Ashton and John Purvey – were none of them of the stuff of which martyrs are made. They were primarily scholars with a social conscience and a sturdy common sense. They were followed by a less intellectual, more fanatical, and therefore in many ways less likeable but more successful, brand of Lollard; and the appeal of their poverty, which eschewed the hypocrisy of mendicancy, won them support in the highest as well as in the lowliest households of the realm. They were protected by nobles like Montague and Salisbury, by gentry like Sir Thomas Latymer of Braybrook and Sir Richard Stury, and they were able to ignore the condemnation of the Church led by the heresy-hunting Courtenay. They were strong in the strength which comes from popular support. William Langland's *Piers Plowman* is full of popular disapproval of monks and friars – 'The Orders that have no pity; Money rains upon their altars. There where such parsons be living at ease, They have no pity on the poor; that is their "charity" '[2] – and he warns that 'Though ye be a Brother of all the Orders Five, though ye have a pocket full, Pardons and Absolutions, and Doubelfold Indulgences, unless Do-well can help you, your patents and your pardons will be worth a pie-crust'.[3] And in another passage can be detected the kind of influence Wyclif had already had amongst the poor and humble: ' "By Peter", quoth a plowman, and forward put his head, "I know Truth as well as scholar does his book. Conscience and my own wit led me to his place".'[4] There was a vast popular literature, of which a fair quantity has survived, to prove that Langland was no isolated critic, and, in more educated circles, there is no need to look further than Chaucer's *Canterbury Tales* for evidence of lay criticism and clerical laxity. The chronicles are equally valid evidence – their orthodox hatred of the new sect can be shorn of its invective yet still leave an interesting picture of these Poor Preachers in long russet-hued gowns with long pockets, staff in hand, preaching in their mother tongue and referring to an English bible[1] in churches and churchyards, at street corners and on fair grounds, and talking privately in the homes of the converted. It is a picture which has its counterpart in the later history of the followers of Wesley.

Immediately after the Peasants' Revolt, the Lollards had been suspected of being its instigators, and the Earthquake Council[2] of the Church at Blackfriars, in May 1382, marked the beginning of open warfare between Courtenay and most of the bishops against Oxford as the centre of Wyclifite influence. Yet when, in July of the same year, a royal ordinance had ordered every bishop to arrest all Lollards, the Commons – either because of anti-clerical prejudice or pro-Lollard sympathy – had secured its withdrawal. From the death of Wyclif, 1384, until Richard's sudden recall from Ireland, the Lollard following in the Midlands, in London, and in the West Country was formidable, and the chronicler Knighton even went so far as to assert that of every two persons you met on the road one was sure to be a Lollard.[3]

What was King Richard's attitude to this new element of disturbance? It is true that his mother had protected Wyclif; but that does not make her son a Lollard. It is true that the retinue of his Bohemian Queen was the likely link between Wyclif and Huss; but that does not make either Anne or Richard a Lollard. It is true that a few members of his household were Lollards, but they only came into the open in his absence. And from Richard's earliest years to the end, the evidence even of unfriendly chroniclers is that he was not merely orthodox but devoutly so.[4] There is no reason to doubt the genuine piety which carved round his tomb in his beloved abbey of Westminster the inscription 'He overthrew the heretics and laid their friends low'. Richard, like the Tudors after him, was fully prepared to represent England faithfully in opposition to papal exactions and papal provisors, but he was much more a 'Defender of the Faith' than the Tudor who was afterwards awarded that title. He was well aware of Lollardism, but, until his Council sent the Archbishop of York and the Bishop of London to urge his immediate return from Ireland, because the Lollards had been so bold as to petition Parliament for direct action against the Church and because they had found supporters within the court circle, he had shown no zeal for supporting the authority of Pope and bishops more than was absolutely necessary. Now his *regalitée* had been touched – the reformers were going too far – and Richard the orthodox returned in tempestuous mood to prove that he was still a mediaeval King, and that, if in ecclesiastical diplomacy he was prepared to fight for English independence, in matters of doctrine he remained a faithful son of the Church.

While Richard had been absent, two Lollards of the Privy Council – Sir Richard Stury and Sir Lewis Clifford – with Thomas Latymer of Northamptonshire and Lord John Montague, brother of the Earl of Salisbury, had brought before Parliament a document which was a complete statement of Lollard views[1] and aims, and called for the urgent reform of the Church. In the eyes of a Lollard, the Church was ruined by its temporal possessions and endowments; its priesthood had no sanction in the New Testament; its vows of chastity were unnatural and a superstition which led to vice and infanticide; its doctrine of transubstantiation made celebrants into idolators; its worship of images, its special prayers for the dead and its pilgrimages were again the accompaniment of idolatry; and its holding of secular office contrary to its true function. The necessity for auricular confession was denied – it exalted the pride of the clergy and afforded too many opportunities for undue influence, and even for 'wowyng'. The Lollards were the forerunners of the Quakers in stating the absolute pacifist position – they argued from the teaching of Jesus that to slay one's enemy in warfare was directly contrary to the New Testament, which was in essence a proclamation of love even to enemies, and which therefore condemned both war and capital punishment.[2] They anticipated the Quakers too in their criticism of luxury in dress and ornament, and demanded the abolition of the crafts of the armourer and the goldsmith, and a return to simplicity in dress and manners. These 'conclusions', which the Lollards placed before Parliament, and nailed to the doors of St Paul's so that the citizens too might read them in their mother tongue, sound mild enough to modern ears (with the possible exception of the conclusions relating to pacifism). But, to orthodox mediaeval ears, they were near to heresy and treason, and it was not to be expected that Richard would tolerate them. Yet,

THE SEVEN QUIET YEARS

although in a fury he might threaten 'the foulest death that may be' to Sir Richard Stury if he ever broke the oath of recantation which Richard insisted upon, there was no attempt at serious general persecution. Heretical tendencies were to be abjured, and the Lollards of the early days showed no desire to invite any kind of death – they were men of shrewd common sense who instead of martyrdom preferred lip-service to orthodoxy, and a continuation of their real purpose underground. It was Henry IV who began the long and bitter history in England of burning for heresy. The Lollards of Richard's reign 'drew in their horns and retired into their shells like tortoises',¹ but their memorial was a tradition of individualist Christianity which prepared the way for Luther.

Richard's personal orthodoxy was coupled with a very proper regard for the independence of England whenever it was threatened with too bold a claim from the Papacy. For two centuries – since the days of Hildebrand – England had been adamant in opposing extravagant papal claims, and Richard maintained that tradition. When the Papacy moved to Avignon and came more directly under the sway of the hereditary enemy in France, its claim to 'provide' archbishoprics, bishoprics, and other benefices with clergy, regardless of the desires of the crown or of the ancient rights of election by the chapters, was staunchly resisted by the English laity. The first Statute against Provisors had been passed in 1351. It had been reissued in 1364, and in 1389 Richard too had to re-enact that 'free elections of archbishoprics, bishoprics, and all other dignities and benefices elective in England should hold' – the Statutes of Provisors were never fully effective. Similarly, in 1353, Parliament had agreed to the first Statute of 'Praemunire'; many more had been necessary, and Richard in 1393 passed the so-called 'Great' Statute of Praemunire, which re-stated the English position quite clearly: –

'A common clamor is made, that the said father the Pope hath ordained and purposed to translate some prelates . . . without the King's assent and knowledge, and without the assent of the prelates . . . so the Crown of England, which hath been so free at all times, that it hath been in subjection to no realm, but immediately subject to God in all things touching the regality of the same Crown, and none other, should be submitted to the

155

Pope . . . If any purchase or pursue in the court of Rome any such translations etc. which touch the King our Lord, against him, his Crown, and his regality, or his realm . . . that process be made against them by praemunire facias.' [1]

Both statutes are famous, not because of their effect when enacted, but because they provided a platform and a background to the lawyers of the English Reformation a hundred and fifty years later. [2] Meanwhile, there was a working arrangement that the Pope would not interfere with appointments to canonries and benefices, but that he would have the nominal right to appoint by Bull candidates to bishoprics already named by the English Crown. Between the claims of the Roman pontiff and the English monarchy there was very little room for the pristine democracy of the early Church, and very little desire for it amongst the clergy. The Monk of Westminster refers to the Statute against Provisors as '*statutum odiosum*', [3] and, although all three estates specifically agreed to the Statute of Praemunire, the clergy realized and resented its implications – which may explain the fact that no contemporary monkish chronicler makes any mention of it. Richard and the English churchmen of his day could combine a detestation of Lollardism with a sturdy resistance to papal overlordship – the middle way of the later English Reformation has roots deep in our history – and references to Richard's regality in the Great Statute of Praemunire were very much in tune both with Richard's personal views and the views of all orthodox contemporaries.

If the Irish expedition had done nothing more it had at least given Richard self-confidence. It had been planned at his instigation, it had been executed efficiently under his personal leadership without help or advice from any of his uncles, and it had met with general approval. Immediately on his return to England he handled the Lollard troubles with firmness and despatch – and without the need for executions or even imprisonment.

The year 1395, therefore, saw Richard at the height of his powers, with noble and villein appeased and tolerably content at home, and the not too distant prospect of a genuine peace with both France and Scotland. Only one gesture revealed that the calm which had succeeded the storm of the First Rebellion was deceptive – and it was a gesture of very profound significance.

Of the three chief victims of the First Rebellion who had escaped abroad, Suffolk had died in Paris, Archbishop Neville had died in Louvain, and Robert de Vere had been killed during a boar hunt near Louvain in 1392.[1] It was de Vere whom Richard now remembered. He obtained special permission to have his body brought back from Louvain and reburied in the de Vere family vault at Earls Colne in Essex. It was no ordinary re-interment. According to the St Albans chronicler, Richard spared no expense in ordaining a solemn and magnificent ceremony, and for a while he gazed on the embalmed face of his friend, and placed on the beloved fingers a ring which was both tribute and pledge. The Archbishop and many of the higher clergy honoured the ceremony with their presence, but the chronicler is careful to note that only a few of the nobility were present, 'because they had not yet got over their hatred of the dead man'.[2] At the ceremony at Earls Colne, Gloucester, Arundel, Warwick and Derby were not present; they at least may have realized what it portended. To those who know its sequel this simple, if somewhat theatrical, act of devotion to a dead friend's memory is a major clue to the understanding of the final years of the reign – it was an act of piety, but it was also the renewal of a private vow.

But Richard's final reckoning still had to wait – there was the affair of peace with France to be concluded first. When Richard had left England for the Irish expedition, and his uncle Gaunt had been despatched to come to terms with his new Duchy of Aquitaine, a final treaty of peace with France had been postponed. Neither the French nor the Gascons were happy about Gaunt's appointment. The loyalty of the Gascons to the English crown, providing that its wearer left them alone and that the wine trade flourished, had become almost proverbial. When Edward III had assumed the suzerainty, he had been careful to do so by virtue of his kingship of England and not of his pretended kingship of France. Now the Gascons were alarmed that their traditional sovereignty had been impugned, because the appointment of Gaunt was not the appointment of at least the heir to the English throne, and had been mistakenly authorized by virtue of Richard's inherited claim to the kingship of France. A mission of protest had failed to alter the terms of Gaunt's appointment – Richard had pleaded in excuse that the appointment was for Gaunt's life only, and involved no permanent alienation from something he valued as part of his regality. The result of Gascon independence, and some diplomatic mishandling on the part of Richard's staff, was that Gaunt was faced with a very awkward situation as soon as he landed on the banks of the Garonne near Bordeaux. By March 1395 he had not only appeased the Gascons by the Treaty of Bordeaux but also had persuaded a French embassy that his intentions were both honourable and peaceful – still more evidence of Gaunt's practical skill as a diplomatist. Where his elder brother the Black Prince had left a bitter memory of massacre and pillage, Gaunt was able in a very short time to create an atmosphere of co-operation and prosperity; where his brother had brought armies and war, he brought a lavish court and all the good business which its banquets and its joustings needed for sustenance and trappings.

The Treaty of Bordeaux needed ratification by Richard, and a deputation of Gascons, with two representatives of Gaunt, left Aquitaine for England. It is our good fortune that about the same time Sir John Froissart,[1] treasurer and canon of Chimay in Hainault, 'had great affection to go and see the realm of England' which he had not seen for twenty-seven years. He carried with him a present for the King whom he had last seen as an insignificant baby princeling at the font in the cathedral of Bordeaux. He had 'engrossed in a fair book well enlumined all the matters of amours and moralities' – and to this jaunt of the great chronicler we owe the lively description of the Irish expedition, a fascinating account of a debate in the Privy Council, and a revealing sidelight on the manners of the English nobility and the interests of Richard himself. He had hoped to meet Richard at Canterbury, where Richard was on pilgrimage both to the tomb of St Thomas and the tomb of his father the Black Prince. When Froissart saw the King and his court, he realized that no one knew him – Gaunt, York, and Gloucester were all absent. He was welcomed however by Sir Thomas Percy, the Seneschal, and rode with him to Ospringe in the hope that an interview with the King could be arranged. There he met Sir William Lisle 'of the King's Privy Chamber' and he pays tribute to 'the gentlemen of England who are courteous, treatable and glad of acquaintance'. He was at last able to hand over his letters of introduction to the Duke of York at Leeds Castle in Kent. York remembered him, welcomed him gladly and ushered him into the royal presence. Richard was equally hospitable, but the chronicler realized that he had come at an awkward moment – 'the King was sore busied there in Council for two great and mighty matters' – the affair of Gaunt's Treaty of Bordeaux, and the project for peace with France which was to be cemented by the marriage of Richard to Isabelle the daughter of the French King. Froissart therefore postponed handing over his gift until a more favourable occasion, which offered itself at the palace of Eltham shortly afterwards. There the King sent for him in his private chamber, where Froissart had placed his book on the bed.

'When the King opened it, it pleased him well, for it was fair enlumined and written, and covered with crimson velvet, with ten buttons of silver and gilt, and roses of gold in the midst, with two great clasps gilt, richly wrought. Then the King demanded me whereof it treated, and I shewed him how it treated matters of love; whereof the King was glad and looked in it and read it in many places, for he could speak and read French very well.'[1]

It was in a gallery of Eltham Palace 'where it was very pleasant and shady, for those galleries were then covered with vines' that Froissart walked and talked with Sir Richard Stury of the King's Privy Council but at the moment in official disgrace for his implication in the Lollard movement. Stury gave the old chronicler an account of a Privy Council meeting, which, though incorrect in detail, provides a revealing picture of the general scene, and in particular a shrewd view of Gloucester. In spite of the charters and documents put forward by the Gascons, Gloucester counselled that the King should not in any way alter his gift to Gaunt, and the rest of the Council, uneasy as they were, 'durst not say against it, the Duke of Gloucester was so sore dread'. Gloucester's purpose was at least clear to Froissart and Stury, 'for he would that his brother the Duke of Lancaster should have bidden still in Aquitaine, for he thought he was over great in England and too near the King . . . for then he thought he (Gloucester) would have shifted well enough in England'. Gloucester's conduct at the Council was both boorish and domineering – he said his say, and then took dinner apart with the Earl of Derby and left before the meeting was over.[1] Froissart reports that the grant of Gaunt's duchy was confirmed but that the views of the Gascons on their inalienable rights were well heard in spite of Gloucester, and the Treaty of Bordeaux was at last approved and filed. With the Gascon episode out of the way, Richard could set earnestly about the business of peace-making with France, and to that end he sent an urgent message to recall Gaunt. Gloucester had again shown something of his old ambitions while Gaunt was away – Richard needed Gaunt at his side in Council and as ambassador-in-chief to the court of France.

Richard's second marriage caused controversy at the time, and has caused it ever since. It seems to have been his own suggestion as his contribution to a peace which was necessary not only to himself but to his realm. The negotiations for a permanent treaty of peace were making no headway, chiefly because France refused England's financial demands and England resolutely refused to surrender Calais, but there was a prospect of a very long truce for which the proposed marriage to Isabelle of France was to be the diplomatic surety. The Princess was only eight years old, and the possibility of her supplying an heir to Richard was therefore very much a hazard of the future. On the other hand, Richard himself was only twenty-nine years old and was certainly no physical weakling. His attachment to the memory of Anne was profound, and the irksomeness of a marriage of convenience may have been more supportable in that its consummation was bound to be postponed for years. Meanwhile the succession to the throne was vested in an adult of whom all spoke well – Roger Mortimer, Earl of March, and heir to Richard by virtue of his mother Philippa of Clarence.[2] He was at the moment the King's Lieutenant in Ireland. There was another point in favour of the French marriage alliance – it was planned to help towards a solution of the Schism in the Church. Richard and Charles VI were to throw over both the Roman and the Avignon Popes, and a Council of the Church was to elect a new Pope, end the Schism, and face the threat from the Ottoman Turks with a united Western Christendom. It was a plan which never materialized, because English diplomacy could not bring itself to admit that it had been wrong in siding with Urban and Boniface; but it was a plan which at least gave Richard's marriage project the full blessing of the Church. The chief objectors were of course Gloucester, Arundel, and their faction. Where the wisdom and experience of a Gaunt could see the necessity for the peace and the desirability of the marriage bond, an irresponsible military baronage could only see frustration, cowardice and the betrayal of a glorious tradition.

Later critics have a more serious charge to make. It has been asserted by no less an authority than Professor Tout that the French alliance was the first obvious step towards Richard's final *coup d'état.*[1] The charge is based on a phrase which occurs in the mandate Richard gave to his ambassadors who were to negotiate the final truce – the French King, his uncle, and his brother were 'to aid and sustain Richard with all their power against any of his subjects.'[2] Was Richard thinking of Gloucester and Arundel, of the Peasants' Revolt, of the contumacy of Londoners, or of the Cheshire Rising? It is the thesis of this book that, since 1388, Richard was *always* thinking of Gloucester and Arundel – they had given him no cause to forget them, and had offered every offence that was in their power. But when Richard finally retaliated and when he finally needed help, there is no reliable evidence which suggests that he ever thought of calling in France to save him. The offending clause seems to have obtained more significance than was warranted, and in effect to have been no more than a mere polite statement of international feudal solidarity rather than the basis of some secret and unholy alliance of Kings against subjects. To the majority on both sides of the Channel it was reasonable that, after over sixty years of indecisive war, peace should be made, and in mediaeval diplomacy a royal marriage was as necessary and as sensible a part of the proceedings as parliamentary ratifications would be in the twentieth century. To Richard, the truce was desirable for both personal and national reasons – there is no doubting the consistency with which he aimed to settle with the Appellants once he could be sure of power at home and peace abroad, and there is no doubt that the constant drain on the Exchequer of an unprofitable war was a powerful economic stimulus to peace on both sides of the Channel. But although Tout's charge of 'subtle autocracy', and of a deep laid plot aiming at unfettered absolutism backed if needs be by French soldiery, is very much overdrawn, there is evidence in plenty that in the seven Quiet Years Richard was building up his own party in the baronage, thinking ahead to the day when he could safely take retribution for the death of his earlier friends, and planning to establish his regality in its fullest mediaeval sense. That is a policy which does not condemn him as a traitor to his country or a murderer of the constitution – it illustrates again that Richard II was a mediaeval King and a human being. On the day when he ousted the Lords Appellant he stood alone – his friends executed or exiled – and, in the seven years which followed, it was only natural that, while he valued the support of his now ageing uncle Gaunt, he quietly gathered round himself new friends and new servants. As well as younger nobles of similar tastes and years to his own – men like Thomas Holland, the younger, now Duke of Kent, and York's son, now Duke of Rutland – he chose as knights of his Privy Council men of the stamp of Stury, Clifford and Dalyngrigge, not mere *duketti* and *novi homines*, but men of excellent birth and ability. The daily work of government[1] was entrusted more to Councils both great and small than to the less efficient method of full Parliaments. The theory which suggests that Richard deliberately 'swamped' the Councils with his 'chamber knights' is answered by the simple explanations that, on the one hand, *maioritas* was not yet identified with *sanitas* (and the Chancellor throughout this period was Archbishop Arundel), and, on the other hand, that Richard's choice of young men was also a preference for efficient and regular attenders. That Gloucester and his friends detested the new *régime* was as natural as Richard's creation of it; and Richard may well have remembered that, even when the Appellants had absolute power, there had still been a body of the Lords well disposed to him and resentful of the overbearing Gloucester. By the time Richard is accused of bargaining for help from France he not only had the firm support of elder statesmen like Gaunt but he had about his person a group of his own generation who were far from being adventurers or 'favourites', and, as his permanent officials, men as capable as de Stafford, his Keeper of the Privy Seal.

The final preparations for the truce and the French marriage needed Gaunt, and in spite of much work still to be done in his Duchy of Aquitaine he obeyed Richard's summons and arrived home at the end of 1395. He presented himself to Richard at Langley, where the court was celebrating Christmas, and then departed to his Lincoln estates where, at the beginning of the New Year, he married his mistress the Lady Catherine Swynford.

She was already the mother of four of his children. According to the English chroniclers she was another Alice Perrers; but according to a more trustworthy witness in such matters, Sir John Froissart, she was *'une dame qui scavait moult de toutes honneurs'*, and, although the marriage caused indignation among such great ladies as the Duchess of Gloucester, the Countess of Derby and the Countess of Arundel, their susceptibilities were probably more political than moral, and the new Duchess of Lancaster was received with all honour not only at Richard's court but also at the court of France during the final negotiations for the truce and the royal marriage.

The terms of the truce were sealed on March 9th, 1396 and Richard's proxy marriage to Isabelle was performed on March 12th. Richard himself paid two visits to Calais before the final celebrations were held in October. They were on a scale which almost equalled the later lavishness of The Field of Cloth of Gold. Richard's court was fixed at Guisnes, and the French court at Ardres. The ceremony was held at a place equidistant from both, and the full panoply of Chivalry was displayed on both sides.[1] Richard was accompanied not only by Gaunt but by Gloucester and Derby, as well as by his own personal entourage. The ceremonies can only have been gall and wormwood to Gloucester, and the presence of the new Duchess of Lancaster[2] may have given Derby food for anxious thought. There is a lengthy description in the chronicles of the magnificence of the ceremonial, the dresses and the mutual exchange of gifts. Richard himself on the first day wore 'a long gown of red velvet, a headdress given to him by the King of France studded with precious stones, and on his breast the hart of his own livery'. His lords-in-waiting were also in long red velvet robes, but with a difference which is strange to a modern eye – they wore the white 'bend' of the livery of the dead Queen Anne. On the second day, Richard wore 'a motely gown of white and red velvet'. Among the rich gifts mentioned are golden vases studded with gems, a picture of the Trinity studded with pearls, a jewelled picture of St George, and the odd gift of a 'certain necklace made with pearls and precious stones which Queen Anne had given him'. To perpetuate the memory of so auspicious an event, both Kings agreed to share in the building of a chapel dedicated to 'Our Lady of Peace' on the spot where their tents had been erected. The climax came with the handing over of the girl Princess, just eight years of age. After somewhat pathetic[1] but gracious speeches she was left in the care of the English peeresses while Richard and Charles attended the final banquet. Princess Isabelle made her state entry into London on November 23rd, and was crowned Queen of England on January 7th, 1397. The truce and the marriage had been both long and costly in their making.[2] According to one account the expenses amounted to £200,000 – a sum which far exceeded the dowry of the new Queen.

At the beginning of 1397, as Richard watched his child Queen's coronation in Westminster Abbey, he had good cause for feeling well pleased with seven years' work as King in the full mediaeval sense of the word. In spite of the war faction, he had engineered a sorely needed armistice with the hereditary enemy. He had built up an able administrative machine, and, as well as being supported by the weight of an experienced Gaunt, he had near to his person friends of his own choosing who were neither idle nor useless. He had carried out a successful demonstration in force in Ireland and had begun a settlement there which promised well, and in civil affairs his administration had survived a formidable provincial rising and the possibility of national disturbances over the Lollard question. The seven Quiet Years were years of experience and achievement – Richard could now turn his attention to more dramatic measures, to that retribution which he had promised himself ever since the day Burley went to the scaffold, and perhaps to the final establishment of that full regality which he had wistfully contemplated for so long.

PART III

Revenge, Tyranny and Abdication

VII

REVENGE

CONTRASTED WITH THE preceding seven years of quiet
preparation, the final three years of Richard's reign were
crowded with dramatic incidents many of which are still
the subject of dispute both as to the facts and their significance.
The contemporary English chroniclers present the partisan case
either for or against Richard (although most are naturally biassed
against him because they had to trim their sails to the wind of
Lancaster) but, fortunately, for the most controversial episodes
there is the more dispassionate evidence of the chroniclers of
France. Superimposed on the testimony of the Lancastrian
chroniclers is the weight of the world's greatest poet, creating
great drama from questionable historical sources and portraying
Richard as spiteful, tyrannical and finally pathetic. There is still
much room for legitimate doubt on many points, and still ample
scope for historians to differ both on matters of fact and especially
on matters of opinion and judgment. But it is now possible to
state some of the facts of Richard's final years without contra-
diction. And where facts are hard to come by it would be cowardice
to shirk legitimate inferences, or to omit judgment where they
demand interpretation.

The year 1397 saw Richard begin to take his revenge. That it
was premeditated is not subject to absolute proof, but the circumstantial evidence[1] leaves no reasonable cause for doubt. That it
was the headstrong act of a neurotic, drunk with power, is at this
distance impossible to prove either medically or legally, and is a
view which must disregard much of the evidence.

What is this evidence? It can be argued that the incident of the
gift of a pair of jewelled slippers to Westminster Abbey in 1390

was nothing more than the courteous paying of a debt. But, when that simple explanation is linked with the name of Sir Simon Burley, and with Queen Anne[1] on her knees to an implacable Gloucester fanatically determined on Burley's execution, it becomes too simple. The story of those jewelled shoes makes sense only as Gloucester's death warrant. Three years later, it was Richard's influence which persuaded the monks of the Abbey of St Mary Graces by the Tower of London, where Burley was buried, to celebrate the anniversary of his death on Tower Hill, and to inscribe his name in their martyrology. That was an act of devotion only recently brought to light[2] – it is yet another link in the chain of evidence. The dramatic scene at Earls Colne, where de Vere had been re-buried in the tomb of his ancestors, seems to have struck even contemporary chroniclers as meaning more than mere devotion to a dead friend. Richard had tried at least once to recall de Vere, but he had quickly realized that he attempted too much. The pomp of the second funeral in Essex, and the ceremony of the ring, make sense as pledge and token of coming vengeance. It is more difficult to understand the obtuseness and miscalculation of both Gloucester and Arundel – they refused to read the signs and still lost no opportunity of insulting and bullying a King they hated and despised; they courted their final destruction.

Richard struck only when he was sure of success. By 1397, he at last had a party of his own, a private army of his own, and the backing of some of the greatest Lords in the land – the triumphant result of seven years' patient political planning.[3] His personal party was no mere caucus of idle favourites, it included a new type of clerical civil servant and a new type of lay official, both of which were hardworking and efficient. Richard's Treasurer, Roger Walden, for example, had served five years as Treasurer of Calais before he had been appointed royal secretary in 1393. He later became Archbishop of Canterbury in place of Thomas Arundel, and it is a tribute to his worth that he survived the deposition of Richard and became Bishop of London under Henry IV. The Lancastrian chronicler Adam of Usk, who knew Walden personally, states that he was 'a modest man, pious and courteous, in speech of profitable and well-chosen words, better versed in things of the camp and the world than of the Church

or the study'.[1] The probability that he was the son of an Essex
butcher does not make him an upstart – the Church was the one
career of the Middle Ages freely open to talent. Edmund de
Stafford was now Richard's Chancellor. The year before, Archbishop Courtenay, who had held the see of Canterbury for fifteen
years since the Peasants' Revolt, had died. The Canterbury
chapter had elected Thomas Arundel, and Richard had not felt
ready to overrule the choice of the brother of one of his most
bitter enemies. On the other hand, the election had left the vital
post of Chancellor vacant, and de Stafford received his well-
earned promotion. In his place as Keeper of the Privy Seal another
clerical churchman was appointed – Guy Mone, who later
became Bishop of St David's. Still nearer to the throne were the
lay members of the household.[2] Sir Thomas Percy, brother of the
Earl of Northumberland had been royal Steward since 1394 –
he was a veteran of the French and Spanish campaigns, and,
although in the crisis of 1399 he deserted Richard, he was loyal
enough to make amends, and to find a soldier's death in the next
reign on the rebel field of Shrewsbury. As Vice-Chamberlain of
the Household there was now William le Scrope of Bolton – a
member of an ancient house, a *protégé* of Gaunt, and a nephew of
the beloved de Vere. As Constable of the Wardrobe, there was
the staunchest veteran of all – Baldwin Raddington – and, in that
he was devoted nephew to Simon Burley, another reminder that
a reckoning was overdue with the manipulators of the Merciless
Parliament. The bench of bishops had five active loyalists,
including Richard's ex-physician as Bishop of Worcester, his confessor as Bishop of Lichfield, Medford as Bishop of Salisbury,
Waldby as Bishop of Chichester, and the most loyal and outspoken of all – Thomas Merke as Bishop of Carlisle. Richard was
therefore well supported by distinguished administrators, by
proved veterans who had known his father and were living re-
minders of dead friends, and by able churchmen. To dismiss such
supporters as mere 'courtier bishops' and 'upstart favourites' is to
mistake propaganda for fact.[3]

Richard's private army is less easily justified. In the time of the
Appellants, Richard had made his first abortive attempt to match
the private armies of the rebel Lords with an army of his own. It
had met ignominious defeat in the mists of the Upper Thames at
Radcot Bridge, but one of the chroniclers mentions that it was at

this time that Richard first embodied Cheshire archers and Welsh pikemen in his bodyguard.[1] The royal connection with the fighting men of Cheshire was hereditary. Richard's father had recruited many of his best bowmen for the Crécy campaign from the warlike Welsh marches, and his mother owned the manor of Macclesfield near which, in Macclesfield forest, the famous 'white hart' may have had its origin.[2] By 1397, Richard had had time to build up, with the help of Baldwin Raddington and such experienced soldiers as Sir Thomas Percy, a force which could be mobilized at need from most of the shires, and which soon had its permanent establishment in the Cheshire Archers of the royal bodyguard who wore the royal livery of the white hart and were rewarded with regular pay and sometimes with pensions and lands. They are described at some length by Walsingham, and, according to this prejudiced witness, they were low-born malefactors capable of every crime who were encouraged to harry the countryside with impunity under royal protection.[3] They were probably neither better nor worse than the average fighting man of the day, and they seem to have earned the friendship of their comparatively cultured and gentle sovereign – from the Kenilworth chronicle we learn that they called him by the friendly nickname of 'Dycun' and were privileged to talk with him *in materna lingua*.[4] It is curious that this first serious attempt to provide for a standing army, with its allegiance to the throne and not to great nobles, was a subject of perpetual grievance at the time, and has been accepted as a weighty charge against Richard ever since. The only final cure for the evils of Livery and Maintenance was a royal monopoly of that custom reformed where it conflicted with justice. It is not likely that Richard in organizing his Cheshire Archers was so far-seeing or high principled that he was planning such an ultimate solution. It is more likely that, having experienced the impotence of an unprotected monarch against over-mighty subjects with their private armies, he was determined to outplay the baronage at its own game – he would have his own private army. The King's private army can be the subject's public safety – it depends how that army is used. The whole question of sovereignty and the rule of law was unsolved throughout the Middle Ages, and in Richard's time, as with so many other questions, the resulting lawlessness and divisions of loyalties had become chronic. It was not until the mutual baronial slaughter of the Wars of the Roses had weakened the feudal baronage beyond recovery that at last the Tudors were able to build a 'new monarchy' whose sovereignty was unquestioned, and whose writs could run without interference from any *imperium in imperio*. The difference between Henry VII creating the Yeomen of the Guard and Richard II mustering his Cheshire Archers is not a difference of kind but of timing. After 1485, the 'new monarchy' could base its sovereignty on King and people; in 1397 the people had not fully emerged, and it was a straight fight between mediaeval regality and feudal oligarchy. To expect Richard to deny himself a privilege which had been used, and abused, by every one of his great nobles is to expect a mediaeval King to be a saint amongst sinners, and it is probable that, if Richard had defeated Henry of Lancaster, his Cheshire Archers would have become as honoured a corps as the Tudors' Yeomen of the Guard. All the actions of Richard in his last three years have been judged in the cruel light of failure – his bodyguard might have been justified and belauded if it had brought him final success, and could have ushered in an earlier 'new monarchy' without the intervening wastage of the Wars of the Roses.

Richard's third line of defence was in the aristocracy. Even at the time of the Merciless Parliament, there had been a certain opposition to Gloucester amongst the Lords. Their leader at that time was the King's ineffective uncle the Duke of York. York's partiality for Richard was probably due to a detestation of his own younger brother Gloucester, and to an indolence of character which preferred an easy loyalty to a bold opposition; Richard had been careful to cement the alliance by showing every favour to York's son. In 1390 this Edward 'Plantagenet' had been made Earl of Rutland. He had later been made sole Admiral of the realm, and in 1396 Earl of Cork. He was younger than Richard and of the inner circle of his personal friends. But this friendship was of far less consequence than the support of Gaunt. Richard, in spite of earlier suspicions and quarrels, was at last fully aware of the value of Gaunt's goodwill, and he was prepared to pay for it handsomely. In the January Parliament of 1397, Richard had granted by letters patent, full legitimization to the offspring of Gaunt and his new wife Catherine Swynford; their eldest son John Beaufort was made Earl of Somerset and a year later was appointed to the office of Admiral. Their second son,

Henry Beaufort, was already started on a brilliant academic career, and was soon to be manœuvred into the bishopric of Lincoln when still in his teens – he was to become Chancellor under Henry V and a Cardinal under Henry VI. Gaunt himself was rewarded in 1398 by the enlargement of his office as Constable and Steward of the royal Palatinate of Chester – it was granted to him and his heirs male in perpetuity. Gaunt was in prestige, in power, in experience, in wisdom, in wealth, in lands, in titles, and in international influence, head and shoulders above any of the baronage: Richard was wise to secure his support, even though by favouring the Beauforts he risked offence to Gaunt's legitimate heir Henry of Derby. For the moment, there were no outward signs[1] that Derby was estranged, and Richard could well afford to honour a loyal father at the same time as he reserved judgment on a son who had been one of the Appellants. At this time too Thomas Mowbray, Earl of Nottingham, was made hereditary Earl Marshal. Although an Appellant in 1386, he had been received back into royal favour and suitably rewarded. Richard seems to have decided that it was impossible or unwise to crush all the Appellants immediately; he could attack their most dangerous leaders first and deal with the lesser rebels at leisure. Richard's half brothers – John Holland, Earl of Huntingdon, and Thomas Holland, Earl of Kent – were consistently loyal throughout the reign, but they carried little weight. John De Montague, Earl of Salisbury, was one of Richard's contemporaries and closest friends. He was the author of many ballads and songs, none of which have survived, and he finally paid both for his friendship with Richard and his support of the Lollards with his life.[2] The Earl of March was heir presumptive and therefore naturally opposed to Gloucester; but he was away from the centre of action attending to his Lieutenancy of Ireland. Of lesser dignitaries, Lords Scrope and Cobham were of the King's persuasion. None of these men could be classed as young and foolish upstarts. Some were very much older than Richard and some few of his own age, but all were by birth of the aristocracy, and the taunt of the chronicler who named Richard a second Rehoboam[3] was mere malevolence. Round his throne, in the convocation of the clergy, and even amongst the nobility, Richard had reasonably sure and able support; he now took steps to manage the third estate, and in this sphere, too, his choice of agents was astute.

For the last two years, Richard had managed without a Parliament. The colossal expenses of his marriage to Isabelle, and the lavishness of his court, had again emptied the royal Treasury, and when a mediaeval English king was financially desperate, the Commons had their uses – and were beginning to find their opportunity. The Parliament of January 1397 illustrates the true status of the mediaeval Commons – their potentialities and their limitations. Richard secured the appointment of Sir John Bushy as Speaker. To the English chroniclers, Bushy was of course 'vicious, grasping, and inordinately ambitious' and a mere creature of the despised Richard, but the facts of his career tell a better story. He was a typical knight of the shire. He had been thrice sheriff of Lincoln, and had represented Lincolnshire in every Parliament since 1386 except the Merciless Parliament. He had been Speaker before – in 1394 and probably in 1395 – and had been appointed a King's knight with a pension of forty marks a year as far back as 1391. It is remarkable that he had been selected by Richard in spite of his earlier support of the Appellants. Even the bitterest of his critics acknowledged his eloquence, and it would appear that, in place of the despicable sycophant of the older history books, a fairer record must substitute a hard-working local legislator with especial skill at managing and persuading his fellows assembled at Westminster. But the Commons of 1397 were not to be easily managed. A royal proposal that funds should be provided, so that Nottingham and Rutland could be sent with an expedition to help the Duke of Burgundy[1] in his war with Gian Galeazzo Visconti of Milan, was rejected out of hand; and, although in other financial transactions the Commons were not ungenerous, they sent a petition to the Lords which included a clause which was the cause of the famous 'Haxey Case', and marks the beginning of the final crisis of the reign. There was nothing extraordinary in the content of this petition – it was merely ill-fated in its timing. Its first clause complained that sheriffs and escheators were continuing in office for more than a year. By an act of Edward III's reign this had been prohibited in the case of the sheriffs, but there had been no mention of escheators. A study of the records reveals that the administration had not broken this statute to any noticeable degree so far as sheriffs were concerned, but that the reappointment of escheators had become more common.[2] Richard replied quite reasonably that there was a good

173

deal to be said for continuity and experience in local government, especially when the illegality of Livery and Maintenance was constantly threatening both local liberty and royal justice. There is evidence to show that a system of rotation in the offices of sheriff and escheator may have been the real abuse at which the Commons aimed – they were protesting against local vested interests, not against royal manipulation. The second clause protested against the inefficiency of the administration in failing to prevent Scottish inroads on the Border – a perennial grievance which Richard was quite ready to remedy if he could. The third clause protested that the abuses of Livery and Maintenance were as frequent as ever – and again Richard would have been as pleased as the Commons if he could have found the right remedy. It was the fourth clause which caused trouble, and yet it had been the subject of innumerable petitions throughout the century – it complained that the King's household was in general too numerous and too expensive, and that, in particular, the King maintained too many bishops and ladies of the Queen's retinue. In its general import such a clause was guaranteed to irritate any mediaeval King – he was likely to be only too well aware of the fact that a privy purse was usually inadequate to support the expenses of a national monarchy. But the particular references to the bishops and ladies roused Richard to an outburst of fury – he took it as a gross affront to his personal regality, he was grieved that his liege Commons should 'misprise and take on themselves any ordinance or governance of the person of the King or his hostel or of any persons of estate whom he might be pleased to have in his company',[1] and asked Gaunt to find out who was the author of so offensive a clause. Speaker Bushy readily obliged and named one Thomas Haxey. A Peter de la Mare might have been bold enough to refuse names, and to plead the ancient right of the Commons to make any petition they pleased; Bushy was no such champion of English liberties. He was a paid knight of the royal household. He accompanied the name of the scapegoat with a grovelling apology to which his eloquence persuaded the Commons to agree.

Haxey was not even a member of the Commons. He was a prebendary of Lincoln and a prosperous King's clerk who was probably only in attendance as one of the proctors for the clergy.

He was brought before the Lords to face the full fury of the King's anger. Richard persuaded his Council to decree that anyone who stirred up the Commons to attack the royal prerogatives should be tried as a traitor. Haxey was duly adjudged to have been guilty of treason, and was condemned to death.[1] But by this time this typical outburst of Richard's anger had spent itself, and a few weeks later Haxey was handed over, as was right and proper, to his ecclesiastical superiors, and released. He was later to become a King's clerk again, and finally even more prosperous as Treasurer of York Minster in the succeeding reign.

The 'Haxey Case' is usually quoted as Richard's first overt act of 'tyranny' – it is better explained as his first tactical error after many years of clever and quiet preparation. His temper had once again betrayed his discretion. On the other hand, he had found out how to handle the Commons and had won the backing of the Lords, and when he realized that he had gone too far he had given way gracefully, and he rewarded the Commons for their sub-servience by withdrawing his proposals for a Burgundian expedi-tion. The persecution of Haxey bears no logical relation to Richard's scheme for final revenge[2] on the Appellants – it was in fact a deflection from that consistent aim – but it might have served as a warning to Gloucester, Arundel and Warwick that, when Richard finally decided to strike, he would not be inhibited from his purpose by any nice calculations either of legality or of pro-priety. From Richard's point of view, the Haxey Case and every act of the Parliament of 1397 – it complacently approved the legitimization of the Beauforts – provided evidence that Parlia-ment (when it was necessary to consult it) could, with the aid of devoted servants like Bushy, be bent to his will. And if, as seems highly probable, the real power behind Haxey was the hand of Gloucester, then the Haxey incident illustrates Richard's formid-able strength at this time and Gloucester's comparative isolation – it was only Richard's excess of temper which had spoilt a good case.

The French war and its expense was over; Gaunt, Nottingham and most of the Lords were now on Richard's side; there were plenty of friends in Church and State; there were other knights, like Sir William Bagot and Sir Henry Green,[3] who could help Sir John Bushy as royal agents 'managing' the Commons; and Richard had all the personal prestige which accrued to him from the seven previous years of comparative peace and prosperity. The opposition of Gloucester and his friends was now without general support. Gloucester himself was persistently rude to the King in the Council. Arundel was openly hostile, but powerless. Warwick had quarrelled with Nottingham over the lordship of Gower, and, having lost his case, he had refused to abide by the judgment and had been fined and disgraced. Derby was again aloof from his fellow Appellants – he could scarcely have openly opposed his own father who was now the chief prop and support of the throne. Nottingham had thrown over his former friends – or been bought over by Richard. The Appellants were now a split and isolated faction.

Richard's sense of power was further reinforced at this juncture by the flattering negotiations with two of the Electors to the Imperial throne, which were now reaching a climax.[1] They had suggested that Richard might displace his former brother-in-law Wenceslas – it was a move in the diplomacy of Pope Boniface to prevent the concerted Anglo-French plan for ending the Schism by deposing both Popes and holding a new election. A similar move in the same cynical ecclesiastical game was Boniface's surprising appointment of Huntingdon, Richard's half-brother, as 'Captain and Counsellor of the Roman Church'.[2] Plans were also discussed for ending the Schism by the more drastic, but now outdated, method of a military crusade. Nothing came of either plan – but the possibility of an invitation to be 'King of the Romans' was enough to rouse the ambition of any mediaeval king, and Richard was never unambitious. It is significant too that at this time Richard was expressing his new-found power in the nobler sphere of architecture. The stately proportions of Westminster Hall and the grandest timber roof in Europe are still with us to bear witness to the breadth of his imagination.

But the household extravagances[3] of which the Haxey petition had complained, the expenses of international diplomacy, and the re-roofing of Westminster Hall did not help Richard's financial difficulties. Later in the summer of 1397, his advisers could see no way out other than borrowing by the irksome method of 'persuading' those with money to part with it. It was not the novel device of a new tyrant – it had been used by the Council when he was a minor in 1379, and the records prove that Richard's loans were all repaid. 'Forced loans' is the tendentious appellation of propagandists who implied something not merely without precedent but little short of robbery and confiscation.

At the end of this spring Parliament of 1397 Richard was at the summit of his achievement.[1] He had built up his strength methodically and successfully, he had isolated the three men he most hated, and, if his handling of the Haxey case had displayed a lack of control, it had also shewn that he was able to repair any damage he had done. It was at this moment that Gloucester chose to invite the fate he had so long deserved.

In April 1397 Richard had handed back the fortress of Brest to the Duke of Brittany. Both the fortresses of Brest and of Cherbourg had been pledged to England for the duration of the war in return for a loan of £20,000, and the grant of Castle Rising in Norfolk and some other lordships to the Duke of Brittany. The loan had been redeemed, and there was a twenty-eight years' truce with France – there was therefore every justification for Richard's action, except in the judgment of Gloucester. In June, Richard gave a banquet at Westminster to which some of the returning Brest garrison were invited.[2] It was over 'wine and comfits' at its conclusion that the Duke of Gloucester began an open quarrel which was soon to cost him his life. He drew the King's attention to the returned soldiers and complained that they had been badly paid and were without hope of further employment. Richard replied courteously enough that they would be paid in full, and that meanwhile they could live at the King's expense in four good villages near London. Gloucester then taunted the King personally; 'Sire, you ought first to hazard your life in capturing a city from your enemies before you think of giving up any city which your ancestors have conquered.' Richard in amazement commanded him to repeat the remark, and then angrily asked him whether he thought he was a merchant or a traitor. 'Thus began the quarrel between King Richard and the Duke of Gloucester,' says the French chronicler.[3] It had begun many years before, but at last it had reached crisis, and, though for the moment and for the sake of propriety 'they separated with civil words before the people', Gloucester retired to his estate at Pleshey in Essex; here was a quarrel which mere words could no longer settle.

Both sides seem to have decided on action, but Gloucester made the first move. A meeting was arranged at St Albans at which its abbot (who was Gloucester's godfather) and the prior of Westminster added the force of significant dreams to Gloucester's anger, and a conspiracy was hatched which summoned the now frightened Appellant Lords to a secret conclave at Arundel. In August 1397 the men of 1388 sat at dinner in Arundel Castle. Gloucester, the Earl of Arundel, Thomas Arundel, Archbishop of Canterbury, the Earl of Warwick, Thomas Mowbray, Earl of Nottingham, and Henry Bolingbroke, Earl of Derby were all present, and, with the blessings of the Church, they swore an oath to stand together until the King and his uncles of Lancaster and York were in prison for life, and the remaining Lords of the King's Council were executed. It was a desperate attempt to forestall Richard's vengeance, and it failed because of Nottingham's treachery. Nottingham repaid recent royal favours by immediately informing Richard of the plot, and Richard acted promptly. He was at dinner in the London mansion of Huntingdon with others of his Council when Nottingham brought the grave news. Richard immediately ordered the arrest of Arundel and Warwick, and, with a strong body of archers and men-at-arms, he himself rode hard to Pleshey where he surprised Gloucester ill in bed. In deference to the Duchess, the arrest was carried out with discretion and fair words – it was couched as a request for his urgent presence at the Council – but Gloucester himself must have realized what was intended. Once out of sight of Pleshey Castle, Gloucester was the King's prisoner, and he was handed over to Nottingham to be immediately shipped to Calais, of which fortress Nottingham was captain. Gloucester was never to return. Meanwhile, Rutland and Kent with another strong force had arrested Arundel; Warwick was similarly dealt with, and both were lodged in the Tower. The three leading Appellants were now in Richard's power. Of the remaining two, Nottingham had turned king's evidence and bought temporary safety, while Derby was after all the son of Gaunt – his turn could wait. It only remained for parliamentary trial and condemnation to cloak with official legality deeds which can be described as judicial murder or just retribution according as Richard's revenge is considered barbarous and unjustified, or stern but inevitable.[1]

Immediately following on the three arrests, Richard took steps to reassure those who might well have been wondering how far his revenge would reach. A proclamation was made that the need for the arrests would be explained in the forthcoming Parliament, and indicated that new offences (and not the old offences of 1386-8) would there be disclosed in full justification. At the same time, the bishops were forbidden to offer prayers or organize processions on behalf of the arrested men. The popularity of all three prisoners with the Londoners was undoubtedly a source of danger to Richard. One chronicler talks of 'public grief', and Froissart emphasizes that Gloucester especially had made it part of a consistent policy to cultivate the Londoners.[1] If the French chroniclers' story of the St Albans plot is accepted, the proclamation was not a blind, and was issued in the hope that, before the trials took place, conclusive proof of the plot would be forthcoming and would suffice to secure conviction. Both the proclamation and the warning to the bishops seem to have been a rather clumsy attempt to prevent any cause of civil disorders before the accused were brought to trial. That Richard was determined on the deaths of all three is quite clear, but he wanted and hoped to have better legal justification than the Appellants of 1386-8.

At a Council held at Nottingham the King's plan for the first act of his revenge was revealed. With grim irony[2] the procedure of the Merciless Parliament was to be followed in every detail, and the first step was the appointment of eight new Lords Appellant – the Earls of Nottingham, Rutland, Kent, Huntingdon, Somerset, and Salisbury, with Sir Thomas Despenser and Lord William Scrope. All of them were of the King's following, but the fact that Nottingham's name appears in the list is evidence either that Richard was still hoping to avoid using the deeds of 1388 as grounds of accusation or that a lack of scruple, which became chronic in the succeeding century, was already manifest – Nottingham was a Lord Appellant for the second time, and he was appealing his old comrades-in-arms! The eight new Lords Appellant were to appeal Gloucester, Arundel and Warwick of treason at the Parliament summoned to Westminster for September 17th, 1397; it was to be a fateful session of what proved to be the last Parliament of the reign.

This autumn Parliament of 1397 has been the subject of much controversy. The assertion of one chronicler that it was a 'packed' parliament is not supported by another chronicler who was actually present throughout its proceedings.[1] Careful modern research finds no evidence to support the charge, and, if it had been 'packed' in the King's interest, there would have been no need for the subsequent threats of the King's bodyguard. The Lancastrian chroniclers also make play with the fact that this Parliament was accommodated in a hall newly built for the purpose with open sides, in order, as they insinuate, that the surrounding Cheshire Archers might overawe the proceedings. The more likely explanation is that, as Westminster Hall was in the hands of the builders, it was inconvenient to disturb them, and a mistake to expose the meeting of Parliament to the exigencies of the weather; a temporary hall was therefore provided. The presence of the Cheshire Archers probably had a darker significance. Richard had hoped for conclusive evidence of the St Albans plot. If he had secured it, trial and condemnation would automatically have followed, and no one would have had a grievance. Three weeks before, he had despatched Sir William Rickhill, one of the King's Justices, to obtain a confession from Gloucester in his Calais prison. He had brought back a general confession of treason and a grovelling plea for mercy, but nothing precise or particular about the recent plot. It was good enough so far as it went,[2] but it was not good enough to enable Richard to implement the promises of his proclamation. When Parliament met, Richard knew that Gloucester was dead; he might well have been anxious as to how his peers, the knights of the shire, and the burgesses of London might receive the news when he deigned to give it them. The presence of the Cheshire Archers was a sign both of an uneasy conscience and a determination that, come what may, he would fulfil his purpose. Richard's private bodyguard of 400 Cheshire Archers had been specially summoned to Kingston-on-Thames on September 15th, but certain of the nobles, including Lancaster, York, Derby, Huntingdon and the other new Appellants, were also permitted to come armed with their retainers. The Parliament of 1397 was to be a show of strength, and Richard had so engineered his affairs that if the show became a show-down his strength would preponderate.

Whether, as Parliament was told later, Gloucester had died of the illness which had kept him to his bed at Pleshey, or whether he was deliberately suffocated on Richard's instructions either by Nottingham or Rutland or some hired murderers, will never be a matter for conclusive proof. Nottingham was the type of mediaeval baron who stooped to anything which might have served his own ends, and at this period his life depended on his atoning for his previous career as a Lord Appellant in 1388. Rutland was at this time one of the King's closest friends, a cousin to Richard, and a nephew to Gloucester. The evidence which attaches his name to the deed is of the flimsiest. On the other hand, one William Serle was later executed by Henry IV for treason; it is significant that after the early part of September 1397, Serle appears frequently as the recipient of lavish gifts from Richard, and was finally appointed one of the executors of his will. He was a more likely assassin. There was, too, a later confession of doubtful authenticity by a man called Halle. These surmises are pointless[1] – the man who must bear the responsibility for Gloucester's death was Richard. It is quite possible that rigorous confinement in a mediaeval fortress prison was the true cause of Gloucester's death; but Richard was responsible for that rigour. It is quite true that if ever a baron deserved no mercy at the hands of the King he had wronged it was Gloucester; but Richard was as certain of a legal conviction against Gloucester as he was against Arundel and Warwick. It has been suggested that murder at Calais was less ignominious than trial and condemnation in England, and a traitor's death on Tower Hill. It is possible that Richard was considering the feelings of his other uncle Gaunt who, as Lord High Seneschal of England, would have to pronounce sentence on a brother; but these are flimsy excuses compared with the weight of Richard's determination to settle accounts with the leader of the original Appellants. In a cruel age let Richard's escutcheon carry the stain of his uncle's murder; it could still claim cleaner colours than those of most of his contemporaries.

The proceedings at Westminster opened with the customary address from the Chancellor, Edmund de Stafford, Bishop of Exeter. On this occasion, it was in the form of a sermon based on the significant text 'One King shall be King to them all' (*Ezek.* 37: 22), and emphasized that anyone who usurped or plotted against the power of the King was worthy of the full penalties of the law. It was therefore this Parliament's special function to enquire into any such usurpation or plot, to determine punishment, and to prevent any possible repetition. The Commons were instructed to produce their Speaker, and on the following day

Sir John Bushy was duly presented and accepted. Bushy, supported by Bagot and Green, seems to have taken a very prominent part in the subsequent proceedings, and although all three are unscrupulously vilified by the Lancastrian chroniclers, the eyewitness Adam of Usk gives no indication that their leadership was resented or questioned. At the petition of the Commons, the acts of the Commission of 1386 were annulled, and the general pardon granted perforce by Richard to the Commissioners was revoked, together with the special pardon granted to the Earl of Arundel in 1394 when Richard was his own master. The bishops seem to have been difficult over these preliminaries, and there is evidence that Archbishop Arundel openly opposed the revocation in defence of his brother the accused Earl of Arundel. It did no good to either. The Commons promptly named the Archbishop as equally a traitor, and, when he rose to reply, he was abruptly silenced by Richard, compelled to withdraw from the Parliament, and commanded to await the results of his impeachment. There was a further ecclesiastical difficulty. 'The judgment of blood' was certain, and, although at first it was arranged that such proceedings might legitimately continue in the absence of the clerics, there was a feeling that this might weaken the validity of the subsequent judgments. The bishops were therefore compelled to nominate a proxy, and Sir Thomas Percy, the Steward of the Household, was duly appointed with full powers of attorney.[1] As the clergy withdrew 'there was, as is wont to be, some bustle. And thereupon the King's archers . . . thought that some quarrel or strife had arisen in the house, and bending their bows, they drew their arrows to the ear, to the great terror of all who were there; but the King quieted them'.[2] Such is the matter of fact description by the eye-witness of a scene which has been magnified by more prejudiced chroniclers and historians into an example of Richard's violent overthrowing of the liberties of Parliament. The charge is vastly overdrawn, and even the Monk of Evesham, who maintains that the Cheshire men actually began to shoot, admits that it was Richard who quietened them, and prevented a tumult.[3]

With the clergy and their scruples out of the way, Bushy immediately petitioned the King to proceed not only against the Lords Gloucester, Arundel and Warwick, but also against Archbishop Arundel. Richard seems to have kept to his main purpose

– the elimination of the three Appellant Lords – but he was quite willing that the gentler process of impeachment should dispose of the Earl of Arundel's ecclesiastical brother, who was so clearly one of the Gloucester faction. It was at this stage that Richard, while adding the Archbishop to the accused, announced that his pardon still held for the other members of the 1386 Commission. In several quarters there was intense relief – his uncle the Duke of York and Bishop William of Wykeham wept for joy 'and fell down on their knees before the King and thanked him for so great a favour'. It was a significant gesture on Richard's part – it indicates that the whole proceedings were aimed solely at personal revenge.

On September 21st the new Appellants, in silken red robes banded with white silk and embroidered with letters of gold, repeated the judicial farce of 1388 and appealed Gloucester, Arundel and Warwick of treason on four points – they had compassed and designed to slay the King, to depose him, to withdraw homage, and to ride against him in war – but the evidence was not new, it related back to the Rebellion of 1386–8.

The Earl of Arundel, in his peer's robes and hood of red, was tried first. Gaunt ordered his belt and hood to be taken off, and there began a bandying of epithets between the two until the King silenced them and ordered Arundel to answer the charge of treason. Arundel had shown his fighting qualities at sea and on land, and now, a doomed man, his courage did not fail him. He demanded trial by battle as Brembre had done in 1388, and, as with Brembre, it was refused him. He then rested his case on the freely granted pardon of 1394, told Gaunt that if treasons were in question Gaunt needed pardon more than he did, and, when Bushy pointed out that his pardon had been revoked by the advice and consent of the faithful Commons, he asked where they were – he could only see traitors. Derby now took a hand – emboldened perhaps by his exemption from the royal proscription list – and reminded Arundel that in 1387 Arundel had urged not the suppression of de Vere but first the capture of the King. Richard revealed a truer charge – 'Didst thou not say to me in the bath behind the White Hall that Sir Simon Burley my knight was for many reasons worthy of death? And I answered thee that I knew no cause of death in him. And then thou and thy fellows did traitorously slay him?' There was no answer to that charge, and Gaunt, as Seneschal of England, sentenced him to death as a traitor with all his properties – entailed and unentailed – forfeit to the crown. Arundel was hurried off to execution[1] – the grosser penalties were excused by Richard on account of his noble birth – on Tower Hill in the presence of his nephew Kent, and his son-in-law Nottingham, who, so Froissart says, actually bandaged his father-in-law's eyes.

The Earl of Warwick's trial was equally dramatic – but it was the trial of a coward. 'Like a wretched old woman,' says the eye-witness, 'he made confession of all . . . wailing and weeping and whining.'[2] The King asked him who had tempted him to treason, and he replied that it was the Duke of Gloucester, the Abbot of St Albans and a monk recluse of Westminster. This was partial confirmation of the St Albans plot, and Richard's extravagant delight was recorded by the chroniclers – 'By St John the Baptist,' he cried, 'Thomas of Warwick your confession is more pleasing to me than the value of all the lands of the Duke of Gloucester and the Earl of Arundel.'[3] There were apparently not enough details forth-coming to make it worth while to change the basis of the published charges, but at least Warwick's confession was valuable enough to purchase his life. His possessions were forfeited, and he was con-demned to exile under the guardianship of Sir William Scrope, Lord of the Isle of Man. Warwick was promised an allowance during his exile but it was never paid, and soon afterwards he was transferred to the Tower where he remained until freed by Henry IV. Richard's delight at Warwick's confession is not easy to explain[4] unless more was revealed than the Lancastrian chroniclers have allowed us to know, and it may be that whatever was re-vealed came at just the right moment to calm the storm caused by Arundel's death and the coming revelation of the death of Gloucester.

Our eye-witness chronicler adds another name to the accused – Sir Thomas Mortimer, an illegitimate son of the second Earl of March. It is a mysterious addition for which no satisfactory explanation has ever been offered, but, judging from a lawsuit which was also discussed in this Parliament between the new Earl of Salisbury and the fourth Earl of March, and the evidence of Froissart who even includes the Earl of March amongst the St Albans conspirators, it would appear that Richard was not at this time by any means sure of any of the March family although the fourth Earl – his Lieutenant in Ireland – was his heir. Sentence on Sir Thomas Mortimer was postponed until the Earl of March could attend the Council.

When the trial of the greatest of the accused was due, it was at last announced that the Duke of Gloucester was already dead. Gloucester's confession, which had been obtained by Sir William Rickhill, was read to Parliament, and it is a convincing document. It confessed fully the treason of 1387–8, it referred to the fact that he 'among other communed and asked of certein Clercs whether that we myght zyve up our homage', and it admitted that he had planned the 'deposail of my lyege loord trewly I knowlech wel that we wer assented ther to for two dayes or thre' – a reference to the meeting of Gloucester and Richard at Eltham in 1386.¹ Here was evidence good enough to justify the proceedings of 1397, and there was even a reference to the St Albans 'clercs', and in general a confession of guilt surpassing that of most traitors. The news of the death of Gloucester seems to have been received with a calm which is a truer reflection of his worth than the adulations of the chroniclers. Richard had already disposed of Gloucester's estates – the first chapter of his revenge was complete.

There was still, however, the case of Archbishop Arundel. He had been dismissed to what would in the twentieth century be called 'house-arrest', and on September 25th he was sentenced as a result of his impeachment – and not by Appeal of Treason – to exile and the forfeiture of his properties, and was replaced as archbishop shortly afterwards by Roger Walden the Treasurer and ex-secretary to Richard. Archbishop Arundel suffered chiefly for his relationship and loyalty to his brother the Earl of Arundel, and Richard does not appear to have borne him any special ill-will. In fact, it is the essence of the second Appellant episode that its objectives were strictly limited. It was a deliberate first stroke against only three of the original Appellants – of the remaining two, Nottingham was a turn-coat and for the moment usefully in Richard's pocket, Derby was son and heir to Gaunt, and Gaunt at this period was an indispensable buttress to the arch of the newly-built regal edifice. There was no repetition of the wholesale proscription of which the Gloucester faction had been guilty. Richard was content with what had already been achieved, and was prepared to bide his time until both Nottingham and Derby could safely be called to account. Accepting the French chroniclers' report that both had been drawn into the St Albans plot and that Nottingham was the informer, and assuming that Warwick's confession revealed more than the chroniclers have permitted us to know, especially in relation to Nottingham and Derby, then Richard's extraordinary manifestation of delight when he heard Warwick's confession becomes less difficult to understand, and the coming quarrel of Nottingham and Derby a less surprising sequel.

Richard's ruthlessness so far compared very favourably with the acts of the Merciless Parliament. One original Appellant executed, one exiled, and one probably murdered before inevitable execution – this was far from the blood bath of Gloucester's brief period of absolutism. Neither was it followed by any such monstrous misappropriation of public funds as the £20,000 extracted from Parliament by Gloucester. On the contrary, Richard wisely gave what was in his power to give to those who had helped him – honours and titles. Five new dukedoms were created – the informer Nottingham became Duke of Norfolk, Derby was reassured by the Dukedom of Hereford, Huntingdon became Exeter, Kent became Surrey, and Rutland became Albemarle (or as Shakespeare called him 'Aumerle'). Such a pride of new dukes roused the sarcasms of the chroniclers – they were laughed at as 'duketti'.[1] Old Gaunt was further honoured in the person of John Beaufort, his eldest son by Catherine Swynford; from Earl of Somerset he was promoted to Marquis of Dorset. The King's lesser supporters were not forgotten – Thomas Despenser took Gloucester's earldom, Ralph Neville was made Earl of Westmorland, Thomas Percy Earl of Worcester, and William Scrope Earl of Wiltshire. The lands of the dead Gloucester and the exiled Warwick helped to endow this galaxy, while the lands of Arundel were added to the royal earldom of Cheshire. For himself, and *ob amorem Cestrensium* Richard took the new title of Prince of Chester. And on September 30th, 1397 Richard staged a memorable scene – his sense of the theatrical was acute. After High Mass in the abbey of Westminster, before the shrine of the saint whose arms he had added to his own,[2] prelates and nobles were individually sworn, and the knights of the shire corporately sworn (by holding up their right hands in consent), to maintain all the acts of the Parliament for ever.[3] The Parliament was then adjourned for a second session to meet at Shrewsbury after Christmas, and, as a dramatic climax to a dramatic episode, a grand review of the armed bands of the

Londoners was held by Richard and Lancaster on horseback, and in the evening there was a 'great court and a sumptuous feast, and at supper the heralds received large gifts from the lords and ladies, and cried "largesse"; and my lady of Exeter received the prize as the best dancer and the best singer'.[1]

On Christmas Day 1397, Richard appeared to be independent, secure and triumphant. He had carried through the major part of his personal revenge for the humiliations of 1386–8 without alienating anyone except the immediate relatives of his victims. If the French chroniclers are right, he had even made a concordat with the Londoners; he had the Pope on his side, with guarantees of excommunication against all opposition; his uncles of Lancaster and York were his staunch supporters; thanks to skilful help he had discovered an excellent technique for managing the unruly Commons – when he needed their help; he had secured a lengthy truce with the hereditary enemy across the Channel; and at the age of thirty he could look forward to a long and prosperous reign, and, in due course, even the problem of a direct heir might be solved to everyone's satisfaction. In ten years, he had risen from the depths of humiliation to a height unrivalled by any other of our mediaeval kings – his court was the rival of His Most Christian Majesty's and, if monkish contemporaries only saw corruption in his luxury, history can see the eternal light of Chaucer, and the twentieth century can still gaze in awe at the roof of Richard's palace hall and in admiration at the beauty of the royal effigies which were at this time commissioned to grace his tomb.[2] Richard had managed the first chapter of his revenge with skill and praise-worthy restraint; in mismanaging the second chapter he was to bring the whole edifice of his power, so patiently built up, crashing in a ruin which not only buried himself but which was never properly rebuilt until Henry VII was able to repair the century of devastations which followed on the usurpation of Richard's throne by Henry Bolingbroke.

VIII

TYRANNY

'WITH SUCH WORLDLY pomp, as ear hath not heard neither hath it entered into the heart of man', so Adam of Usk tells us,[1] the adjourned Parliament met at Shrewsbury on January 28th, 1398. There has been much conjecture as to why Richard chose the Welsh Marches for this famous session. One of the chroniclers suggests that it was to punish the pride of the Londoners; but this suggests a breach which is difficult to reconcile with another chronicler's report of the royal review of the Londoners,[2] and the general goodwill with which the first session had been concluded. One reason cannot be doubted. Near Cheshire, Richard was in very friendly territory, and his bodyguards were very much at home: and, in spite of the new goodwill of the Londoners, he knew well enough that both Arundel and Gloucester had been popular with the London citizens. Richard had two objectives at this time – to reckon with the remaining Appellants of 1388, and to buttress his power with essential finance. The full toll of his reckoning had to wait on the right opportunity; finance might be more quickly and conveniently arranged away from London. Meanwhile, the cost of supporting so lavish a court as Richard's could be temporarily met by a change of pasture – Shrewsbury was honoured by the King's presence, but its citizens soon found that it was a costly privilege.[3]

The financial concessions obtained from this Shrewsbury session were substantial. Richard was granted not only generous subsidies, but, more prolific and quite unprecedented, the duties on wool, wool-fells, and leather *for life*.[4] It meant that Richard had temporarily solved his more pressing financial problems, and even secured his financial future, by obtaining a war subsidy in time of peace. Adroit management further obtained Parliament's agreement to some less spectacular items in the royal programme.

188

Sir Thomas Mortimer was condemned in absence; Lord Cobham, who had foolishly allowed himself to be a member of the hated Commission of 1386, was mercifully banished to Guernsey; and all the acts and judgments of the Merciless Parliament were repealed and a general pardon proclaimed. But there was a financial twist in the tail; all previous pardons were renewable at a price, and – a move which must have worried many guilty consciences – there were fifty unnamed exceptions. This seems to have roused even Bushy to a mild show of protest, and Richard's reply, to the effect that to have published the names of the exceptions would merely have expedited their escape, was both lame and over-ingenious.[1] There were two of the five Lords Appellant still to be dealt with, and, though he was not yet ready to name them, he was certainly not prepared to pardon them. The final reckoning was nearer than he realized.

Like Gloucester before him, Richard was anxious to secure his new position by every possible mechanism – parliamentary and otherwise. In the September parliamentary sessions, 1397, oaths of loyalty had been sworn on the shrine of St Edward at Westminster. At Shrewsbury, the cross of Canterbury served a similar purpose for Lords and bishops, while the Commons, clerical proctors and knights stood round the King and swore on oath, while raising their right hands, to maintain the judgments of 1397–8 for ever. The judges and the serjeants-at-law had been consulted as to the best means of establishing what had been done, and they had replied that 'the greatest surety that can be is what is established ordained and affirmed by Parliament', but they had also advised a renewal of the oaths sworn at Westminster. The full sovereignty of Parliament was clearly not recognized either by King or Parliament at this time, and there was still a pathetic belief that the oaths of one generation could bind the next. Richard went further. Anyone who attempted to reverse the acts of his revenge Parliament would be guilty not only of treason, but would suffer spiritual as well as physical condemnation – he told his Parliament that he was writing to the Pope to ask that decrees of excommunication should be promulgated against any man who broke his oath, and, when letters apostolic finally arrived, they were duly publicized at Paul's cross and other public centres.[2]

There was one personal oath taken at Shrewsbury which is

puzzling. Roger Mortimer, Earl of March, who as the King's Lieutenant in Ireland had been unable to attend at Westminster, had been specially summoned to Shrewsbury to take the oath of loyalty to Richard and the acts of the 1397-8 Parliament. Adam of Usk maintains that he was suspected by Richard, and one of the French chroniclers suggests that he was implicated in the St Albans Plot. Usk describes how 20,000 of Shrewsbury's citizens went out to greet 'the noble knight, clad in hoods of his colours, red and white, and hoping through him for deliverance from the grievous evil of such a King'.[1] Mediaeval Shrewsbury must have been more than empty if Usk's figures were right, and, if his description of popular feeling was correct, then Richard may have had good grounds for suspicion. But Usk's admiration for March is perhaps explained by his own admission that he owed his first step in preferment to March's father, while Usk's contempt for Richard can be explained by the fact that he was writing as a civil servant to Henry IV. March seems to have conducted himself with considerable circumspection – he quietly took the oath on the first day of the Shrewsbury session, and immediately returned to Ireland confirmed by the King's authority. The simplest explanation of March's special journey to Shrewsbury is that, as he was the heir presumptive and had not been present at the Westminster oath-taking, it was both convenient and proper that he should take the oath at Shrewsbury. His murder by rebel Irish later in the year was the prime cause of Richard's second Irish expedition, and it is unlikely that Richard would have gone to so much trouble to avenge the death of a relative he seriously suspected of treason.

Shakespeare, with a dramatist's eye for the dramatically significant, opens his *Tragedy of King Richard II* with the quarrel between Thomas Mowbray, now Duke of Norfolk, and Henry Bolingbroke, now Duke of Hereford. That famous quarrel was in its sequel to bring Richard down from the peak of his power to bitter humiliation and an obscure death within a period of a mere eighteen months. The quarrel was first publicized at this Shrewsbury session of the Parliament of 1398.

Their three comrades-in-arms during the Rebellion of 1388 were already disgraced – one in exile and the other two in traitors' graves. Why had Norfolk and Hereford been spared? It is inconceivable that Richard had forgiven either; but Norfolk had turned king's evidence, and if not Richard's actual instrument he had at least acquiesced in the fate of Gloucester, while Hereford was the son and heir to 'Old John of Gaunt, time-honour'd Lancaster', now one of the most famous knights in Christendom, and Richard's eldest and most powerful supporter. While Norfolk was useful the King could dissemble his real feelings; while Gaunt was alive the King was wise to try to postpone a reckoning with Hereford. But it was Hereford who forced the pace; his attack on Norfolk may have seemed to him the best form of defence in a situation which in any event might have appeared to foretell his doom. To Norfolk the quarrel and its publicity must have come as a rude shock when to all appearances he had at last found his way back to royal favour and perhaps pardon, even if he had passed by the murder of a former friend and colleague on the way.

Hereford accused Norfolk of treason. His story,[1] as told to Richard prior to the Shrewsbury session, was that he and Norfolk met while riding to London a month before, and that Norfolk had asked him whether he realized how perilously they both stood. Hereford had professed that he did not understand, and Norfolk had reminded Hereford that it was more than likely that their behaviour at Radcot Bridge and afterwards had not been forgotten by Richard. Hereford had protested that they had both been pardoned; to which Norfolk had pertinently replied that so also had Gloucester and Arundel, that the King's younger friends were daily urging their master to secure his position by disposing of the two survivors of the original five Lords Appellant, and further that Hereford's father Gaunt was also marked down for destruction. They had better take action before it was too late. Hereford alleged that he had indignantly refuted Norfolk's insinuations, and had refused to be a party to such treason.

The story bears the stamp of truth, except that the suggestion of treason was probably Hereford's gloss on a narrative which merely shows Norfolk as over-worried, conscience stricken, and very indiscreet. Hereford's action in betraying to the King a conversation which was confidential as between brother knights in equal danger was a breach of the code of Chivalry so gross that it suggests that Hereford himself fully realized the truth of Norfolk's analysis of the situation. He had therefore seized this opportunity of avenging his uncle Gloucester's death, for which Norfolk as captain of Calais was officially responsible, of finally putting himself right with Richard, and of securing the royal favour and security which so far only Norfolk had been able to win. That in so doing he broke the knightly code could not have unduly worried Hereford – throughout his life he was a man who calculated without any care for conscience. This time he had miscalculated – the quarrel delivered both remaining Lords Appellant into Richard's power. If Richard refused to believe Hereford, and Hereford were unable to substantiate his charges, Hereford would be branded and disgraced as a perjuror. If Richard believed Hereford, and Hereford proved his charges, Norfolk could be disposed of as a traitor without public complaint. Richard seems to have hesitated between the two courses, either of which would have suited a part of his purpose, and only after some deliberation did he plan a deeper scheme.

There is evidence[1] that Richard at first attempted to reconcile the disputing Lords, but it was of no avail. Hereford was instructed to put his charges into writing and was informed that they would be dealt with by the Parliament now adjourned to Shrewsbury. Meanwhile both disputants – each accusing the other of treason – were placed under arrest. Hereford found bail in his father, his uncle York, his cousin Albemarle and Surrey – he was therefore free to attend the Shrewsbury session in person. Norfolk was significantly unable to find bail – he was committed to Windsor Castle, and was immediately replaced as Marshal by Surrey, and as Captain of Calais by Exeter – and was therefore not present at Shrewsbury. On January 30th, 1398, in full Parliament, Hereford repeated the story he had already betrayed to Richard. On January 31st Richard dissolved Parliament, and the Norfolk-Hereford dispute was referred to the usual parliamentary Committee which had to deal with any outstanding business.

This parliamentary Committee of 1398 was used as deadly evidence against Richard after his fall. We are told that 'the fatal subservience of Parliament . . . by delegating its powers to a Committee of members, struck at the root of representative government',[2] that 'the Parliament of Shrewsbury, although it sat only four days, made Richard to all intents and purposes an absolute monarch',[3] that 'the nation was furious at this betrayal of its rights',[1] that 'it seemed as if he (Richard) had succeeded in inducing Parliament to commit suicide'.[2] It is odd that reputable historians have accepted such obvious propaganda as fact, and that phrases proper to the days of the Stuarts and later Kings have been admitted into criticism of a Plantagenet. Discounting such anachronisms, what truth is there in the contemporary charge? There were precedents for such a Committee in 1371, in the Merciless Parliament of 1388, and there was a similar arrangement later in 1437[3] – none of these Committees have roused contemporaries, or modern historians, to the extravagant charges to which the Shrewsbury Committee gave rise. It is only when seen in the light of Richard's own extravagant insistence on his regality that the Shrewsbury Committee can seem sinister. Yet there is no evidence that Richard had any hope of doing without Parliament, although there is plenty of evidence that he was determined to use it, as and when his regality thought fit – he never pretended to be more than a mediaeval king, but he was aiming at nothing less.

The actual record of this parliamentary Committee's activities is the best answer to those who have regarded it as a dastardly attack on 'the constitution'.[4] Eighteen members were appointed on the last day of the Shrewsbury session with full parliamentary authority to perform two specific duties: first, to deal with outstanding petitions; second, to deal with the Norfolk-Hereford dispute. Its membership included the seven new Appellants together with Lancaster, York, March and Northumberland, six knights of the shire, and the Earls of Worcester and Wiltshire as clergy's proctors. A quorum of any six Lords and any three knights was to be sufficient for the first part of their duties; the same quorum plus one of the clergy's proctors was stipulated for settling the second part. True, the members of the Committee were chiefly of the King's party, including the chamber-knights Bushy and Green, but Bagot, who is usually considered their leader, was not included, and Lancaster, York and Northumberland were too old and independent to be classed as mere royal nominees. To expect any different complexion for such a Committee is to imagine an opposition which no longer existed, and to forget that the only possible leader of an opposition was at this time on his own request at the bar of judgment.

The Committee's first meeting was in March 1398 at Bristol,

whither Richard had moved his court. It duly and legally dealt with a few outstanding petitions of no great consequence, and then, as instructed, proceeded to deal with the Norfolk-Hereford quarrel. Hereford had now added to his first charges two further counts: that Norfolk had been responsible for the murder of Hereford's uncle Gloucester, and that Norfolk had misappropriated public funds entrusted to him as Captain of Calais for the pay of the garrison. The Committee decided that, if Hereford could not substantiate his charges by conclusive proof, the whole question should be referred to the *curia militaris*, or, in other words, to trial by combat. In April 1398, the Committee met again at Windsor, decided that Hereford had not proved his case, and therefore made arrangements for a judicial combat at Coventry on September 16th. Both at Windsor and at Coventry, the Committee was reinforced by so large a muster of the greater Chivalry of England that it was almost indistinguishable from a Great Council. Thus far its acts were legitimate, reasonable and in no sense suggest that Richard was using it as an alternative to Parliament. That Richard did misuse it later is true, but, before that sorry tale was told, the Lists of Coventry had been erected, and the stage set for Richard's decline and fall.

Between the first publicity given to the Norfolk-Hereford dispute at Shrewsbury and the final sentences at Coventry, Richard had first tried a scheme of reconciliation, and only when this failed had he gradually swung round to a policy which he hoped would rid him of the remaining two original Appellants for ever. Froissart records that the necessity for a show of impartiality was impressed on Richard by counsellors who feared Hereford's popularity with the Londoners, and that the final decision to get rid of both the disputants before they met at Coventry was counselled by Huntingdon, the Archbishop of York, and the Earl of Salisbury. The effort at reconciliation could never have had much hope of success, and, although it is impossible to decide at this distance whether the final outcome was Richard's own impromptu invention or the product of earlier consultation with his inner circle of friends, there is no question that it was in many ways a masterly plan . . .

The Lists of Coventry were heralded throughout the country.[1] Two of England's most famous knights, including one of royal blood famed for his prowess in arms throughout Europe, were to meet in a fight to the death before the assembled Chivalry of England. Both had been granted the customary facilities to prepare for battle. The King's armoury was placed at their disposal, royal painters of escutcheons were supplied, and armourers summoned from the Duke of Milan to assist Hereford and from Germany to assist Norfolk emphasized the international character of contemporary feudalism.

On the day before the duel, Hereford rode out to take official farewell of Richard, who was lodged in the castle of Baginton which belonged to his friend Sir William Bagot. Norfolk went through a similar ceremonial early on the day itself. The setting for the combat had been arranged with a lavishness befitting so dramatic an event, and the chroniclers mention not only the magnificence of English Chivalry but the presence of 'foreigners from over sea, as well as a Scottish knight who was called Walter Stuart'. The Duke of Hereford as challenger was the first to enter the lists; he was 'mounted on a white courser, banded with greene and blew velvet imbrodered sumptouslie with swans and antelops of goldsmiths woorke and armed at all points'. Next, King Richard entered into the field with great triumph accompanied 'with all the peers of the realm', and took his throne on the great dais. Now Norfolk appeared, 'his horse being banded with crimson velvet embroidered richly with lions of silver and mulberie trees'. While the Earl Marshal examined and matched their lances and the other preliminaries were settled, the two dukes dismounted and sat on chairs at opposite ends of the lists. The dukes were next mounted and lances couched in rests. A trumpet sounded, and the charge was begun. The herald's trumpets immediately sounded a different warning, the duellists reined in their steeds, and the amazed concourse turned from the lists to the royal dais. King Richard had cast down his staff, the duel was stayed.[1] Lances were reclaimed by the Marshal, the duellists were dismounted and ordered back to their seats, and for two hours they sat amid a hubbub of rumour and counter-rumour, disappointment and speculation, while Richard took private counsel with his assembled peers. At length, Sir John Bushy, who now appeared as the King's secretary, mounted the tribune of the lists and read the judgment of King and Council from 'a large roll of writing a full fathom long'. Henry of Derby, Duke of Hereford, was sentenced to exile for ten years. A tremendous uproar greeted this announcement. Thomas Mowbray, Duke of Norfolk, was sentenced to exile for life, and to the confiscation of all his property save for an annual allowance of £1,000. And again there was a roar from the assembly. The two Lords were summoned to the royal dais and commanded to avoid any meeting during exile under pain of forfeiture. The Lists of Coventry ended in a scene which to the populace was a galling anticlimax, but which to Richard must have been one of the sweeter moments of his life – in one crushing and surprising judgment he was ridding himself of the two remaining Lords Appellant without loss of blood. His revenge was complete.

Shakespeare as a dramatist is right in saying

> '*O, when the King did throw his warder down,*
> *His own life hung upon the staff he threw;*
> *Then threw he down himself*'
>
> (*Henry IV*, ii. iv. 1)

but *post hoc* is not necessarily *propter hoc*, and the famous 'Judgment of Coventry' deserves closer analysis before it can be dismissed as the reckless act of a tyrant verging on insanity. There appears no reason to doubt that Richard was genuine in his first attempts to reconcile the two dukes. While Gaunt was alive, drastic action against his son was difficult, and it was plainly in Richard's interests that the affair of Gloucester's death, with which Hereford accused Norfolk at the Windsor committee meeting, should not be too openly ventilated or too closely investigated. It was only after much cogitation, and probably after much consultation with his closest friends, that the deeper scheme of Coventry was evolved. He was certain to rid himself of one Appellant, why not two? The Trial by Battle would at best only get rid of one – and, as Hereford according to the best critics was the better and more experienced jouster, it would probably be the less important. If, by some accident, the stronger man lost and was slain, the blow to his uncle Gaunt would be bitter, and might weaken a support Richard had given much to obtain. On the other hand, if Hereford won, the glory of so great a victory would increase his already established popularity, and make the consummation of Richard's final vengeance more difficult. The suggestion that Richard might halt the combat before blood was shed was therefore both welcome and ingenious. It was not a revolutionary or unheard of suggestion – royal intervention to prevent two valiant knights from slaughter had happened before, and it was to happen again.[1] The only difficulty was to find a justification for the sentence which would satisfy Chivalry while also satisfying Richard's determination to rid himself of two powerful Lords who had damned themselves for ever in his eyes when they first linked arms as Lords Appellant in 1386. The life-exile of Norfolk was easy to explain – he had in fact confessed to plotting against Gaunt, but had pleaded subsequent pardon. But, if Norfolk were guilty, Hereford had accused him rightly, and therefore deserved praise rather than blame. That was legal logic: but it is probable that in that two hours' Council at Coventry (which had to persuade Hereford's father Gaunt to agree) a much more realistic view of the whole affair was put forward. The argument might well have been that here was a case where two ex-Appellants, while discussing what steps they should take in view of the fates which had overtaken their comrades, had fallen out; that the less scrupulous had taken the unchivalrous step of denouncing the other to the point of accusing him of a 'treason' which any lord in a similar dilemma might well have been contemplating. They were therefore both guilty in varying degrees. The English chroniclers make much play with the general unpopularity of the verdict, and especially with the supposed injustice to Hereford. But the English chroniclers were monks writing for Lancastrians, and, in an affair which was properly an affair of Chivalry, it is as well to take notice of the chronicler of Chivalry. Froissart tells us that the Lords present at Coventry were well enough pleased: 'My Lord of Derby', they said, 'can go and play and fight out of the kingdom for two or three years. He is young.' And it must not be forgotten that Hereford's father Gaunt, while he was personally hurt by the judgment, did not disagree with it, and it was a graceful act of Richard's to remit four years of Hereford's sentence in deference to Gaunt's plea for mercy. No doubt the blood lust of a holiday crowd was disappointed to the point of fury, but such emotions do not last and do not shake thrones. The judgment of Coventry was not the cause of Richard's fall though the sequel was its proximate cause: the true causes were deeper and less spectacular, and the final events both unpredictable and very much at the mercy of that chance which has ever been one of the most neglected of historical causes.

The sentences were implemented forthwith. The rival dukes took polite and almost sentimental leaves of their King, and were granted safe conducts and letters of protection. The Duke of Norfolk sailed from the Suffolk coast to Holland, and thence made pilgrimage to Jerusalem. Exactly a year after leaving England, he died at Venice 'of a broken heart'. The Duke of Hereford was made of sterner stuff, and was given a farewell which may have been the beginning of temptation. It was said that 40,000 Londoners saw him depart for the Kent coast, and mixed their farewells with tears and lamentations. He sailed from Dover to Calais, and thence made his way to Paris and the royal court of France. Neither duke was ungenerously treated so far as money was concerned. Norfolk was to have 10,000 nobles per annum, although his lands were forfeit to the King to reimburse the money that he had received for the pay of the Calais garrison – an explanation which indicates that this was the proved charge that justified the severer sentence of exile for life. Hereford was allowed £2,000 per annum,[1] and received the more important promise that he would enjoy his father's possessions should they fall to him in absence[2] – did Richard in the excitement of victory forget that Gaunt was advanced in years, and that Hereford was heir to vast Palatinate powers?

With the last of the Lords Appellant out of the way, Richard at the end of September 1398 could have looked about him and found most things good. A year later, Richard was deposed and succeeded by the exiled Duke of Hereford. These twelve fateful months have given us one of Shakespeare's most popular and fascinating tragedies, they have set historians a puzzle almost impossible to solve from the data of contemporary documents, and they have provided every moralist since with the most poignant example of pride preceding a fall. They are the twelve short months – even shorter if the four months of the second Irish expedition are subtracted – of what is known as Richard's 'tyranny'. It is a word which to English ears is sufficient justification for, and explanation of, the worst of fates. If the charge of 'tyranny' can be proved against Richard, then Henry IV was no usurper but rather the defender of English liberty. If the charge is groundless, then Richard II was a martyr, sacrificed to the ambition of a selfish baron. If the charge is not-proven, then Henry IV was responsible not merely for the death of his King but for nearly a century of bloodshed. Richard II was either a King who misplayed his hand or a King who was the victim of one of Fortune's most tragic mis-deals.

Was there a personal tyranny? We are told by most of the chroniclers of Richard's violent outbursts of temper, and there is no need to doubt them: on the other hand, most of these outbursts can be explained if they cannot be excused, and in a violent age he was not singular in giving vent to outraged feelings. But one chronicler registers something more serious: he tells us that, about this time, Richard set up a special throne in his chamber on which he sat from dinner time to evensong 'spekynge to no man, but overlokyng alle menn; and yf he loked on eny mann, what astat or degre that ever he were of, he moste knele'.[1] It is a description without confirmation elsewhere; but, when coupled with the persistent evidence of the magnificence of Richard's court since the peace with France, with the story of the extraordinary festivities of the Christmas feast of 1398[2] (when 26 or 28 oxen and 300 sheep and innumerable fowls were consumed daily), with the new interest in the pomp of heraldry and Richard's adoption of the rising sun as an emblem,[3] it is reasonable to admit that here are at least the trappings of absolutism if not the substance. Richard has usually been condemned as a tyrant out of his own mouth. His determination to break down the established laws of real and personal property is proved when he said, 'The lives lands properties goods and chattels of my subjects are mine'; his deliberate intention to set himself above law is proved when he said '*vultu austero et protervo*' that the 'laws were within his own breast and that he alone could change and make the laws of his realm'; his dictatorship is proclaimed when he announced 'I am entire Emperor of my Realm'.[4] But the evidence for the first two phrases is only contained in the Articles of Accusation by which he was finally condemned, and the third phrase can have a perfectly 'constitutional' significance when read in its correct context – the legitimization of the Beauforts. An indictment without supporting evidence is not proof. On the other hand, absence of proof does not necessarily show that the indictment is false; and there is recorded in the Rolls of the Parliament of 1397 the words of the opening address by the Bishop of Exeter, Richard's Chancellor, which derive added significance from the events which followed. His speech was on the theme of monarchy. A mixed monarchy is anarchy, a true king must be strong to rule, the laws must be lawfully executed, the duty of all subjects is obedience, the king is the father of his subjects and the fountain of law and justice, and the first duty of his Parliament is to watch over and protect the royal prerogative and all that it implies. Here was the state sovereignty of Marsilius of Padua joined with Wyclif's theory of Dominion, and presented to an intelligent mediaeval monarch at the very moment when such theories could have their maximum effect and their most obvious temptation. Here was a plain statement of the theory of monarchy as practised later by the Tudors and as over-exploited by the Stuarts, but under Richard it lacked the buttresses of popular support, of spectacular successes on foreign fields, and of personal popularity. Richard, in seeming to anticipate the New Monarchy, was merely being logical about a truly mediaeval monarchy, and logic is perhaps the least important technique in the art of government. When all that was required of a king was leadership in successful war and strength in the enforcement of rough justice, a conqueror and a lawgiver need never have feared for the security of his throne; but when a king found himself the heir to this tradition and at the same time the keystone in a crumbling economic arch which was trying to support the weight of a developing civilization without reasonable financial abutment, the mediaeval theory of monarchic sovereignty broke down. The Tudor theory of government needed a century of internecine civil war, and a century of prosperous economic expansion, before it could hand on its glories to a Stuart monarchy. This in turn fatally substituted logic for the finesse of government; and the gradual emergence of a parliamentary monarchy involved yet another civil war, the public execution of an anointed King, and yet another revolution, before its theory and its practice could be reconciled and accepted by a 'constitutional' King, Parliament and people. Richard had from his earliest years imbibed from his mother, from his uncle Gaunt, and from his tutors the correct logic of mediaeval kingship; it was only in the last year of his reign, when for the first time he found himself with the necessary power, that he attempted to put it into practice. In doing so, he was neither destroying the constitution nor breaking his oaths, he was merely taking theory a step too far. In achieving the fullness of his revenge on those who had so wounded, thwarted and humiliated him, Richard's most fatal step was not an infringement of popular rights but an arbitrary act of confiscation against the most powerful of his barons, and therefore a threat to the propertied 'liberties' of every baron in the land. When the reply to that arbitrary act culminated in rebellion, usurpation and murder, it was as well for the future development of an English constitution that such crudities were cloaked with liberal principles and semi-democratic theories, but it has long been one of history's most unhistorical judgments that Richard should be condemned on evidence which is only contained in a usurper's indictment, on grounds which were still doubtful in the seventeenth century, and on charges which were wholly unsubstantiated in the fourteenth.

But there is evidence of acts which by any standards of judgment can be termed tyrannical, and they can be fairly admitted without in so doing agreeing that here was a conscious attempt at a *system* of tyranny – that would be as absurd as submitting that a tyrant who at times uses the technique of the democrat is in fact aiming at setting up a democracy.

Let Richard plead guilty to a love of pomp and ceremony. The first English King to indulge in the luxury of a personal bodyguard, the diplomat who anticipated the glories of the Field of Cloth of Gold, the first English King who was not only the moulder of courtly and knightly fashions but second to none in his appreciation of the highest culture of his time and place, the lover of the arts of the goldsmith, the jeweller and the embroiderer, the patron of architects, artists and sculptors of genius... there is ammunition in plenty for anyone who is willing to condemn culture in a savage age as the mere extravagance of a tyrannical lunatic. Richard had inherited a resplendent crown, and he tried to live up to its splendour. In this last year of his reign, when he had reached the prime of manhood, and power at last was his to command, his sense of majesty had been still further flattered by the tentative suggestions that, as well as King of England, he might one day be Emperor of the Holy Roman Empire.[1] But Richard's dream of empire was not the wish-fulfilment of a thwarted imperialist – it was a quite reasonable and pleasant excitement at the prospect of a possible honour to himself and his country which in mediaeval Europe's international feudalism might quite easily have come his way. In the event, the overtures had led to nothing, and the incident has been given too much significance. Richard can plead guilty to a love of colour, of magnificence, of art, of poetry, of manners, and of all the glories of a great position and a dazzling inheritance: in doing so he is not automatically to be condemned as a tyrant.

Let Richard plead guilty to high-handedness against the Church in one much publicized act of this period – he forced Gaunt's legitimized son Henry Beaufort into the bishopric of Lincoln at the age of eighteen in spite of the not unnatural opposition of Bishop Buckingham, who was ejected into the lesser see of Lich-field. It was a precipitate act, for the favour he did for his ageing uncle gave his enemies in the Church a useful handle when they joined the baronial opposition. But Richard of all the kings still stands unchallenged as one of the most devout and loyal sons of the Church. His affection for his favourite Abbey of Westminster is witnessed throughout the chronicles, and not least by the spleen of a Walsingham who clearly demonstrates the jealousy of a monk of St Albans; and Richard's many visits to the shrine of St Thomas and the grave of his father at Canterbury are equally well-attested. The patronage of Beaufort was headstrong and unwise, but at least it was picking out for early distinction a churchman who was soon to show signs of greatness, earn himself a Cardinal's hat, and hold the highest position in the land below the monarch. The Beaufort incident is the flimsiest of all the evidences of tyranny.

Let Richard plead guilty to outbursts of violence and of temper throughout his reign, and, during this final year, to a high-handedness with his Council and courtiers which surprised enemies who during the Quiet Years had thought him timid and cowed. But a hot temper goaded by galling irritation, and a lordliness tempted by the first enjoyment of real power, do not condemn Richard as a tyrant. Few monarchs throughout history could escape a similar condemnation.

But there are two graver charges: there are the unpleasant facts of forced loans, crooked pardons, blank charters, and the grim joke of '*le plesaunce*', and the crowning act of folly which in con-fiscating the Lancastrian estates cost him his throne and his life.

Oath after oath was enforced on Richard's subjects of every degree in an attempt to perpetuate his position as established by the Parliament of 1397-8. Richard went further, and a copy of a writ, recently come to light,[1] addressed to the Bishop of Norwich shows that he attempted to obtain special pledges from all his subjects so that the deeds of his revenge Parliament and its special Committee could be ratified for ever. The general pardon issued on the last day of the Shrewsbury session had excepted all who had sided with the Appellants in 1387-8, unless they came to somewhat stringent financial terms with the King by June 24th, 1398. On February 27th, 1399 the general pardon was renewed again, with the exception of those who had ridden to Waltham Cross and Radcot Bridge against de Vere. And now a new gloss was added by Richard – the seventeen counties which had supported the Appellants were condemned, compelled to submit themselves 'like traitors', and to buy back the pleasure (*le plesaunce*) of the King by huge fines amounting to £1,000 or 1,000 marks for each guilty shire. One example of a resulting petition from London[2] and the south-eastern counties, couched in the most grovelling terms and sealed amongst others by Richard Whittington as Mayor of London, has recently been printed – it can have been no easy document to endorse. A further device was next invented. Although the seventeen counties had bought back the King's *plesaunce*, their proctors were compelled for surety's sake to seal blank charters into which the King might write any price he chose. Richard's strength at this time was such that his demands were met in full, and the '*albae cartae*' were not declared null and void and destroyed until the first Parliament of the succeeding reign. On the other hand, the letters of submission were returned to their authors just before Richard sailed for his second Irish expedition, when he was presumably anxious to leave behind him as few enemies as possible. The irritation of the succession of oath-takings, the crooked pardon which condemned the seventeen richest counties of England to ignominious submission and weighty fines, the blank charters which committed the richest of his citizens to unknown penalties for unknown crimes – here was a technique nearer to folly than to tyranny. The reasons for such acts are clear. Richard's expenses far outran his income, and moneys he could not find through his Parliament he had to find by more onerous means. Throughout the later Middle Ages, and well into Tudor and Stuart times, this same problem faced succeeding monarchs, and Richard's *plesaunce* was no worse than Morton's

Fork or Charles' Ship Money; but it was no better. It might also be fairly argued that if money had to be raised it was reasonable that those who had earlier shown themselves capable of treason should be the ones to provide it – a rough justice but not out of step with contemporary thought and an extremely practical way of demonstrating that disloyalty to the Crown had to be paid for in the end. The blank charters, again, are easily explained – they were a reasonably good form of surety when financial securities had already been given and taken. Their folly was in that, when Richard's power had crashed in ruin, the blank charters could be filled with all the malevolence that sycophants of the succeeding *régime* could invent. They were soon to make the utmost use of their advantage.

But Richard's final act of folly – his sequestration of the Lancastrian estates – has a long history which needs telling before it can be judged objectively.

When Roger Mortimer, Earl of March, returned to Ireland after the Shrewsbury oath-taking to resume his duties as the Lieutenant of a Richard who was proud of his hereditary title 'Seigneur d'Irland', he found the Dublin Pale reverting to its former state. It was again being harried by Art MacMurrough, King of Leinster, who had broken his oath of fealty given in all solemnity to Richard during the first Irish expedition of 1394. Mortimer determined to bring MacMurrough to justice, but on July 20th, 1398 at the battle of Kellistown (or Kells) in Carlow he was defeated and slain. When the news reached England some time in the autumn of 1398, Richard immediately recognized Mortimer's young son Edmund as presumptive heir to the throne, and began planning a second Irish expedition which would avenge Roger Mortimer's death and complete the work so well begun four years before. An Irish expedition necessitated even greater expenses than a French expedition. Across the English Channel was a rich country on which an army could live, and a wealthy aristocracy which could make campaigning a paying proposition if victory were won and prisoners could be held to ransom. Across the Irish Sea was a poor land where an ill-provisioned army might easily starve, a half-savage clan system which could yield no worth-while spoils, and a terrain of bog and forest which would involve difficult and wasteful skirmishing in the wettest of climates without ever providing the opportunity for a pitched battle to reward the prodigious efforts of knights and soldiery. Richard and his advisers had had bitter experience of what an Irish campaign involved, they knew that moneys and provisions were even more important than men-at-arms. But Richard's treasury was never over-full, and the planning of his second Irish expedition must have revealed the need for drastic methods if its financial backing was to be assured. This compelling need may well explain Richard's subsequent actions.

To those who know its sequel, the second Irish expedition must always seem a fatal mistake. But to Richard's eyes it must have appeared both obligatory and offering a reasonable chance of success. After twenty years, he had finally overthrown the baronial opposition and could claim to rule in the sense that his grandfather had ruled. The Lords Appellant were dead or in exile. Round him were able men of his own choosing and a court which shared his cultural tastes. In his child-bride he had found an outlet for a nature starved of natural affections since his first wife and his earliest friends had died. He had fought one successful campaign in Ireland, saw no reason why he might not fight another, and, in achieving that martial glory which every knight of Chivalry pursued, he might also not only avenge the death of his heir but make Ireland for the first time a profitable apanage to the crown.

But while these great preparations went on apace,[1] his father's brother and comrade-in-arms was slowly dying – old John of Gaunt had reached his favourite castle of Leicester for the last time; neither he nor his son would sail to Ireland. Shakespeare's death-bed scene of John of Gaunt is wholly the dramatist's invention, and its portrayal of Richard as a cynical monster is directly at variance with the only mention of any visit of Richard to Gaunt's death-bed in any of the chronicles. A kindlier Scottish chronicler writes:

> 'The King com til hym bodely
> And til hym spake rycht curtasly,
> And gaive hym consale of dysporte
> Wytht plesaund wordis of comfort.'[2]

There had been many times when Richard had suspected Gaunt of ambitions which threatened his own life and throne, but since Gaunt's return from Guienne he had every reason to be grateful to an uncle who was now a tower of strength to him, and he had indeed taken the rashest of steps to prove his gratitude. On February 3rd, 1399 John of Gaunt died, Duke of Lancaster, father-in-law to two monarchies, but father to an heir condemned to six years' exile. The never-crowned King of Castile had a sad and weary death-bed, but Richard did not make it sadder, and only the Fates could have appreciated the irony of the scene – within a few months the son of John of Gaunt was to be King of England.

Richard was now faced with a fateful decision. In the previous October, he had authorized the exiled Norfolk and Hereford to appoint attorneys to receive any inheritances which might fall to them in exile. The death of Gaunt meant that Richard's greatest surviving enemy was rightful heir to the Lancastrian estates – to hundreds of manors spread throughout the land, to an ecclesiastical patronage almost as vast and important, to over thirty castles, and to that '*imperium in imperio*', the County Palatine of Lancaster, where as Duke of Lancaster he would have his own Chancery and his own justices and where the royal writ did not run.[1] In five years' time, Richard would be faced with a Duke of Lancaster whose widespread wealth might easily outrival his own resources without his national commitments. It was a situation which called for deliberation and for boldness. The theory that Richard had been hoping that Gaunt would die quickly so that he might immediately sequester the Lancastrian estates has no factual support; nor was Richard's decision the reckless gesture of a maniac. Richard's generosity to the father had now made the son heir to wealth, privileges and jurisdictions which were far in excess of what any centralized monarchy could be expected to tolerate – he was being asked to pay a bitter price for the folly of a dotard Edward III, and for excess of his own generosity. His first care was to ensure some kind of authoritative support, and he resurrected the celebrated parliamentary Committee of 1398, which had been created to terminate outstanding petitions and to deal with the Norfolk-Hereford quarrel. Its terms of reference were clearly not wide enough to cover a revocation of the writ which specifically allowed Hereford to receive inheritances in exile. Richard's extremity drove him to forgery. The Parliament Roll recording the establishment of the Committee was altered so that 'to terminate petitions' now read 'to terminate petitions *and all other matters and things moved in the presence of the King in accordance with what seems best to them*'.[2] The next step was for the Committee to find sufficient reasons for cancelling the grant of powers of attorney, and the Chancellor obliged. It was announced that legal opinion had decided that the grant had been made 'inadvertently', as it could not be legally reconciled with a sentence which had in effect declared both Hereford and Norfolk traitors – a traitor could not inherit what should normally have been forfeit to the crown. It is impossible to excuse such legal chicanery, still less the clumsy alteration to the Rolls of Parliament, but both the forgery and the excuse prove that the decisive sequestration of the Lancastrian inheritance was at least carefully pondered and carried out with the support of the Council. That it was not a mere reckless act of tyrannical robbery, but a premeditated attempt to meet the gravest threat to his throne since the day at Eltham when Gloucester threatened him with the fate of Edward II, is further attested by the fact that Hereford's exile was extended to a life-term, while a long list of pensions and grants to Gaunt's dependents was promptly confirmed.[1] The confiscation of March 18th, 1399, however justified, was Richard's greatest political mistake, and, though it gave Richard's resources immediate aid in men, wealth and financial credit, it made the exiled Henry, now Duke of Lancaster, the champion of any Lord great or small who might have cause to fear the security of his property and title. The sharp horns of the King's dilemma have never been sufficiently appreciated. If he had allowed Henry to succeed to the Lancastrian inheritance, a future, which while Gaunt lived seemed so rosy and secure, was doomed in five short years to be at the mercy of an enemy more powerful than any of his uncles had been – for Henry had added by marriage half the Bohun inheritance to the castles, the broad acres and the palatinate regality of Gaunt. If he could exile Henry for life, and try his present strength so far as to consolidate in his own hands the royal and the Lancastrian inheritance by sanction of a parliamentary Committee, and a trifle of forgery by the way, then the major threat (not only to himself but to his country) might be averted, and his position of supreme power maintained in spite of anything that Henry might threaten from overseas. In choosing the horn of confiscation he was to impale himself within twelve months – but that event was by no means certain; if he had chosen the horn of acquiescence he might have saved his throne, but he would certainly have lost his power and his pride within five years. It was a portentous decision, and

Richard realized something of its implications. The chronicler tells us that the King was asked one day why he was sighing, and he replied that not only was he nervous about the outcome of the Irish war, but he was nervous about an exasperated populace at home: 'Do you wonder then that I sigh, I who am fated to so many unavoidable evils'.[1] The decision of March 18th merely revoked the letters of attorney to the exiled Appellants, it was not until Richard was on his way to Ireland at the end of May that the sequestration of the Lancastrian estates, and the perpetual banishment of Henry, were publicly proclaimed by the Regency – it sent a thrill of fear through every man of property in the land. The only remaining acts of the parliamentary Committee were the post-mortem condemnation of Sir Robert Pleasington, who had been the Chief Baron of the Exchequer and the Appellants' spokesman in 1388, and the condemnation of a favourite clerk of Hereford's – one Henry Bowet – who had gone into exile with his master.[2] Richard had only misused this Committee in the last resort; and there is no evidence that he ever intended it as a permanent substitute for either his Council or for Parliament. The surreptitious addition to the parliamentary Rolls is as much evidence on behalf of Richard's respect for the weight and authority of Parliament as for the theory that Richard was deliberately aiming at a tyranny.[3] He was not the first or the last English King who only wanted a Parliament when he had a financial use for it, and who preferred to manage with a high hand rather than be subservient to its whim. The Committee had completed with its authority the full measure of Richard's revenge – it had done all that was required of it, and it was promptly allowed to lapse.

Richard had been comparatively merciful: as Oman put it succinctly 'he frightened all men though he struck down but few'.[4] Had Richard been cast in Gloucester's mould neither Hereford nor Norfolk would have escaped death – either judicial or arranged; and, judged by the standards of his own day, Richard's mercy was exaggerated to the point of foolhardiness. He was so convinced of the strength of his position and the completeness of his victory that he persisted in his second Irish expedition before he knew what Henry's answer to the sequestration of his inheritance would be, and before he could judge the full effect of this dramatic act on a nation already harried by forced loans, crooked pardons, *le plesaunce*, and a repetition of costly oaths. He was taking with him to Ireland a formidable army – and by so doing he exposed the very heart of his kingdom to easy attack. No wonder Richard sighed.

On April 16th, 1399 Richard made his will. He asked to be laid to rest beside his first Queen, the revered Anne of Bohemia, and he revoked all his bequests if the acts of his last Parliament were not upheld.[1] The men and provisions for Ireland were slowly assembling at Milford Haven, but before he set out Richard went to Windsor Castle to say farewell to his child-Queen Isabelle. There had been some trouble within the Queen's household concerning the fitness of the Lady de Corcy to be her guardian, and Richard took much trouble to find out the truth. The Lady de Corcy's extravagance seems to have shocked even an extravagant court, and, on the advice of the Queen's Chamberlain and his own physician, the Lady de Corcy was firmly but politely dismissed, and in her place he appointed the widow of Roger Mortimer – another piece of evidence to show that Richard's regard for Mortimer was genuine. The final leave-taking seems to have been both sincere and pathetic – Richard had taken a great liking to his child bride; 'I never saw so great a Lord make so much of nor shew such great affection to a lady, as did King Richard to his Queen', says the French chronicler.[2]

On May 29th, 1399 King Richard and the main body of his army set sail, and after a two day crossing – so speedy, the chronicler adds, because of such fine weather – they landed at Waterford. Meanwhile, in France, Henry of Lancaster, Archbishop Arundel, and a bevy of Lancastrian Lords were planning the final rebellion which was to reclaim for Henry Bolingbroke the Lancastrian inheritance and change the dynasty.

Richard's so-called 'tyranny' had lasted some eight months. It had displayed him in pride of place as the triumphant but by no means bloodthirsty judge of the men who had ruined his youth, murdered his friends, and insulted his first Queen. It had shown him capable of the shrewdest judgments and the most reckless generosity. It had seen him stoop to any expedient to find money for his treasury, and even to forgery, that he might fend off for ever the appalling threat from the power of Henry of Lancaster. His 'tyranny' was the sum total of the acts of a mediaeval king, true to the traditions of his time but with rather better morality than usual. He showed too some of the instincts of a Renaissance 'Prince', who, having sworn to avenge the murder of his rightful heir, kept his promise at the very moment when his own title was most in jeopardy. Yet Richard's second expedition to Ireland has never been fully explained. It has been suggested that Richard was deliberately running away from the unpopularity of his own exactions and leaving his friends to face the gathering storm. It was a curious form of cowardice which avoided a political storm at home to weather the Irish Sea in a small open sailing ship, and face the rigours of a second military campaign in the mists of a difficult and almost unknown country. It has been suggested that Richard was simply mad, and over confident; but there was nothing insane about his planning, even if there was misjudgment in his reckoning of risks. As events turned out, the second Irish expedition was a fatal move: but neither Richard nor anyone in England knew that an heir who might justifiably claim his inheritance would speedily become a usurper who would seize the throne. It is even doubtful whether Hereford himself, plotting in Paris, was as yet seeing himself King of England. It is easy for the historian to be wise after the event; the men who make history, but do not write it, are usually opportunists rather than planners.

IX

ABDICATION

RICHARD'S SECOND IRISH expedition had not been planned without some consideration for the dangerous possibilities at home. As head of the State in Richard's absence there was no suitable peer available other than his last surviving uncle the Duke of York. Of the colourful race of the Plantagenets he was the most colourless. While Gaunt was fighting for kingdoms, and Gloucester scheming to chain a King, Edmund of Langley was content to be merely a baron of the blood royal. In his younger days, he had seen fighting under his father in France, and he had shared with his famous brother, Edward the Black Prince, the infamy of the sack of Limoges. Since then he had taken part in one rather insignificant campaign against the Scots, and had acted as Regent during Richard's first Irish expedition in 1394, but otherwise he had not figured prominently in the major crises of the reign, and his only excitements seem to have been the pursuit of stags, and, as rumour had it, of women. Even his final treachery was unspectacular.

The day-to-day administration of affairs was left to the competent Sir John Bushy, Sir Henry Green and Sir William Bagot, with the Marquis of Dorset as Admiral, Sir William Scrope as Treasurer, Edmund de Stafford, Bishop of Exeter, as Chancellor, supported by the very capable civil service which had been created during the Quiet Years. But by now it was a highly unpopular government. The squeezing of all classes, in order to finance the Irish campaign and the normal (and abnormal) expenses of the royal household and the royal government, had roused a mood of exasperation, while the likelihood of glory and booty from an Irish campaign was remote. There is no mistaking the bitterness of one of the popular songs of the day which has survived: –

'There is a Bush that is overgrown
Crop it well and keep it low
Or else it will grow wild

The long grass that is so Green
It must be mown and raked clean.
For it hath overgrown the field.
The great Bag that is so mickle
It shall be cut and made little,
Its bottom is nearly out . . .'

So the simple allegory goes on, slandering the royal ministers as a popular ballad should, but with an air of cocksureness, an assumption that now that the 'Heron is up' (Henry of Lancaster) the Bush, the Green and the Bag will get their deserts – York is not even favoured with a mention.[1] There is no doubt that Richard and his advisers had completely underestimated the volume of discontent, but to call it 'popular' discontent is to mislead. Throughout the Middle Ages, every tax, tallage and fine was considered unnecessary and unreasonable, and it was the King's duty either to 'live of his own' or to find recompense for himself, and opportunity for his peers, in victories on foreign fields. The discontent against the Bush, the Green and the Bag was the discontent of barons of an older lineage, of peers who had had no ransom money for thirty years, and now of men of property who feared a theory of monarchy which admitted the expropriation even of a Lancaster. The enmity of the people – the popular discontent – was rather aimed against the rapacity of friars, the falsehoods of summoners, the frauds of pardoners, the laxities of monks, and the rascalities of millers. The complaints of William Langland and Chaucer's Pilgrims are not against king and government, but rather against extortionate officials of both Church and State and the misdemeanours of fellow citizens. It was not Richard's unpopularity with the populace that was to hand over the kingdom to Lancaster, it was his determination to rule in his own right on principle, and through his own ministers; but above all because in the pursuit of that aim he incurred the hostility of the most powerful baronial group in the kingdom supported by the wealth and power of the great merchants of the capital.[2]

The Irish expeditionary force was a royal army led by the King in person with a few of his trusted barons, and it was accompanied by much of the trappings of the court. The Duke of Surrey, who had been appointed the King's Lieutenant and Justice in Ireland in succession to the slain Earl of March, had been sent on ahead. With the main body sailed the Dukes of Exeter and Albemarle, the Earls of Worcester, Gloucester and Salisbury and Sir John Stanley – King's friends all. The clergy were well represented: Bishop Merke of Carlisle, Burghill of Lichfield, Mone of St David's, Medford of Salisbury, who was also titular Treasurer of Ireland, and Braybroke of London, who was also titular Chancellor of Ireland. The staff of the Wardrobe went over, and one chronicler[1] affirms that the crown jewels and treasure went too – a phrase which to modern ears conjures up an unpleasant picture of a thriftless king about to scuttle the ship of state and escape to a well-provided security on some foreign shore. Richard needed 'treasure' to pay his soldiers, and he might well have needed a crown if the campaign had been fought to victorious conclusion and he had had to receive rebel homage ceremonially in Dublin. Fortunately for the modern student, a French esquire named Creton sailed with Richard, and his story has come down to us in the elegant rhymed verses in which he sang of his love for Richard, and his rage at his betrayal.[2] He tells us with evident relish that Richard took with him not only soldiers but minstrels.[3] Four young Lords were virtually compelled to accompany the expedition. The young Henry Beaufort, Bishop of Lincoln, was hostage for his elder brother the Earl of Dorset, the young Henry, son to Henry of Lancaster (and future King Henry V), was hostage for the exiled Duke, the young son of the late Duke of Gloucester and son of the executed Earl of Arundel were considered hostages enough for the hatred of the rest of the Lancastrian faction. It was a miscalculation: Henry of Lancaster was not the man to be stopped by danger to hostages, and, unfortunately for himself, Richard was not the man to take full advantage of what little power they gave him. There was too one great family represented neither at home with the Regency, in Ireland with Richard, nor in France with Lancaster – the great House of Northumberland. The Percies were summoned to the royal mobilization in South Wales, but to Richard's annoyance made excuses for absence. They had been appalled by the treatment of Lancaster, and preferred to await events in their northern fortresses. The private armies of the greater baronage of England were left largely untouched: it was a second miscalculation.

From Waterford the royal army marched inland some fifty miles to Kilkenny, preparatory to engaging the rebel King of Leinster in his wild haunts in the Black Mountains. The army had already been delayed six days at Waterford waiting for Albemarle, and at Kilkenny a further fortnight was lost for the same reason. Creton, who knew the sequel, draws the moral: he hints that Albemarle's treacherous course began at Waterford:

> *'That shifty Duke whose guile forever hid*
> *The harm he did.'*

It was at this time that the future Henry V of England received his knighthood from King Richard[1] – the ironies of history are stranger than those of fiction. As Creton rode through the bogs and forests in the King's retinue, he had ample opportunity to study Richard, and the picture he gives is a pleasant one of a King who shared the burdens of his army and who knew how to lead. MacMurrough again adopted the traditional tactics of all guerrillas. He avoided pitched battles, picked off stragglers, and ambushed foraging parties. As the English army marched through the Wicklow mountains their sufferings increased. Envoys sent by Richard to MacMurrough offered a pardon for submission, but the King of Leinster merely returned a haughty defiance, in spite of the fact that his son and cousins were hostages in England. For nearly a fortnight more, the English army struggled to bring him to terms, suffering all the pangs of semi-starvation in a poor and hostile land, where every shrub might conceal an enemy and no prosperous villages provided food 'for noble or hind'. Creton tells us that he saw with his own eyes how six men contrived to share a loaf a day and still keep on, and there were some 'even gentlemen' who did not eat a morsel for five days. It was finally decided that, while Richard and the main body pushed on to Dublin, where they might expect supplies, a special embassy should accept an invitation from MacMurrough to a parley. The young Earl of Gloucester (Thomas Despenser) was chosen to represent Richard with an escort of 200 lancers and a thousand archers, and Creton accompanied them. He describes the famous meeting 'in an unnamed glen', and cannot withhold his admiration for the King of Leinster and especially for his horse. 'His carriage mightily contented me,' he writes, and describes how MacMurrough sat a beautiful horse without saddle or saddlecloth and armed only with a spear. The embassy was fruitless. MacMurrough repeated his defiance. When Richard, now in Dublin with an army restored to vigour and optimism by the arrival of Albemarle and a hundred barge-loads of supplies, heard the message, his patience was ended, and he swore by St George and St Edward to take MacMurrough dead or alive, and offered a reward for anyone who would compass it. For six weeks Richard and his army had been cut off from news from England – the Irish Sea had been too stormy for mediaeval ships, and in those six weeks Henry of Lancaster had taken those first fateful steps which so rapidly led him to the throne.

Since his banishment after the Lists of Coventry, Henry had been living in Paris, where he was well received by the French nobility, and where he had set up his establishment at the Hôtel de Cluny. He had been accompanied into exile by a small group of personal friends and retainers and had soon been joined by Thomas Arundel, the son and heir of the executed Earl of Arundel who had escaped from safe-keeping in the house of the Duke of Exeter. The attitude of the King of France was non-committal. When he was consulted on the project of a marriage between Henry and Mary, the daughter of the Duke of Berry, he correctly referred the affair to his son-in-law King Richard, and the alliance never materialized. It was not long before Henry received a visit from the banished ex-Archbishop Arundel, who had been dividing his time between Utrecht and Cologne, and plans for returning to England to claim the Lancastrian inheritance followed rapidly on the death of Gaunt and Richard's sequestration. We are told that the Duke of Brittany was visited by both Henry and the Archbishop, and that the conspirators were rewarded with ships, men and weapons. Froissart reports that to this material aid the Pope added spiritual blessings, and that Arundel was duly furnished with a papal Bull.

Towards the end of June 1399, when Richard and the royal army were struggling through the Wicklow mountains, Henry and his friends sailed from Vannes for England.[1] Henry was accompanied by the ex-Archbishop Arundel, young Thomas Arundel, Lord Cobham, Sir Thomas Erpingham (an ex-Lollard whose name is perpetuated in the beautiful gateway to Norwich Cathedral), Sir Thomas Rempston, John Mowbray, a few more knights and squires, and enough retainers to fill no more than three ships. It was scarcely an armada; but what seemed a very hazardous adventure was to take place at precisely the most propitious moment for success, and the hundred who sailed from Vannes were counting on thousands of friends when they reached England. The Lancastrians seem to have sailed up the south and east coast of England touching here and there to sound opinion, and on July 4th Henry of Lancaster landed at Ravenspur – at the northern point of the Humber estuary – within easy reach of the hereditary strongholds of his father, and the expected aid from the northern Percies and Nevilles. The castles of Pickering, Knaresborough, and Pontefract were promptly occupied, and at Pontefract the rallying of rebels to Henry's standard began. The Earl of Northumberland and his son Henry Hotspur were the first of the great nobles to side with this armed rebellion, and they were quickly followed by the new Earl of Westmorland. Henry laid his plans well. He had been in constant communication with the growing discontent before he set sail, and even had correspondence with the newly created Marquis of Dorset, the elder Beaufort. It was from Pontefract that he now issued cunning invitations to revolt.[1] Letters were addressed to citizens, prelates and Lords. To the citizens, he maintained that the King was plotting the death of their chief magistrates and a burden of taxation greater than they had ever feared. To the prelates and Lords, he maintained that the King was plotting the sale of Guienne and Gascony for private gain. He even warned the villeins that under Richard they were doomed to be kept 'in greater subjection and harder bondage than any Christian King had ever held his subjects'.[2] At Pontefract too the legend that Edmund Crouchback, son of Henry III, was the elder brother of Edward I and had been put aside on account of his deformities was publicized afresh, so that even Richard's title might be called in question as well as his governance. All was grist to Lancaster's mill; he was even ready to swear an oath to the hesitant Northumberland that he had only come to claim his rightful inheritance, and that Richard should reign till his life's end.[3] Nothing was defined as to what might happen then, but the bloody field of Shrewsbury and the death of Hotspur were to prove that the Percies took this oath seriously. In these dramatic weeks of July 1399 Henry of Lancaster showed himself the shrewd planner, the able opportunist and the unscrupulous politician; his plan of action was as masterly as his propaganda, and within a fortnight a great army of rebels was mustered at Doncaster.

The Regent, York, at first made a show of energy and sense. Sir William Bagot was immediately despatched to Ireland to warn Richard of Henry's landing, and the shire levies of the Midlands and the south were promptly summoned to St Albans. The levies responded loyally, but there was a significant lack of response from the gentry, who provided the lances of a mediaeval array, and even the rank and file had little stomach for a fight against a Lord who, so men said, had merely come to claim what was so obviously his own. Moreover their King was in Ireland. Had he fled in cowardice to avoid the reckoning with so famed a knight as Lancaster? Ugly rumour was a mighty ally of the Lancastrian cause, and Henry exploited it to the full. Recruits for the rebels arrived in such numbers that they became an embarrassment; many had to be sent home for lack of commissariat.[1]

Lancaster's plan of campaign was a good one; throughout, he was acting on reliable information and marching on interior lines. He decided that he could afford to ignore the royalist St Albans muster and strike for the west, where Richard was bound to arrive sooner or later from Ireland. The loyalists came to the same conclusion and also made for the west, but with rapidly dwindling forces and morale. There was no sign from Richard or his army, and Lancaster proceeded to deal with York's army before Richard arrived. Between Bristol and Berkeley, on July 27th, the huge army of Lancaster made contact with the already disheartened loyalists. Only Despenser, Bishop of Norwich – still a fighter in spite of his ill-fated crusade in Flanders – and Sir William Elmham showed any zeal for battle. York's men deserted to Lancaster, and the Regent tamely followed their example,[2] attempting to save his face by making a show of being satisfied that Lancaster was still a loyal subject to King Richard. Scrope, Bushy and Green realized that no mercy was to be expected at the hands of Lancaster – they took refuge in Bristol Castle. It was a very brief respite. The governor, Sir Peter Courtenay, promptly surrendered without a blow, and the three royal ministers were handed over to Lancaster's lynch law. They were summarily executed without even the pretence of a trial, and their heads in a white basket were sent to London to lend point to a letter which formally announced Lancaster's arrival to take his rightful inheritance, and to ask the citizens 'to let me know if you will be on my side or not; and I care not which, for I have people enough'.[1] Within three weeks, Lancaster had most of England behind him, including the Regent York, Beaufort, his step-brother, Marquis of Dorset, all the great barons who had not gone to Ireland, and the capital city of London. Richard and the royal army could only count on Cheshire and the Welsh Marches – and there was still no news of his arrival. Lancaster could afford his cocksureness.

About July 10th Sir William Bagot reached Dublin with the news of Henry's muster in the north of England. There was no faint-heartedness in Richard's wrath as he cursed the fact that he had ever been persuaded to allow Henry of Derby to escape death. A Council was hastily summoned. Richard was for immediate departure to North Wales, but the majority of the Council urged that Salisbury should be despatched forthwith to raise and rally the loyalists of Cheshire, while the main army should return to Waterford and thence to South Wales. There are obscurities in this story. The treacherous Albemarle is said to have been responsible for the advice to delay and embark from Waterford; but it may have been prompted by the very good reason that there was insufficient shipping at Dublin, whereas the royal fleet was available in Waterford's estuary. Unfortunately Creton, 'for the sake of merriment and song', chose to accompany Salisbury, and we therefore lack an eye witness's account of exactly what happened between the receipt of the invasion news and the embarkation at Waterford. Richard's forces were in any event not all in Dublin – they were scattered in the search for Mac-Murrough, and for troops fighting in the Leinster mountains a concentration at Waterford was not very much more difficult than a concentration at Dublin. Albemarle's subsequent treachery was flagrant – his guilt in Ireland is not proven. The royal army, after forced marches, reached Waterford; but the journey took a week, and it was about July 25th before Richard at last reached Milford Haven. On landing, Richard immediately had confirmation of the fall of Bristol, the defection of his Regent York, the execution of his friends and counsellors, and the triumphant progress of

Lancaster now encamped at Bristol with an overwhelming and jubilant army. Richard's own army was riddled with disloyalty; the Lords Scales and Bardolf deserted, to be followed shortly by Thomas Percy and the recreant Albemarle. There was only one chance of saving his throne, and Richard took it. Abandoning his personal baggage, plate, chapel furniture and other encumbrances, he set out immediately for the loyal Salisbury and the loyal army he had every reason to expect in North Wales. The Lancastrian version is that Richard deserted his men and fled in disguise to the north. The more likely version is that, in face of a rapidly disintegrating army, and in full knowledge of the position of Lancaster and the treachery in his own nearest circle, Richard did the only sensible thing, and, with a few staunch friends, made for the one spot in England where true loyalty might still be found. He had a hard journey of some 160 miles along the Welsh coast – and he seems to have accomplished it with creditable speed. The story of the dazed wanderings of an enfeebled and terrified King is a fiction which cannot stand up to investigation. 'Pale with anger'[1] is a more likely description of Richard at this time than the moaning dotard of the Lancastrian legend. And even more bitter news awaited his arrival at Conway Castle.

Salisbury had managed to gather a substantial army from the Welsh and the men of Cheshire. But Creton tells how the absence of the King added to the difficulty of keeping it together. Salisbury has been accused of incompetence at this stage,[2] but it is not easy to see why. His duty was to summon all loyalists to North Wales and to hold on until Richard and reinforcements arrived. By remaining on the North Wales coast he had the advantage of magnificent castles and a possible retreat by sea if the worst should happen. If he had attempted a sortie from this strategic base he would have been promptly annihilated; and his failure to hold the wild Welshmen together, in the absence not only of the King but of news of the King, was not blameworthy under the circumstances.

Richard's dash to Conway seems to have been well reported to Lancaster by traitors, and, again moving on interior lines, the Lancastrian army moved north along the Welsh Marches to Chester. Adam of Usk had joined the rebels at Bristol, and he describes the march with a shocked eye for the atrocities committed by ruffians who saw in rebellion at least a temporary opportunity for robbery and rapine.[1] Henry and the Lancastrian army reached Chester on August 9th, and celebrated their capture of the town by the summary execution of Sir Perkin de Leigh the leader of the King's party in Cheshire; and it was about August 11th that Richard reached Conway to find Salisbury deserted by his army, and left with perhaps a score of loyal servants. It was a situation which might have daunted the most valiant, but Richard still had the stout castles of Carnarvon, Beaumaris and Conway, the Welshmen might still be remustered, and he still had that confidence in the sanctity of his own kingship which never left him. In a gloomy council of war there was no talk of surrender, still less of abdication; on the contrary, it was decided to try the arts of diplomacy in the absence of the means of dealing out justice to rebels and traitors. It was decided to despatch Exeter and Surrey as ambassadors to Henry, with authority to offer him his lands and titles but to ask what further he wanted, and why he continued in open rebellion. Henry refused to answer, and kept both Exeter and Surrey as hostages while awaiting news of a more cunning embassy which he himself had devised and instructed.

Ex-Archbishop Arundel and the Earl of Northumberland had been despatched by Henry to secure Richard's person by persuasion or, if necessary, by guile and force. The Lancastrian version of this embassy has long been accepted by subsequent historians: it is an unconvincing story which portrays Richard as a poltroon bewailing his woes, begging for his life, offering to abdicate 'provided his life were spared', and accompanying the embassy in the best of spirits to greet his noble cousin at Chester.[2] Richard's position was certainly desperate. He had lost two armies, and was cut off by Henry's strategy from the rest of England. On the other hand, he held the almost impregnable castles of North Wales, and there was nothing to prevent safe retreat by sea to his father-in-law's court in France, to Bordeaux, or, for that matter, back to Ireland. An offer to abdicate at such a moment needs more confirmation than is afforded by chroniclers whose paramount duty was to whitewash a usurper; both the French chroniclers and two independent English chronicles, which have only come to light in recent years, give the lie direct to the Lancastrian story.[3] The revised version of these events is well authenticated, and makes sense. Henry's ambassadors took with them four hundred lancers and a thousand archers, but only a tiny deputation actually

presented itself at Conway – the main body lay in ambush somewhere in the mountains between Conway and Rhuddlan. Northumberland seems to have been the spokesman. He offered comparatively reasonable terms. Richard could keep his throne on
condition that he declared for a free Parliament, righted Henry's
wrongs, and surrendered to Henry's mercy Exeter, Surrey, the
Bishop of Carlisle and his own clerk Maudeleyn. The negotiations
which followed may have lasted as long as three days, but at least
there was no hasty and immediate answer. Richard took counsel,
and, instead of a cringing coward, we have the picture of a very
angry man bowing to force of circumstance but swearing that, as
soon as Fortune's wheel took a turn for the better, he would 'flay
some people alive'.[1] The Council at Conway decided that Henry's
offer should be accepted, with the secret reservation that, as it was
accepted under duress, it could be withdrawn as soon as circumstances permitted. Even to modern morality this was a reasonable
and justifiable plan. There was the added security of an oath which
to mediaeval minds was much more binding than any treaty –
Northumberland swore over the Host that Henry had no treasonable intent; it was an oath that Northumberland's conscience
could not forget. Richard and his tiny troop of friends rode in
confidence with the embassy towards Chester. Their confidence
was short-lived. As the cavalcade entered the wild glens behind
the coast, the glint of armour and spears all about them told
Richard that he was betrayed. King Richard reached Flint as
Northumberland's prisoner, captured by as low a piece of
treachery as ever stained a mediaeval escutcheon; at Flint Castle
Henry's army finally made sure of their prize, and returned in
triumph to Chester. Again there are two versions of how Henry
received Richard, and how the cousins rode to London. That
Richard should have been cheerful about the situation is as unlikely as the story that Henry treated him 'reverenter et honeste'.[2]
Creton was an eye-witness of this journey, and his story is that
Richard was treated with shameful indignity, and that somewhere
between Lichfield and Coventry there was a serious attempt at
rescue either by the men of Cheshire or by Welshmen or quite likely
by a mixed band of both. The rescue attempt is also mentioned
by the Lancastrian chronicler – and men do not fight to rescue
a King who travels to London cheerfully and of his own
accord.[3]

From the moment Henry had Richard in his power, there began a consistent and successful process of glossing over illegalities and smoothing the path which led Henry to the throne. At Chester, writs were issued in Richard's name for a Parliament to be held at Westminster on September 30th, and a proclamation, also in Richard's name, was issued to the sheriffs giving them a polite Lancastrian version of recent events, and commanding them to restore order and await events at Westminster. Richard's last journey as King 'guarded as strictly as a thief or a murderer' [1] took him through St Albans to London. On reaching London the cavalcade divided. Henry left Richard in the charge of Gloucester, Arundel and the Mayor and chief citizens of London, while he set off to enjoy his own triumphal entry through the Ludgate up to St Paul's. 'And the bells of the churches and monasteries rang so merrily that you could not even hear God thundering' is the double-edged comment of the French chronicler. [2] Richard, who was mounted on a tiny nag and clothed in a plain black gown, was escorted to the palace of Westminster for the night; early the next morning he was allowed to hear mass in his beloved Abbey for the last time before being taken to the fortress of the Tower. He had first spent anxious days there when the men of Kent and Essex were hunting Lancastrians to death. This time the Londoners were demanding his deposition and the elevation of a Lancaster. They had arrested the few friends he had in the city, and had even sent a special deputation to Henry as he marched south demanding Richard's instant execution. Within five weeks, Henry of Lancaster had conquered England, and now held its legitimate King a defenceless prisoner.

For four weeks – from September 2nd, 1399 to September 30th, 1399 – England was without an effective head of the State. All necessary proclamations and statutes were issued in the name of King Richard, but the business which really occupied men's minds was how to depose an anointed King, and elevate Henry of Lancaster to the throne with a sure and just title. Henry was thus faced with two urgent tasks – the reorganization of officialdom following on the casualties of the rebellion, and the determination of procedure for carrying out his now avowed policy of ascending the throne in Richard's place. For the moment, Henry stepped warily – there was no wholesale proscription or violent purge.

Wiltshire, the Treasurer, had been executed at Bristol – he was succeeded by John Norbury, who had been a companion of Henry's exile and of whom otherwise little is known. De Stafford, the Chancellor, was compelled to relinquish his office but was not disgraced – he survived and was reappointed in 1403 to the post he had filled with such skill for the last three years of Richard's reign. His assent to Richard's deposition was not so much the act of a traitor to a benefactor as an early example in the history of that tradition of the civil servant which puts loyalty to governments before loyalty to personalities. Richard's Keeper of the Privy Seal – Clifford, Dean of York – was a clerical civil servant whom Henry wisely retained, and who was to serve his new master faithfully in the persecution of Lollard heretics. Richard's surviving 'duketti' were soon to lose their dukedoms but resumed their original titles, so that the confusion of the chronicles becomes worse confounded by Albemarle reverting to Rutland, Surrey to Kent, Exeter to Huntingdon, Dorset to Somerset, and Gloucester to plain Despenser. The exiled Earl of Warwick and Lord Cobham were naturally recalled, and restored to their patrimonies. Norfolk of course was not recalled – he died a few weeks later at Venice. The Earl of Salisbury, who had been with Richard at Conway, was imprisoned – but he was released in time to seal his loyalty with his blood at the Rout of Cirencester. Northumberland's help was rewarded by the office of Constable and Westmorland's by the office of Marshal, while Thomas Percy's services to Richard lost him no more than his office of Steward. Even Sir William Bagot, who had found refuge in Ireland, and had therefore escaped the fury of the Bristol men who murdered Bushy and Greene, was merely imprisoned, and later released to die in peaceful retirement. Nor was there immediate persecution of the loyalist bishops; for although Walden was forced to surrender the archbishopric of Canterbury to the returning Arundel, he was soon compensated by the bishopric of London. It was a most reasonable settlement, and its reasonableness sadly misled the rebels of the early years of Henry's reign into underestimating his strength. For the moment, Henry was shrewd enough to wear the velvet glove: his claim to the throne was neither framed nor published, for the reactions both of the Northumberland group and of the King of France were doubtful and dangerous.

Henry's second problem was not so easily solved – on what

223

foundation of fact or theory could he now proceed to claim the throne? His first step was to appoint a Commission of 'sages in the law' (of whom the chronicler Adam of Usk was one) to sift the evidence procured from all the scriptoria of all the important monasteries. Their report was bitterly disappointing to Henry: they gave him no support for hereditary claims, but merely stated that Richard's 'perjories, sacrileges, unnatural crimes, exactions from his subjects, reduction of his people to slavery, cowardice, and weakness of rule' were cause enough for setting him aside, and that he should be deposed 'by the authority of the clergy and people'.[1] Henry persisted in pressing his hereditary title, and only buttressing it with his claim by right of conquest. It was asking contemporaries to believe in the Crouchback Legend.[2] If the legend were true, the first three Edwards and Richard II were not legitimate Kings, and Henry of Lancaster was the rightful King through his mother Blanche of Lancaster. There is no reliable evidence to support this story, and it does not read convincingly in the contemporary Lancastrian chronicles. But Henry used it because the only other cover for the nakedness of his sword was 'the authority of the clergy and people'. Henry, who in some constitutional histories is featured as the first King of 'the Lancastrian constitutional experiment', was casting himself in a much more mediaeval role. He stuck to his legend, was proud of his conquest, and preferred the magical discovery of the true sacred oil for his coronation to any new-fangled notion of kingship by consent of Parliament.

If the theory behind the usurpation was full of obscurities, pretences and potential disputes, the procedure for ensuring Richard's abdication was even more obscure,[3] more coloured by subsequent propaganda, and more pregnant with future disasters. The Northumberland faction held that Henry had sworn a solemn oath not to claim the crown – they did not remind Henry of it yet, because of the treacherous oath of their own leader in North Wales; but neither Henry nor Northumberland could have been blind to its consequences. There were not only Richard's personal friends but there was the Duke of York and the Nevilles who, however much they might have objected to Richard's government, were nevertheless reluctant to depose a legitimately anointed King in order to promote the son of John of Gaunt. But time was in Henry's favour. By September 30th, Richard's writ for a Parliament demanded an urgent reckoning. The key situations in the capital, and the greatest concentration of armed might, were held by the Lancastrians, supported by Archbishop Arundel and the power of the Church. Henry determined to ignore argument, and to claim the throne, first, by right of descent from Henry III, and, second, by right of conquest. Yet, discernible through the mists that shroud these final and decisive weeks is the first appearance of what has since become the sovereignty of Parliament. Men seem to have expected at least a trial of Richard, even if the result were already determined, and they seem to have looked to a Parliament as the right and proper mechanism for the making and unmaking of Kings. Even Archbishop Arundel[1] seems to have been uneasy about Henry's plans; he would have preferred that Richard should name Henry as his heir, that Richard should willingly abdicate in face of the complaints of Parliament, and that therefore automatically Henry would ascend the throne as legal successor, as the head of a State where Parliament could control kingship. Such a plan needed a complaisant Richard and a subservient Henry – an unlikely combination. There were two further objections to Arundel's policy: first, the claim of the eight-year-old Edmund Mortimer, Earl of March, was better than Henry's, on the assumption that his father Roger Mortimer had actually been approved by a Parliament in 1385 as Richard's heir presumptive – an assumption of which there is no conclusive proof; second, if Richard abdicated, his writs for a Parliament were vacated, and there would be further dangerous delay during which Richard's friends, and those of Northumberland's persuasion, might the more easily foment trouble. Henry persisted in his own more mediaeval technique, and the plan of Arundel was not accepted although it survived in the records to cloud the picture ever since.

The official story of Richard's abdication is recorded in the Rolls of Parliament, and in most of the Lancastrian chronicles. On the day before Parliament had been summoned to meet, a deputation, which included Northumberland and representatives of the Church and the Law, called upon Richard in the Tower and suggested that, in accordance with the supposed agreement at Conway, he should abdicate. Richard asked for time to read what he was about to sign, and also for an interview with Henry. Both requests were granted, and, later in the day, Henry and

Archbishop Arundel went to the Tower for the final scene. Twice in a few sentences the official version[1] tells us that Richard cheerfully (*'hilari vultu'*) signed away his crown, surrendered his signet to Henry, and immediately afterwards appointed the Archbishop of York and the Bishop of Hereford to be his proctors in the forthcoming Parliament, in which his abdication, and his recommendation that Henry should be his successor, should be read aloud to the assembly. This is the story which has found general acceptance until very recent times: it is an edged fiction.

A week before the abdication, Adam of Usk – whose political sympathies were on Henry's side – describes how he was present at Richard's dinner, and how he marked 'his mood and bearing'. The passage is eloquent of truth at a time when falsity was a political necessity:

> 'And there and then the King discoursed sorrowfully in these words, "My God! a wonderful land is this, and a fickle; which hath exiled, slain, destroyed, or ruined so many Kings, rulers and great men, and is ever tainted and toileth with strife and variance and envy" . . . Perceiving then the trouble of his mind and how that none of his own men, nor such as were wont to serve him, but strangers who were but spies upon him, were appointed to his service, and musing on his ancient and wonted glory and on the fickle fortune of the world, I departed thence much moved at heart.'[2]

It is a description which cannot tally with the 'cheerful countenance' of the official abdication scene, and of which Usk makes no mention. The Evesham chronicler also ignores it. The French chronicler presents a much more likely version.[3] He speaks of an interview in the Tower at which Henry, the Duke of York and his son Rutland (recently Albemarle) were present. Henry first summoned Richard to his presence, and Richard haughtily refused. Henry and the others then waited on the King. At the sight of Rutland, Richard's anger could not be contained – he charged York as a villain and his son as a traitor. Rutland threw down his bonnet as a challenge, and the King kicked it away in his wrath. Henry, acting a part of sweet reasonableness, ordered Rutland to be silent, and explained to Richard that he was still King but that 'the Council of the realm have ordered that you should be kept in confinement until the day of the meeting of

226

Parliament'. Richard next asked that he might see his young wife. Henry again replied that the Council would not permit it. At that point again Richard lost his temper, and, after an impassioned speech, flung down his bonnet in challenge to knightly combat. Henry besought him 'to be quiet till the meeting of Parliament', and, when Richard put in a last plea for a fair trial, the evasive reply was, 'My lord, be not afraid, nothing unreasonable shall be done to you.' This is an inset picture which fits easily and naturally into the general picture of Richard's reign as we now know it. The tempers and the challenges of an overwrought King are easier to accept than the 'cheerful countenance' of a feckless poltroon. The *Dieulacres Chronicle* again makes no mention of the official version, but simply states that Richard resigned the crown to God – and not to Henry. The French Chronicles, the *Dieulacres Chronicle* and *Giles' Chronicle*[1] all make mention of Richard's demand for a fair hearing and a public trial. The official version makes no mention of this, and refers to the agreement at Conway as not only a fact but a fact accepted by Richard. The agreement at Conway was a piece of calculated treachery, and Henry's parliament roll was a deliberate tampering with the truth – it distorted the Conway incident, it painted a false picture of the King's demeanour in the Tower, it is silent about the demand for a fair trial, and it also ignores the one courageous protest made in Richard's defence by his friend the Bishop of Carlisle at the subsequent deposition session in Westminster Hall. The author of this 'tainted and partisan contemporary evidence'[2] can be excused as any politician in a quandary expects to be excused, but the virtues of a Henry have for so long been contrasted with the vices of a Richard that the more complicated picture of a mediaeval opportunist taking shrewd advantage of a King who believed in mediaeval mystical kingship is overdue for acceptance as authentic.

On Tuesday, September 30th, 1399 there was a large and tumultuous assembly in Richard's great hall in the palace of Westminster. There were representatives of the 'estates of Parliament' but also a great crowd of the London citizens, and, although the assembly had been summoned by King Richard, the throne was empty. Constitutional and legal historians have pointed out that this assembly cannot properly be called a Parliament – it ignored such customary procedure as the presence of the King, the

THE HOLLOW CROWN

opening speech or sermon of the Chancellor, the choice of a
Speaker by the Commons, the appointment of receivers and triers
of petitions, and the usual judicial functions of a 'correct' Parliament. But Henry was in a hurry. The procedure of Parliament
was still elastic, there was certainly no written constitution, and
the authorities' search for precedents and legal guidance had
proved fruitless and even disconcerting. It was an *ad hoc* assembly
of most degrees of a mediaeval society determined to end a situation which could not last long without disaster in an age when
civil obedience was a comparatively new experience. All those
present knew what was about to be done, some of them had their
fears and reservations, but Henry of Lancaster without fear or
reservation proceeded to act as he had determined.

The King's request for a fair and open trial was ignored. The
abdication signed by Richard was read in Latin and in English
and 'accepted' by each of the 'estates' and by 'the people', and
the justification for this act was then made clear in the reading
aloud of thirty-three articles of accusation – the celebrated
'gravamina'[1] which for so long have condemned Richard unheard. Richard had squandered his possessions and therefore laid
grievous burdens on his people by taxation; at Shrewsbury he had
wrongfully accused his peers and by bribery and tyranny ensured
their condemnation; he was directly responsible for de Vere's
'rebellion'; in spite of his express pardon the Lords Appellant had
been done to death or exiled; he had overawed Parliaments by a
'great crowd of malefactors from the county of Cheshire' and had
never punished their violent excesses; he had lied in his proclamation as to the reason for arresting the Lords Appellant; he had
resorted to illegal financial extortions from those he considered
should ask pardon for the deeds of 1386–8; by a subtle move he
had tricked Parliament into surrendering its powers to a Committee
in his own despotic control; to complete this ruse he had even
tampered with the Rolls of Parliament; he had weighted the scales
of justice against Hereford in the dispute with Norfolk; he had
humiliated England by applying to the Pope for confirmation or
his statutes; his officials were his creatures and not the elect of the
people; he had bilked his debts; he had been incapable of living
'of his own' and moneys granted for war purposes had been
squandered in other directions; he had said 'that the laws were in
his own mouth and frequently in his own breast and that only he

himself could change and make the laws of his realm'; he had craftily evaded the binding powers of statutes; he had kept his sheriffs in office for over the scheduled year; he had corrupted the elections to Parliament and had contrived to obtain the grant of the wool tax for life; he had ignored the traditional doctrine of the seals by misusing his private signet; he had been guilty of avarice and extortion in condemning whole counties to be fined for treason; he had used the device of blank charters for further extortions; he had wrongfully despoiled the Church; he had taken the royal treasury and jewels out of England and ordered the records to be destroyed; he had been deceitful and personally offensive to his Council; he had been guilty of the constitutional heresy that he had absolute power over the life and property of his subjects; he had misused the court of the Earl Marshal contrary to Magna Carta clause 13; he had employed forced oaths; contrary to Magna Carta he had tampered with ecclesiastical justice and had wrongfully exiled an Archbishop of Canterbury; his will proved that he was determined to uphold illegal statutes; he had revoked his special pardon of his uncle Gloucester and was responsible for his cruel murder; he had tricked Archbishop Arundel into not attending the Parliament which condemned him to exile; and throughout his reign he had broken his coronation oath.

The 'estates of the realm' decided that there was sufficient proof in this indictment, and forthwith agreed that Richard should be deposed. Commissioners were appointed to pronounce sentence, and Richard was formally deposed as being 'utterly unworthy and useless to rule and govern the realm'. Henry of Lancaster then stood up so that he could be seen by the people, and, after making the sign of the Cross, he challenged the throne speaking 'in lingua materna':

'In the name of Fadir, Son and Holy Gost, I Henry of Lancastr', chalenge yis Rewme of England and the Corone, with all ye membres and ye appurtenances ther to, als I yt am disendit be right lyne of the Blode Comyng fro the gude lorde Kyng Henry therde, and thorghe yat ryght yat God of his grace hath sent me, with helpe of my Kyn and of my Frendes to recover it; the which Rewme was in poynt to ben undone, for defaut of Governance and undoyng of the gode Lawes.' [1]

He reinforced his challenge by displaying the signet Richard had

given him in the Tower. Without scruple or delay, the estates of
the realm agreed the claim, and the Archbishops of Canterbury
and York placed Henry of Lancaster on the throne amid the
applause of the assembly. Archbishop Arundel then preached a
sermon on the significant text *'vir dominabitur populo'*. Henry, to
quieten any doubters, then gave thanks:

> 'Sires, I thank God and zowe Spiritual and Temporel and all
> the Astates of the lond; and do yowe to wyte, it es noght my
> will that no man thynk yt be waye of Conquest I wold disherit
> any man of his heritage, franaches, or other ryghtes, that hym
> oght to have, ne put hym out of that that he has and has had
> by the gude lawes and customes of the Rewme; Except thos
> persons that has ben agan the gude purpose and the Commune
> profyte of the Rewme.[1]

The chronicler explained that Henry had been persuaded not to
claim the throne by simple right of conquest because Chief Justice
Thirnyng had objected to its implications. Some new appointments were then announced, a Parliament was summoned for
October 6th at Westminster, and arrangements were made for the
official coronation ceremony on October 13th. The Deposition
Parliament ended with a great banquet in the White Hall of the
palace, while 'Sir Richard of Bordeaux, a simple Knight'[2] waited
for news in his prison in the Tower.

The Lancastrian story carefully omitted one significant incident.
A vague reference is made to the objections of Thirnyng and to
other doubters, but there is no mention of vocal opposition to the
elevation of Henry to the throne – all is done smoothly, quickly,
and with the utmost goodwill. Less prejudiced evidence supplies
the omission.[3] There was one, bolder than the rest of the doubters,
who raised his voice in protest. Thomas Merke, the Bishop of
Carlisle, a man, as Hall remarked, 'which was both well learned
and well stomacked', rose and said:

> 'My Lords, consider well before you give judgment upon what
> my Lord the Duke has set forth, for I maintain that there is not
> one present who is competent and fit to judge such a sovereign
> as my Lord the King whom we have acknowledged our Lord
> for the space of twenty years and more, and I will give you my
> reasons; there never was, nor is in this world, any false traitor

nor wicked murderer, who, if he be taken prisoner by the hands of justice, is not, at the least, brought before the judge to hear his sentence. My Lords, you have well and truly heard the accusations that my Lord the Duke has made against King Richard; and it appears to me that you are about to give judgment, and to condemn King Richard, without hearing what he has to answer, or even his being present. Moreover, I say that my Lord the Duke has more erred and offended against King Richard than has the King against him; for we know full well that my Lord the Duke was banished ten years by the Council of the realm, and by the consent of his own father, for the great crime which he and the Duke of Norfolk committed; and he has returned to the country without the King's permission: and moreover I say he has done still worse, for he has seated himself on the throne, where no Lord ought to sit other than the lawfully crowned King of England; wherefore I declare that you ought to bring King Richard in presence of the full Parliament to hear what he has to say, and to see whether he be willing to relinquish his crown to the Duke or not.'

It was a brave speech but a useless one – Merke paid for his courage by immediate imprisonment and the subsequent loss of his bishopric; he had to wait two years for his pardon. All other doubts were drowned in the general rejoicing. And Richard's defence was never heard.

On the day following, October 1st, Sir William Thirnyng headed the proctors of Parliament in a visit to Sir Richard in the Tower. He first quoted his authority, and Richard replied that he knew they would speak nothing but as they were bidden. Thirnyng then reported the act of deposition and the renunciation of allegiance; to which Richard replied that 'he hopede that hys cosyn wolde be good Lord to hym', but, when Thirnyng pointed out that this involved the renunciation of all the honours and dignity appertaining to a King, Richard made one final objection. He could not, he said, renounce that spiritual essence of kingship conferred upon him by the mystery of the coronation anointing, and, when Thirnyng countered that he had already confessed himself unworthy to reign, Richard denied it and maintained that his downfall was simply due to the fact that his government had displeased the people. And again the chronicler takes pains to add that the interview closed with Richard 'showing a cheerful countenance'.[1] From the Lancastrian point of view it was essential that the story should have a happy ending – they could not foresee that it was simply a tragic beginning, that the story was to spin out in bloodshed and vendetta over nearly a century, until Henry Tudor trampled another crown in the mud of Bosworth field.

On the whole, King Henry the Fourth of Lancaster had handled a tricky situation conspicuously well. A wave of impatience, and the fears of affronted men of property, had swept him into power from exile with astonishing speed. He may not have sought such power, but he was not the man who would fail to extract the utmost from opportunity. He may have landed at Ravenspur genuinely determined merely to claim his birthright; but he did not hesitate a few weeks later, in spite of sacred oaths to his northern friends, to claim the throne. Disregarding the opposition of his own legal theorists, he placed first his right by descent, second his right by conquest, and took good care that no statement of his could carry the implication that he was finally enthroned by kind permission of Parliament. On the other hand, he took the greatest care to carry Parliament with him; to censor its Rolls in accord with his own interests; and to publicize a list of charges against Richard which were to be a mine of precedents for checking monarchy in the future. The 'gravamina' were special pleadings, they were a speech for the prosecution with no defendant to answer them, and a jury already most notably prejudiced; they served their purpose for the moment. But in one way they were a concession for they implied that the new King had first to justify himself before Parliament; they were in essence a confession that he was a usurper, and that, if the immediate sanction of his authority was force, the ultimate sanction was in the growing power and the increasingly recognized rights of Parliament. The constitutional implications[2] of the fall of Richard and the usurpation of Henry were momentous, but their record belongs properly to a history of the Houses of Lancaster and of York, and not to a history of the last of the Plantagenets.

The coronation ceremonies of Henry IV although necessarily hurried were performed with the most scrupulous regard for precedent, and with the utmost splendour. But one more invention betrayed the weakness of Henry's position. Richard had insisted throughout his reign, and still insisted in captivity, on his inalienable majesty conferred on every true King by the anointing ceremony. Henry was not to be beaten by a flask of oil, and it was more than a providential coincidence that in time for a usurper's coronation the true sacred oil of Edward the Confessor in the eagle-shaped ampulla was miraculously re-discovered and duly used.[1]

The coronation ceremonies over, the new régime appeared to have only one problem before it – the prisoner in the Tower: while that prisoner lived, Henry sat uneasily on a shaky throne. The story of the charges and countercharges of rival baronage attempting to find favour by challenging traitors belongs to a history of Henry IV, and the full epilogue to Richard's life and death is a part of the savage story of the next eighty-five years. But the account of the four months that intervened between Richard's deposition and his death shatters the pretty picture painted by the Lancastrian apologists. There had been only one outspoken objector in the deposition Parliament, but within a few months there was an armed rising pledged to restore Richard to his throne, and three years later Hotspur was to die on Shrewsbury field challenging the usurper who had broken his oaths, and who had so carefully tried to disguise his illegalities behind a façade of pious right.

On October 28th, 1399 Sir Richard of Bordeaux was forcibly disguised as a forester, taken secretly first to imprisonment in Leeds Castle in Kent, and from there to Henry's castle at Pontefract.[2] Henry prepared to keep his first Christmas as King in the royal castle of Windsor, and after the feast there was to be a magnificent 'mumming' on Twelfth Night. It was at this early juncture that Richard's supporters planned a counter-stroke. Rutland, Huntingdon, Kent, Salisbury and Despenser plotted with the Bishop of Carlisle, Walden lately Archbishop of Canterbury, the Abbot of Westminster and Sir Thomas Blount to storm Windsor Castle and capture Henry and his eldest son dead or alive. The conspirators were to concentrate at Kingston-on-Thames with Maudeleyn, Richard's secretary, who was said to resemble him in looks and stature, to play the part of Richard; they had then arranged the betrayal of Windsor Castle through a confederate within the walls. Once again the name of Rutland becomes associated with treachery, though once again definite proof is lacking. It was said that he confessed the plot first to his father the Duke of York, and secondly to the new King himself.[1] Henry was saved by a few hours. He escaped with his son to the friendly shelter of the walls of the City of London, while the frustrated conspirators captured Windsor Castle. Henry, ever the man of action, rapidly mobilized a formidable army, and at Colnbrook it seemed that a pitched battle was inevitable. Whether the conspirators had lost heart after the disappointment at Windsor, or whether they judged their forces totally inadequate to face Henry's, or whether once again Rutland was their evil counsellor, cannot be known. They determined on a hasty retreat to the west,[2] and, thanks to a brave stand by Kent at the bridge of Maidenhead, they reached Cirencester still an army; but with Henry's superior forces in hot pursuit.[3] Kent and Salisbury lodged in the chief inn, but the bulk of their forces were quartered in the surrounding countryside. They had reckoned without the citizenry. At dawn, the inn was surrounded by an armed mob, and the two Earls were forced to surrender. When the remaining Lords heard the news they lost their nerve, and fled for safety. Meanwhile, one of Kent's chaplains had tried to fire the town and draw off the citizens to the protection of their homes. It was a ruse that failed – Kent and Salisbury were brutally beheaded in the market place, and we are told that Salisbury, poet, scholar, soldier and Lollard, refused the ministrations of the priest, and preferred his own prayers as he waited for death. Despenser escaped to Cardiff but was recognized and shipped to Bristol where the citizens beheaded him without trial. Huntingdon, who had attempted to stir up a rising in London while the rest of the conspirators stormed Windsor Castle, tried to escape down river to the sea. He was unluckily driven on to the Essex coast and was captured and slain by a mob outside Pleshey Castle. Henry, who had halted at Oxford, executed twenty-six knights and squires,[4] and several others were hanged in London. One man he spared – John Ferrour who had saved his life from the mob who surged through the Tower shouting death to any Lancastrian and thirsting for the blood of Archbishop Sudbury in 1381. Bishop Merke was spared his life though condemned to be translated to a see 'in partibus infidelium', but Sir Thomas Blount and Maudeleyn were executed.

The 'slaughter at Cirencester' was not merely a tragic failure, it gave Sir Richard of Bordeaux his sentence of death. There is a minute of Henry's Council dated February 8th which runs 'if

Richard the late King be alive, as it is supposed he is, it be ordered that he be well and surely guarded for the salvation of the state ... but if he be dead, that then he be openly shown to the people, that they might have knowledge thereof'.[1] A week later Richard was dead. The Lancastrian story was that he had starved himself to death; Adam of Usk says that he perished heartbroken, fettered, and 'tormented by Sir Thomas Swinford with starving fare';[2] the French chroniclers give the story of his murder by Sir Piers Exton, which Shakespeare followed.[3] The truth will never be fully known, but in 1871, when Dean Stanley examined the skeleton of Richard in the tomb at Westminster Abbey, he found no marks of violence on skull or frame.[4] On the other hand, a mediaeval prison in mid-winter in Pontefract Castle might have killed stronger men than Richard without the need of hunger-strike, and there is the sinister minute of the Council to lay his death, however encompassed, at Henry's door. After the shock of the duketti's rebellion, Richard's death was a political necessity for Henry, and, as the French historian Wallon wittily put it, *'on l'avait fait mourir naturellement'*.[5]

The corpse of Richard was taken by easy stages to London, its face exposed to the people, so that all men might know that Henry was unchallenged King. At every chief town on the way a halt was made until the procession finally reached Cheapside and St Paul's, where in two days some 20,000 people saw the last of Richard. The body was buried without state ceremony in the Dominican priory of King's Langley in Hertfordshire, and it was only received into Westminster Abbey by permission of Henry V in 1416.

In spite of careful propaganda, Henry was plagued throughout his reign by the legend that Richard was not done to death at Pontefract but was still alive. Most of the English chroniclers are agreed that starvation was the cause of death, but they hedge with either an *'ut fertur'* or a *'deus novit modicum'* when they repeat the story that it was enforced starvation. The French chroniclers preferred the Exton story – or they may even have invented it to suit French politics for their Princess, Richard's widow, was still in English hands. But the French chroniclers are largely responsible for yet another version. Richard was supposed to have escaped from Pontefract to Scotland. The Scottish chroniclers support this version with evidence of a person who was assumed to be

Richard but who was mad, and who finally died in peace in Stirling Castle. There are several curious facts which lend a certain credence to this legend.[1] When Henry heard that Richard's friends had risen against him, and that Richard himself was at their head, he swore that 'if I should meet him, one of us shall die'. Did he accept the fact that Richard had already escaped from Pontefract. And had the ruse of passing off Maudeleyn as Richard deceived Henry into giving himself away? The Pontefract prison was a secret, perhaps he had hoped that the escape might be also secret? But, once Maudeleyn was captured, it was essential immediately to kill the escape story, and the only certain way to do that was to kill the true King and display his corpse to any doubters. But was it Richard's corpse? A wealth of evidence suggests starvation as the cause of death, and the accepted date of death is Valentine's Day, February 14th, 1400. Yet the body was exposed in order to be recognized by many who had seen Richard, and was not finally buried until a month later on March 12th. Only the face was visible to the populace – the rest of the corpse was sealed in lead. Was another face – perhaps even the face of Maudeleyn – used to cheat the ravages of decay and deceive many who may have heard of the escape to Scotland? On the other hand, in France, where the legend of Richard's survival was most likely to find friendly ears, there was the esquire who had known and loved Richard so well – Creton. Creton joyfully believed the Scottish story and joined with his rhymed welcome to the news a challenge to the French nobility to avenge the son-in-law of their King. Creton was despatched to Scotland to discover the truth. There is no trace of his report; but there is the evidence that on his return he again issued a call to action – but this time to avenge the blood of Richard. If Richard were alive and sane in Scotland, Creton was the one Frenchman who would have made sure and left the King of France in no shadow of doubt. If Richard were alive but insane, he might well have preferred to keep silent, and leave the legend to stimulate revenge. The French court, however, certainly assumed Richard's death, because in 1404 Richard's widow was married to the son of the Duke of Orleans very shortly after the return of Creton's deputation to Scotland. The legend, however, persisted in England. In 1402 Henry had to issue a proclamation to all the shires urging them to beware of the Scottish rumours, and to arrest anyone who propagated them – it resulted in the death of one Roger Clarendon (an illegitimate son of the Black Prince) and nine Franciscan friars. In 1403 the Percies, whether they believed it or not, spread the rumour that Richard was still alive, although they were careful in their challenge to the throne merely to accuse Henry of Richard's death, and Henry Hotspur paid for his loyalty to Richard with his life. In 1404 William Serle, Richard's Chamberlain, was executed for announcing that Richard was still alive. In 1406 the Commons petitioned the King to issue a statute against the rumour mongers who spoke of 'this madman in Scotland'. In 1405 and 1408 Northumberland took up arms in Richard's name. In 1415 the revolt of the Earl of Cambridge against Henry V kept the legend alive, and as late as 1417, Cobham's heir, Sir John Old-castle, the Lollard martyr, protested even before the flames that he could not recognize his judges as long as his liege-lord Richard was alive in Scotland. The secrecy of Richard's final imprisonment was Henry's greatest mistake. Afraid of the divinity which hedges a true King, and nervous of a popularity which he was at such pains to deny, he insisted on that secrecy which rumour feeds on, and which fostered a legend which even outlived himself. It would have been better for Henry to have tried Richard openly and executed him publicly, just as it would have been better for Richard if, instead of the subtlety of Coventry and the cunning of exile, he had substituted the crudity of an appeal of treason and the brutality of a traitor's death for Henry. The legend remains a legend; Richard died when Henry was crowned.

It is another of the ironies of history that the reign of Richard II saw the first brilliant flowering of the English genius, and at the same time saw the enactment of a personal tragedy which has absorbed students of human nature ever since. In the beginnings of so many significant movements Richard played a prominent part. As a youth he had found the common touch and that genius for leadership which Henry VIII and Elizabeth I[1] were to practise to perfection in easier circumstances. As a man he had stood up to the most powerful concentration of baronial opposition and won the day. The years of his personal rule saw the development of a sound governmental machine, and his choice of servants and of friends was so shrewd that even Henry of Lancaster acknowledged it by continuing so many of them in office and honour. His theory of kingship was always in conflict with economics – like the Stuarts he could not reconcile a divine right with the human need for living of his own – but he was not the only mediaeval King to find that problem beyond him. He was certainly the first mediaeval English King to anticipate some of the techniques of those Renaissance 'Princes' whom historians so unanimously acclaim.[1] It is a somewhat unfriendly modern historian of Richard's reign who wrote: 'The period of Richard's personal rule – thanks to the peace policy which he so successfully pursued and for which he is seldom given full credit, the finances of the Crown at that time achieved a prosperity and buoyancy unequalled in the whole Middle Ages.'[2] He saw his regality threatened with subservience to a brutal and domineering baronage – he fought successfully for some years but finally was overthrown because he had not learnt the Tudor trick of playing off populace against aristocracy, and subduing both to royal will and guidance. But the true picture of Richard's reign cannot be found in the documents of constitutional history alone. Richard's personality even in defeat is the colourful warp to the woof of events. Here was a prince weighted down in his youth by the tradition of a dead hero, and thwarted by the rivalries of ambitious uncles. As he grew to manhood, he saw his closest personal friends hurried to the block or to exile, and his beloved young wife insulted by his own uncle – these were experiences he never forgot, and the story of Richard's revenge is one of the most dramatic narratives in English history, and in a brutal age it was Richard's humanity which was outstanding. He may have been sickened by the sight of death when forced to witness the St Albans gallows after the Peasants' Revolt, and certainly he never indulged in massacre when finally he had the Appellants in his power. He was responsible for the execution of Arundel and the death and perhaps the murder of Gloucester, but neither of these barons deserves sympathy and England was well rid of both. His temper was capable of the most extravagant threats, but his actions for the most part showed his good sense. Only at the last, when, in persisting in his second Irish expedition he exposed his throne almost undefended to the might of Lancaster, did he make his fatal mistake, and for that mistake the opportunist ambition of Henry of Lancaster compelled him to forfeit not only his power but his throne, and not only his throne but his life.

Of Richard's personal appearance we have excellent evidence. Archbishop Sudbury said of him as a youth that he was the very image of his father Edward, Prince of Wales, and he 'was fair to look upon'. Adam of Usk at the end of the reign tells us that Richard was 'fair among men even as another Absalom'. In the Westminster Abbey painting, there is discernible through the grime and over-painting of centuries an intelligent and handsome face. Richard was apparently six feet in height: the fact that in 1383 he rode all night by relays from Daventry to London without stopping shows that he had considerable powers of physical endurance. The splendid effigy on his tomb shows no brutal tyrant but the gentleness of wisdom and the serenity of scholarship. The painting in the National Portrait Gallery is by an indifferent hand and its air of strain and mental stress may reflect the artist rather than the sitter. There is a miniature in Corpus Christi College library at Cambridge which is not flattering but which is merely an incident in the art of the illuminator and hardly an attempt at accurate portraiture. On the other hand, in the Wilton Dyptych, Richard, in the prime of young manhood, recalls the fulsome praise of Usk who was writing when the call was for calumny rather than flattery.[1]

Of Richard's love of the arts and of the culture of his time we have excellent evidence. He was the patron of Chaucer, of Gower, and of Froissart, and we have Froissart's word that he was a charming conversationalist in perfect French. He was the employer of Henry Yevele,[2] the greatest of English mediaeval architects; his reign is the golden age of the arts of the brass engraver, the mural painter, the glazier, and the sculptor of effigies in the round. Three small sidelights on Richard, the man, enable us to imagine a pleasing picture of the whole: Richard was the first King of England to sign his own letters.[3] He was probably the inventor of the handkerchief;[4] and the first English cookery book was specially compiled for him.[5] But the finest testimonies to Richard's love of the arts are still at Westminster. In the Abbey is the superb tomb he ordered for himself and his first wife, and across the way is the great roof of his Westminster Hall.

The reign of Richard of Bordeaux saw the first appearance of the English people: on the one hand, as peasants and artisans in savage mood questioning every current axiom; on the other, as citizens and participators in Parliament of growing substance able to bargain with their social superiors, and turn royal and baronial needs to their own advantage. There was now a Bible in the people's tongue to provide a source-book of questions to which the ultimate answers were given by the English protestant reformers, and there was now an elegant literature which was herald to the achievements of the Elizabethans.

In the centre of so crowded and so exciting a stage was Richard himself; and personality in the Middle Ages was still paramount. Was he simply a spiteful tyrant, who tamely and even gladly surrendered before striking a blow in self-defence, and who finally starved himself to death, a self-pitying weakling, or, in modern terms, the victim of an oedipus-complex and nothing more than a mumbling neurotic?

The brutalities of Richard's peers had asked for the retribution he calculated and achieved with such cautious skill. The logic of his heritage demanded that mediaeval kingship should be established above Lords and Commons, and, in achieving this for a time, he not only summed up his mediaeval past, he anticipated some of the later doctrines of the Divine Right of Kings. His autocratic acts – and there were many towards the end – were not the wilful misdeeds of a savage dictator, they were urged upon him by force of circumstance at a time when mediaeval kingship still had to fight baronial oligarchy, and when neither had yet succumbed to the sovereignty of Parliament.

Richard

FURTHER READING

There are detailed bibliographies for the reign of Richard II in the *Cambridge Mediaeval History*, Vol. VII, and in *The Fourteenth Century* (Oxford History of England) by M. McKisack. At the end of C. Oman's *Political History of England*, Vol. IV is an essay on authorities which brings bibliography to life, and at the end of A. Steel's *Richard II* is a review which brings Oman up to date.

For the general reader who may wish to delve into the original sources the notes will help, and here is a brief survey of the main chronicles for further guidance (where details of publication are not given they will be found under Abbreviations, p. 243): –

FROM THE LANCASTRIAN POINT OF VIEW: –

(1) *Chronicon Anglie* for 1377–1388.
    Historia Anglicana for the whole reign.
    Annales Ricardi II et Henrici IV from 1392.
    All three are the work of Thomas Walsingham, a monk of St Albans Abbey, who is always antipathetic to both John of Gaunt and Richard. (See *EHR* Vol XLVII, pp 12–29.)
(2) The Continuator of *Henry Knighton's Chronicle*, an admirer of John of Gaunt. His account ends in 1395.
(3) The Continuator of the *Eulogium Historiarum* who covers the whole reign.
(4) The Monk of Evesham who wrote the *Historia Vitae et Regni Ric II*, and, who up to 1390, follows Walsingham, and then writes his own bitter version of the last years.

FROM THE LOYALIST POINT OF VIEW: –

(1) *Froissart, Jean.* The notes quote the one-volume Globe edition. The full edition is in 25 volumes, ed Kervyn de Lettenhove, Brussels, 1870–7.
(2) *Chronique du Religieux de St Denis* (1380–1422), ed, with French translation, L. F. Bellagnet, Paris. He was a constant visitor to England throughout the reign.
(3) *Chronique de la Traison et Mort de Richard II* whose title betrays bias, but it is nevertheless invaluable – it sums up the French attitude.

(4) *Creton.* A metrical chronicler who was an eye-witness of the Irish expedition and a devoted Ricardian.

(5) *The Anonimalle Chronicle* which is invaluable for the Peasants' Revolt and the final deposition scenes.

(6) The Continuator of *Higden's Polychronicon* who is known as the 'Monk of Westminster'. On the whole, his work (which ends in 1394) is friendly to Richard, who was a staunch patron of Westminster Abbey.

(7) *The Dieulacres Chronicle* which in its account of the deposition is entirely free of Lancastrian bias.

FOR SIDELIGHTS: –

(1) *Adam of Usk* who, although very Lancastrian, was an eye-witness whose evidence at the end gives the lie to parts of the official Lancastrian version.

(2) *John Hardyng* who, writing in verse under Henry IV, incidentally contradicts parts of the Lancastrian version.

(3) *The Kirkstall Chronicle* which is very Ricardian in dealing with the Appellant episode and Richard's revenge policy, but holds the balance with a damning account of Richard's autocracy in his final years.

(4) *Chronique de Jean le Bel*, ed J. Viard and E. Déprez, 2 vols, Paris, 1904–5; and
Chronique de Richard II by Jean le Beau, ed Buchon; Collection des Chroniques Françaises. Vol XXV, suppt. ii, Paris, 1826–8. Both for specialists.

NOTES

ABBREVIATIONS

The following abbreviations are used in the Notes:

Adam of Usk *Chronicon* (1377–1404), ed E. Maunde Thompson (with translation), London 1904 (2nd edition).

Annales *Annales Ricardi II et Henrici IV* (1392–1406) in *Chronica Johannis de Trokelowe*, ed H. T. Riley (Rolls Series) London 1866.

Anon. Chron. *The Anonimalle Chronicle* (1333–1381), ed V. H. Galbraith, Manchester 1927.

Chron. Angl. *Chronicon Anglie* (1328–1388), T. Walsingham, ed E. Maunde Thompson (Rolls Series) London 1874.

Creton *French Metrical History of the Deposition of Richard II*, ed J. Webb (with translation), London 1819. In *Archaeologia* Vol XX.

D.NB *Dictionary of National Biography.*

Dieulacres *The Deposition of Richard II* by M. V. Clarke and V. H. Galbraith, Manchester 1930.

EHR *English Historical Review.*

Eulogium *Eulogium Historiarum*, ed F. S. Haydon, 3 vols (Rolls Series) London 1858–63.

Evesham *Historia Vitae et Regni Ric II a monacho quodam de Evesham*, ed T. Hearne, Oxford 1729.

Fasc. Ziz. *Fasciculi Zizaniorum*, ed W. W. Shirley (Rolls Series) London 1858.

Hardyng *Chronicle*, John Hardyng, ed Henry Ellis, London 1812.

Higden *Polychronicon Ranulphi Higden, 1381–1394*, Vol IX, ed J. R. Lumby (Rolls Series) London 1886.

Hist. Angl. *Historia Anglicana, 1272–1422*, Thomae Walsingham, ed H. T. Riley (Rolls Series) 2 vols, London 1863–4.

Kirkstall *The Kirkstall Chronicle, 1355–1400*, ed M. V. Clarke and N. Denholm-Young, Manchester 1931.

Knighton *Chronicon Henrici Knighton*, Vol II, 1337–1395, ed J. R. Lumby (Rolls Series) London 1895.

Rot. Parl. *Rotuli Parliamentorum*, 1278–1503, 6 vols and index, ed J. Strachey, London 1767–83.

Traison *Chronique de la Traison et Mort de Richard II*, ed B. Williams, English Historical Society, London 1846.

243

NOTES

CHAPTER I

Page

3 (1) See Froissart, who was present, in *Chronicles of Froissart* (Globe Edition) Macmillan 1913, 165; but on 472 he says the birth was at 10 o'clock on a Tuesday morning. My references for Froissart are from this single volume edition of the classic English translation by Lord Berners (c 1525). The masterly but massive French editions by Kervyn de Lettenhove, Brussels 1863–77, are not easily available to the general reader.

(2) The first known mention of Edward, Prince of Wales, as the Black Prince is in Grafton's *Chronicle* (1569) London 1809, I 388. There is no reliable evidence as to why Grafton used this nickname. Did he invent it? If so, it was brilliant journalism in that it has outlived the Prince's true name. To his contemporaries, the Prince was known as Edward of Woodstock or simply *'le Prince d'Angleterre'*. See *History* XXIV, No 93, 1–15.

(3) In heraldry a *lion léopardé* was a *lion passant guardant*. 'A leopard of England is a golden lion walking and full faced on a red field': *Leopards of England*, E. E. Dorling, Constable 1912.

(4) See Anthony Steel's *Richard II*, Cambridge 1941, *passim*. Although his judgments suffer from the jargon of psychology his is a scholarly political study of the first importance.

(5) See genealogy on p. xii and *DNB* under Joan, Princess of Wales, and Edward, Prince of Wales. Also H. Wallon's *Richard II*, Paris 1864, I, 4. See *Univ. of Birmingham Hist. Journal* I (1947–8) 13–50 for the theory that Joan was the romantic lady in whose honour Edward III founded the Order of the Garter.

4 (1) The story is told in *Froissart*, 252.

(2) *Froissart*, 205.

5 (1) For Spanish affairs throughout the reign see P. E. Russell's *The English Intervention in Spain and Portugal in the Time of Edward III and Richard II*, Oxford 1955.

6 (1) Fiction can contain accurate history, and the reader is recommended to enjoy *The White Company* by Sir A. Conan Doyle.

7 (1) She was pensioned by Richard in 1378 and married Walter Rauf of Witley, Richard's tailor. *Calendar of the Patent Rolls, 1377–81*, 609.

(2) 'It was great pity to see the men, women, and children that kneeled down on their knees before the Prince for mercy; but

Page

he was so inflamed with ire, that he took no heed to them, so that none was heard, but all put to death, as they were met withal, and such as were nothing culpable ... I trow they were martyrs'. *Froissart*, 201. But for a less emotional view see A. Leroux, *Le Sac de la Cité de Limoges*, Limoges 1906.

8 (1) *Froissart*, 206 and 262, where he adds 'he was merry, true, amorous, sage, secret, large, prewe, hardy, adventurous and chivalrous'.

  (2) All the books were in French save one romance in English. See M. V. Clarke, *Fourteenth Century Studies*, Oxford 1937, 117–22, based on PRO *Liber Forisfacturarum* ff 17–19 E. 154/1/24.

  (3) See *Hardyng*, Pref. i and ii quoting *Lansdowne* MSS 200 f 12, and for the manners, and especially the table manners, of the time, see the amusing collection by F. J. Furnivall, *The Babees Book* (E.E.T.S.) London 1868.

9 (1) See *D.N.B.*

10 (1) '*in eo Parliamento quod "Bonum" merito appellatur*'. *Hist. Anglic*, I 343.

  (2) See A. F. Pollard, *The Evolution of Parliament*, Longman 1926, and Faith Thompson, *A Short History of Parliament 1295–1642*, Minnesota 1953.

  (3) See J. G. Edwards, *The Commons in Mediaeval English Parliaments*, Univ. of London 1954.

11 (1) 'Magnates' is the chronicler's Latin for 'Greater Barons'. The literal English translation 'magnates' is not confusing to students of mediaeval history but its modern derogatory sense (eg 'industrial magnates') necessitates avoiding it as much as possible for the general reader.

  (2) See the fascinating account in *Anon. Chron*, 79 *et seq*, and Intro xliii–xlv. Also *Rot. Parl*, II, 321–30.

12 (1) The Staple was a fixed and continuous market (as opposed to a periodic fair) where all wool and woolfells produced in England had to be inspected, taxed and sold. Staples were ordained in the thirteenth century at a number of important towns in England, later at various towns in the Low Countries, and finally at the end of the century at Calais, where it remained until the loss of that fortress in 1558. The system was run by the privileged traders with capital known as the Merchant Staplers. It enabled duties to be levied efficiently and both prices and quality to be kept high. It was a restriction to free trade, a protection to mediaeval England's richest industry and at times a useful economic weapon in diplomacy. See E. Lipson's *Economic History of England*,

Page

London 1937, I 471–86, and Eileen Power's *Mediaeval English Wool Trade*, Oxford 1941, 66–123.

(2) *Anon. Chron*, 83.

13 (1) See G. R. Owst's *Literature and Pulpit in Mediaeval England*, Cambridge 1933, 576 *et seq*.

(2) Edward was 'Hector' to one chronicler and 'Alexander' to another. See *Chron. Angl*, 88–9.

14 (1) In fitting Gaunt into my picture of Richard, I have not hesitated to use to the full the balanced and brilliant *John of Gaunt* by S. Armitage-Smith, Constable 1904.

15 (1) *Rot. Parl*, II, 330.

16 (1) *Froissart*, 205.

17 (1) *Anon. Chron*, 102.

(2) *Chron. Angl*, 111, and Armitage-Smith, *Op. cit.* 145–7.

19 (1) A 'liberty' in mediaeval connotation is a 'privilege' in modern connotation. Hence so much misunderstanding of charters (including Magna Carta) which secured 'liberties' but did not therefore grant 'freedom'. Nevertheless, documents which used the word 'libertas' were useful to Jacobean lawyers and Whig politicians in thwarting theories of monarchy which refused to reinterpret mediaeval Latin and French to suit new theories of constitutionalism and freedom.

(2) W. Hardy, *The Charters of the Duchy of Lancaster*, London 1845. Cap. IX.

(3) Armitage-Smith, *Op. cit.* 208. His whole Chapter X is invaluable for a true appreciation of the power of the House of Lancaster.

20 (1) *Hist. Anglic*, I 326, and Appendix to *Chron. Angl*, 400.

(2) *Hist. Anglic*, I 328.

(3) *Chron. Angl*, 142–6 and *Hist. Anglic*, I 327.

21 (1) *Chron. Angl*, 150.

22 (1) *Chron. Angl*, 199–200, and *Hist. Anglic*, I 331 and II 384.

(2) *Hist. Anglic*, I 332 *et seq*, and *Anon. Chron*, 107 *et seq*.

23 (1) *Hist. Anglic*, I 333, and *Anon. Chron*, 109–10.

(2) 'jure hereditario ac etiam voto communi singulorum'. *Knighton* II, 125. It is clear from *Anon. Chron*, 110, that the Commons' assent was only asked *after* the oath had been administered; cf the Archbishop of Canterbury's speech at the opening of Richard's first Parliament – p. 27 below and note.

NOTES

CHAPTER II

Page

25 (1) *Hist. Anglic,* I 331.

(2) *Adam of Usk,* 3 and 140; *Eccles,* X 16.

(3) 'All the passages of the realm were stopped; for they would not that the death of the King should be so soon known in France, till they had set the realm in some order.' *Froissart,* 206.

(4) 1379 – 'The thyrde pestilence reigned in England so sore that moste part of the people clene dyed awaye . . .' *Hardyng,* 338.

(5) *Hist. Anglic,* I 340 *et seq.*

26 (1) eg Edward III, the Black Prince, the Lord Captal de Buch and Lord de Spenser.

(2) Rymer, *Foedera* IV 30.

(3) *Froissart,* 205; G. M. Trevelyan, *England in the Age of Wycliffe,* London 1909, 71, and *Cambridge Mediaeval History,* Cambridge 1932, VII, 456.

(4) *Hist. Anglic,* I 339–40.

27 (1) *Rot. Parl,* III 3 and Stubbs, *Constitutional History of England,* Oxford 1875, II 464.

(2) Trevelyan, *Op. cit.* 73–4.

28 (1) *Rot. Parl,* III 5; Armitage-Smith, *John of Gaunt* 193.

29 (1) '*Volo esse christianus ex integro*'. *Fasc. Ziz,* 245.

30 (1) For Wyclif I have used H. B. Workman, *John Wyclif,* Oxford 1926; G. V. Lechler, *John Wycliffe and his English Precursors* tr. Lorimer, London 1884; my own notes of unpublished lectures by Miss M. V. Clarke and R. Lane Poole of Oxford (1922); and the evidence of the *Fasc. Ziz., Knighton* II and *Hist. Anglic.* all in the Rolls Series. Rashdall's article in the *DNB.* is still the clearest summary, but K. B. Mcfarlane's *John Wycliffe and the Beginnings of English Nonconformity,* Oxford 1952, is now the standard authority.

(2) *Fasc. Ziz,* 245.

(3) The Bull is dated 1299 and concludes 'we declare announce and define that it is altogether necessary to salvation for every human creature to be subject to the Roman pontiff'. Henderson, *Select Historical Documents of the Middle Ages,* London 1912, 435–7.

31 (1) *Defensor Pacis* written c 1324. See summary in *Harvard Theological Studies* No 8, 1920, and the translation by A. Gewirth, *Marsilius of Padua,* Columbia 1955, II.

(2) See *DNB.* He died c 1349. Marsilius and Ockham were fellow scholars in Paris. See G. Lagarde, *La Naissance de l'Esprit Laique,* Paris 1934.

247

NOTES

Page

(3) See *DNB*. He died c 1360 and was not only a scholar but a popular preacher both in England and Ireland. His sermons are in the Bodleian. C. W. A. Pantin, *The English Church in the 14th Century*, Cambridge 1955.

(4) Wyclif's Theory of Dominion is explained in two documents – his *De Dominio Divino* of 1376 and his *De Dominio Civili* of 1381. Both are summed up in the answer he made to the Parliament of 1377. See *Fasc. Ziz*, 245–57.

32 (1) *'Deus debet obedire diabolo.'* *Fasc. Ziz*, 278.

(2) Wyclif's *De officio Regis* is a subtle defence of absolute kingship; but see J. N. Figgis, *Divine Right*, Cambridge 1914, 2nd edition 66–80.

(3) *Hist. Anglic*, I 356.

33 (1) *Hist. Anglic*, I 375–9 and 411–12. Also *Anon. Chron*, 121–3 which also mentions that Richard heard Wyclif's testimony to Parliament.

34 (1) *Hist. Anglic*, I 79.

(2) See E. Perroy, *L'Angleterre et le grand schisme d'Occident*, Paris 1933.

36 (1) See G. G. Coulton's *Mediaeval Panorama*, Cambridge 1943, Cap. XXXIX, for a brilliant condensation of many scattered sources. The standard work is E. Perroy's *The Hundred Years War*, London 1951.

(2) But see p 154 and note.

37 (1) Even by 1327 the truly feudal army was obsolete in England and was being superseded by recruitment by indenture. See M. McKisack, *The Fourteenth Century*, Oxford 1959, cap IX.

40 (1) *Hist. Anglic*, I 372.

41 (1) *Hist. Anglic*, I 405.

(2) *Hist. Anglic*, I 419–25. Arundell was more of a fop than a soldier – he lost 52 suits of clothes *'vel aureos vel auro textos'* in the wreck.

(3) *Adam of Usk*, 8 and 148–9 draws a different moral from that of the monk Walsingham – he blames the disaster on high and unjust taxation!

42 (1) *Hist. Anglic*, I 369–71.

43 (1) Philpot was told *'non licuisset benefacere Regi vel regno sine consilio Comitum et Baronum'*. *Hist. Anglic*, I 371.

(2) See A. F. Pollard, *Evolution of Parliament* cap IV; J. F. Willard W. A. Morris, *The English Government at Work*, Cambridge Mass. 1947, I.

45 (1) See A. Steel, *English Government Finance 1377–1413* in *EHR*, LI,

NOTES

44–8, and the same author's brilliant *The Receipt of the Exchequer, 1377–1485*, Cambridge 1954.

(2) The Mayor of London paid the same as an earl or a bishop, justices of both benches and of the Exchequer were rated above earls, and the aldermen and mayors of the larger towns paid the same as barons. All foreign merchants were taxed, and the greatest were rated as high as knights bachelor. It was *'une subside si mervaillous qe tiel ne fuist unqes veu ne oie'*. *Anon. Chron*, 172. For the full scale see Adams & Stephens *Select Documents of English Constitutional History*, New York 1921, 140–1.

(3) *Rot. Parl*, III 90; *Hist. Anglic*, I 449.

(4) *Hist. Anglic*, I 407–8.

CHAPTER III

48 (1) *Froissart*, 250.

(2) Even Bishop Stubbs writes 'The rising of the Commons is one of the most portentous phenomena to be found in the whole of our history.' Stubbs, *Constitutional History*, II 471.

(3) I have not given many references for my brief summary of the social life of the period – the notes would have become too voluminous. I recommend the general reader to G. G. Coulton's *Mediaeval Panorama*, Cambridge 1943, or his *Chaucer and his England*, London 1908. Also to L. F. Salzman's *English Life in the Middle Ages*, Oxford 1941, G. M. Trevelyan's *English Social History*, London 1944, and E. Rickert's *Chaucer's World*, Oxford 1948.

(4) See J. H. Clapham, *Concise Economic History of Britain to 1750*, Oxford 1949, and M. McKisack, *The Fourteenth Century*, cap XI.

(5) In Kent and East Anglia there was less villeinage than elsewhere, and recent research proves that the revolt was not exclusively a villeins' revolt. Nevertheless, its moving spirits were close to the villeins and its rank and file largely composed of villeins. See M. McKisack, *loc. cit.*

49 (1) The 'ease and riches' which struck Froissart also attracted the strictures of William Langland, who complains of landless labourers who 'deigned not to dine on day-old vegetables' but demanded richer fare, and, unless they had high wages, cursed King and Parliament 'that makes such laws to keep the labourer down'. Langland also scourges 'wastrels' who

refused to work and became vagabonds content with nothing less than 'clean wheaten bread' and 'no halfpenny ale but of the best and brownest'. See *Froissart*, 250; Langland, *Piers Plowman* (Everyman edition) 117.

(2) See Lipson, *Economic History* I, cap III.

(3) 'Commutation' was the system of accepting cash in lieu of service.

50 (1) See C. Petit-Dutaillis, *Studies Supplementary to Stubbs*, Manchester 1908–29, II, 264 *et seq*. The first Statutes of Labourers were enacted in 1349 and re-enacted at intervals throughout Edward III's reign.

51 (1) *Statutes at Large*, Ric. II, VI preamble 207.

(2) J. J. Jusserand's *English Wayfaring Life in the Middle Ages*, tr. Lucy Toulmin-Smith, London 1892, *passim*.

53 (1) The best and perhaps most typical surviving example is in the church of St Thomas in Salisbury.

(2) See G. R. Owst, *Literature and Pulpit in Mediaeval England*, Cambridge 1933, and cf *Froissart*, 251, and *Hist. Anglic*, II 32–4.

54 (1) *Hist. Anglic*, I 452. '*Infinitam pecuniam sic collegit*', Adam of Usk, 3 and 140.

(2) The title of the standard French work on The Peasants' Revolt is *Le Soulèvement des travailleurs de l'Angleterre* by A. Reville, Paris 1898.

55 (1) Even Walsingham makes this point – *Hist. Anglic*, I 454.

(2) C. Petit-Dutaillis, *Op. cit.* 278; G. M. Trevelyan's *England in the Age of Wycliffe*, 99 and 103–205.

(3) See Trevelyan, *Op. cit.* 202–4.

56 (1) *Anon. Chron*, 134.

(2) *Froissart*, 252.

57 (1) *Knighton*, II 138–40. *Hist. Anglic*, II 33–4.

58 (1) See *Froissart's* lurid story of the 'Jacquerie', 136–7.

(2) *Hist. Anglic*; I 454.

(3) *Anon. Chron*, 136, whose excellent factual reporting I have followed faithfully. Froissart is, however, a better guide to contemporary reactions.

59 (1) 'Many of the people loved him', *Froissart*, 251.

60 (1) *Anon. Chron*, 138.

(2) See M. V. Clarke, *Fourteenth Century Studies* 95–7; *Hist. Anglic*, II 11.

(3) *Froissart*, 252.

61 (1) '*Velut stertentes*': *Hist. Anglic*, I, 455.

(2) *Froissart*, 254.

Page

62 (1) *Froissart*, 251 says that it was the discontented Londoners who invited the rebels to London. This is not incompatible with the usually accepted story in the text.

(2) *Anon. Chron*, 139.

63 (1) *Froissart*, 251.

65 (1) 'Certes Jacke Straw, and his meinie, Ne made never shoutes half so shrille Whan that they wolden any Fleming Kille, As thilké day was made upon the fox!'. Chaucer, *Nun's Priest's Tale* 4580.

68 (1) *Anon. Chron*, 143.

(2) *Anon. Chron*, 144–5 says it was Tyler, but other versions say that Tyler led the attack on the Tower; cf Reville, *Op. cit.* 195.

70 (1) See *American Hist. Rev*, VII 254–85.

(2) See *Monk of Evesham*, 27.

71 (1) *Anon. Chron*, 146.

72 (1) 'The Law of Winchester' substituted the mutilation and blinding of felons for common hanging, and was a coveted privilege in early borough charters. *Anon. Chron*, 196.

73 (1) No one has ever explained why Richard was not used as a hostage by the rebels.

74 (1) *Anon. Chron*, 150.

(2) Although Tyler's reign in the capital was ended on June 16th it took five days before the news of his death reached Norwich.

75 (1) *Hist. Anglic*, II 20–1.

76 (1) *Hist. Anglic*, II 18.

(2) *Knighton*, II 150.

(3) *Hist. Anglic*, II 20.

(4) *Hist. Anglic*, II 22–30 and 35–41.

77 (1) 'Hurling' meant 'shouting', see Trevelyan, *England in the Age of Wycliffe* 366 note.

(2) *Anon. Chron*, 151 explains that the first savagery of judicial revenge was succeeded by a more lenient policy, and the issue of new charters and pardons by the King '*pur luy fair riche*', but cf *Hist. Anglic*, II 13–14 and *Camb. Med. Hist*, cap VII, 738.

(3) See Ramsay's *Genesis of Lancaster*, Oxford 1913, II, 176.

(4) See Petit-Dutaillis, *Op. cit.* II 303 and Trevelyan, *Loc cit*, 252–5.

78 (1) A poll-tax was levied in 1513 and the method was also used by the Stuarts. The last poll-tax was in 1698. See S. Dowell, *History of Taxation and Taxes in England*, London 1888, III 85 *et seq.*

Page

    (2) See Rymer, *Foedera* IV 125 – a denial which confirms the fact but not the truth of the rumours.

CHAPTER IV

81 (1) There was a minor upheaval in Norfolk in 1382 (*Chron. Angl*, 354). Lewes Castle was sacked in 1384, and there was further trouble in 1390 (*Higden*, IX 220). But cf Lipson, *Economic History*, I 128.

82 (1) cf Armitage-Smith, *John of Gaunt* 248–58.

83 (1) John of Gaunt's *Register* (Camden Society), II 410–11 and Armitage-Smith, *Op. cit.* 257–8.

84 (1) See *DNB*.

    (2) Oman refers to him as 'a veteran official'.

85 (1) See T. F. Tout, *Chapters in Mediaeval Administrative History*, Manchester 1920–33, III 404.

    (2) He was a nephew of Burley's. See N. B. Lewis in *EHR*, LII 662–9.

86 (1) See below p 111 and note.

87 (1) *Hist. Anglic*, II 46. *Adam of Usk* 3 and 140; *Knighton*, II 150; *Higden*, IX 12.

    (2) She possessed the gospel written in Bohemian, German and Latin, and Archbishop Arundel remarked that 'in the reading of godly books she was more diligent than are the prelates themselves'. It is Stowe in his *Survey of London* (B 206) who accuses her of being to blame for introducing into England the 'piked shoes tied to their knees with silken laces or chains of silver and gilt'. In the following reign the length of these 'pikes' had to be restricted by Statute. See *Traison*, 134 note.

89 (1) *Froissart*, 291.

90 (1) cf Tout, *Chapters* IV 207, and M. V. Clarke, *Fourteenth Century Studies* 39.

91 (1) cf Armitage-Smith, *Op. cit.* 279–82.

92 (1) For the Salisbury Parliament see *Higden*, IX 33 *et seq.*

    (2) The story, so often repeated, that Richard threw his cap and shoes out of the window in his temper, has to be abandoned. It was the friar who feigned madness by this display. See the brilliant essay by L. C. Hector in *EHR*, LXVIII 62–5.

93 (1) cf *Higden*, IX 33–40; *Monk of Evesham*, 50–2, *Hist. Anglic*, II 112–15 and *Chron. Angl*, 359.

    (2) '*Dementia instigatus*' is the comment of two contemporaries, and see note on p 92 above.

    (3) cf G. M. Trevelyan, *History of England*, London 1926, 314 note

– he reminds his readers that, in the last year of the reign of Henry VIII, the Chancellor and the Solicitor General of England with their own hands turned the screws of the Tower rack to torture a confession from the Protestant martyr Anne Askewe. She survived only to be burnt to death at Smithfield.

94 (1) *Hist. Anglic*, II 96–7 is Walsingham's scornful commentary on the court circles. It begins with a description of a royal tour visiting his abbey '*non offere sed auferre*', and concludes with a diatribe on the Queen '*cum suis Boemiis*', and the words of the Preacher (*Eccles*, X 16) '*Vae terrae cuius rex puer est*'.

(2) For the complicated London politics of the reign, see Ruth Bird's *The Turbulent London of Richard II*, London 1949.

95 (1) See above p 89.

96 (1) *Higden*, IX 46.

97 (1) *Higden*, IX 58 and Armitage-Smith, *Op. cit.* 290–1.

(2) *Higden*, IX 58–9.

98 (1) cf Armitage-Smith, *Op. cit.* Appendix ii 437.

99 (1) *Hist. Anglic*, II 131–2, *Higden*, IX 65. *Monk of Evesham*, 61–3.

100 (1) *Rot. Parl*, III 204–13, secs 32–8.

102 (1) It was to her that Chaucer dedicated his *Legend of Fair Women*.

CHAPTER V

104 (1) *Anon. Chron*, 138.

(2) The 'Merciless Parliament' of 1388 was named the 'Wonderful Parliament' by Thomas Favent, a clerk to the diocese of Salisbury, who wrote its history with all the circumstantial detail of an eye-witness. By a curious misreading, the name 'Wonderful' has since been applied to the Parliament of October 1386. See Camden *Miscellany*, XIV (1926) ed Miss M. McKisack. For the Wonderful Parliament and the Lancastrian Faction see M. V. Clarke, *Fourteenth Century Studies* 36–52.

105 (1) *Knighton* II, 215 *et seq*.

(2) *Hist. Anglic*, II 150.

(3) *Knighton*, II 216–20. He is much the best chronicler of this episode.

106 (1) See N. B. Lewis, *EHR* XLII, 402–7, and Tout, *Chapters* III 412–14.

107 (1) cf E. C. Lodge and G. A. Thornton, *English Constitutional Documents 1307–1485*, Cambridge 1935, 67; J. E. A. Jolliffe, *Constitutional History of Mediaeval England*, London 1937, 470.

Page

(2) cf Lodge and Thornton, *Op. cit.* 25; *Rot. Parl,* III, 224–350; *Knighton,* II 216–20.

(3) *Statutes at Large,* 10 Ric. II, cap. I, 1386, 280–4; *Rot. Parl,* III 227.

108 (1) *Hist. Anglic,* II 147.

(2) *Hist. Anglic,* II 153–6 expatiates on the contrast between these successes and the misdeeds of the King's friends who were '*plus valentes in thalamo quam in campo*'.

(3) cf G. G. Coulton, *Chaucer and his England* 58–9. Chaucer's other patron, Gaunt, was absent in Spain.

(4) Tout, *Chapters* III 418–21.

(5) *Higden,* IX 94.

109 (1) *Higden,* IX 99–101; Lodge & Thornton, *Op. cit.* 25–6.

110 (1) *Hist. Anglic,* II 161.

(2) E. Perroy, *Schisme* 296–301.

(3) cf M. V. Clarke, *Op. cit.* 115–45.

(4) Half-hanging, disembowelling while still alive, then beheading and quartering is the strict definition of a traitor's death in the fourteenth century.

111 (1) *Higden,* IX 103.

(2) cf M. V. Clarke, *Op. cit.* 118.

(3) See The *Dieulacres* Chronicle, page 45 of *The Deposition of Richard II* by Clarke & Galbraith, Manchester 1930. The note on the same page is unkind to de Vere in that it applies a nineteenth-century standard of morality to the fourteenth. De Vere's offence to the fourteenth century was not that he changed partners with or without legal approval but that he preferred a landless and foreign maid-of-honour to a granddaughter of Edward III.

(4) *Hist. Anglic,* II, 165.

112 (1) cf M. V. Clarke, *Op. cit.* 134 and 135, and for his treatise on Trial by Combat see E. Rickert, *Chaucer's World* 151–6 or *Archaeologia,* LVII, 62–6.

(2) *Higden,* IX 106.

(3) Richard obviously feared a parliament 'packed' by Gloucester.

113 (1) *Higden,* IX 109–10.

(2) cf J. N. L. Myres, *EHR* XLII 20–33, for this short campaign.

(3) *Adam of Usk,* 6 and 145.

114 (1) *Knighton,* II 246–7, and *Higden,* IX 114.

(2) See *DNB.*

115 (1) cf M. V. Clarke, *Op. cit.* 91–5.

(2) See T. Favent *Historia Mirabilis Parliamenti* in Camden Miscellany, XIV (1926). The Monk of Westminster's version

NOTES

Page

is in *Higden*, IX 119–40: see also *Hist. Anglic*, II 172 *et seq.*, and *Rot. Parl*, III 228–56.

117 (1) cf Lodge & Thornton, *Op. cit.* 156–7, and for the legal problem at this time see Steel's *Richard II* 150–3 and 178–9.

(2) Notably Tout, *Chapters* III 432–3.

118 (1) The whole subject of the 1388 trials is admirably dealt with by M. V. Clarke, *Op. cit.* 114–45.

(2) 'Tanquam nix' Favent, *Op. cit.* 16 and cf *Higden*, IX 166.

119 (1) Favent, *Op. cit.* 17, and *Higden*, IX 167. Later in his chronicle the Monk of Westminster reports the confession of a servant of the abbey, one John Paule, who when on the scaffold for murder admitted that he had betrayed Tresilian and had therefore offended against the privilege of sanctuary; cf *Higden*, IX 271.

(2) *Higden*, IX 168.

(3) *Hist. Anglic*, II 174.

121 (1) *Rot. Parl*, III 250.

(2) This phrase is the opening title of the Second Statute of Westminster (1285) which established perpetual entail. If heirs failed, the property reverted to the grantor; cf Stubbs *Constitutional History*, II 122.

(3) *Higden*, IX 154.

123 (1) cf Ramsay, *Op. cit.* II 259–61.

(2) *Higden*, IX 189–98.

124 (1) *Higden*, IX 192–6.

125 (1) *Statutes of the Realm*, II 59.

126 (1) In fairness it must be mentioned that our first detailed knowledge of the working of the mediaeval Chancery dates from the documents of one of the Appellants' special commissions. cf Tout *Chapters*, III 443–9.

(2) cf Armitage-Smith, *Op. cit.* 301–36.

127 (1) *Hist. Anglic*, II 181.

128 (1) Tout, *Chapters* III 454.

(2) For a close parallel in France where King Charles VI triumphed in a similar situation see H. Wallon, *Op. cit.* II 17–19.

CHAPTER VI

131 (1) Suffolk died in Paris in Sept 1389; de Vere died at Louvain in 1392 as the result of an accident while boar-hunting; Archbishop Neville died as a parish priest in Louvain in 1392.

In Suffolk's obituary notice, written by the pious Walsingham, is an amusing example of how little the mediaeval monk cared for the charity he preached: 'That sewer of treachery, that sink of avarice, that charioteer of treason, that coffer of vice, that inventor of hate, that fabricator of lies, that vilest of informers, that most expert of forgers, that most accomplished of slanderers, that traitor to his fatherland, Michael de la Pole, Earl of Suffolk, Chancellor but evil councillor of the realm, died at Paris deservedly giving up his faithless ghost in a foreign land'. *Hist. Anglic,* II 187.

(2) He became Bishop of Exeter as a reward from Richard ten years later.

132 (1) Rymer, *Foedera* VII 641.

(2) *Higden,* IX 218. *Rot. Parl,* 23 Ric. II part ii.

(3) cf Armitage-Smith *John of Gaunt* 341–2.

(4) Tout calls it a 'curious comedy'; see his *Chapters,* III 460 ff.

133 (1) W. Hardy, *Charters of the Duchy of Lancaster,* London 1845, xiv. Rymer, *Foedera* VII 659–63. *Rot. Parl,* III 263. *Higden,* IX 73 wrongly dates this event to the time of Gaunt's last Spanish expedition (1386).

134 (1) *Hist. Anglic,* II 195–6.

(2) *Hist. Anglic,* II 196. The *Annales* give a little more information. The insurgents were apparently craftsmen, and of sixteen taken prisoner at Croydon three were later executed. But it was all taken as a matter of course. cf *Annales,* 220.

(3) *Higden,* IX 222–4.

(4) *Higden,* IX 222–3.

135 (1) *Higden,* IX 238–9.

(2) *Higden,* IX 241, and see Henry Newbolt, *The New June.* In *An English Chronicle,* ed J. S. Davies, (Camden) 1856, 6, the chronicler describes Richard's livery as 'white hertis, with cronnez aboute thair neckis, and cheynes of gold hangyng thereupon, and the cronne hangyng lowe befor the hertis bodye, the whiche hert was the Kyngis liverey'.

136 (1) cf Wallon, *Op. cit.* II 40.

(2) Tout, *Chapters* III 474, and *Rot. Parl,* III 284–99.

137 (1) Walsingham reports that a royal demand for horses and money from St Albans was settled '*caritatis intuitio*' by Gaunt. *Hist. Anglic,* II 199.

(2) cf Armitage-Smith, *Op. cit.* 346 (note) *et seq.*

(3) The complete poem by Eustache Deschamps is in Wright's *Political Poems* (Rolls Series) I 99 and 300–1.

139 (1) *Hist. Anglic,* II 207–11; *Higden,* IX 267–70 and 272–8.

NOTES

Page

(2) One 'Ricardo Whityngton' was among the City's representatives. *Higden,* IX 270.

140 (1) cf Tout, *Chapters* III 482–4; *Annales,* 159–62 and 166; *Hist. Anglic,* II 214; *Higden,* IX 239–40 and 265–81, and *Rot. Parl,* III 309–23.

141 (1) But Gloucester may also have been puzzled – Mowbray was also an Appellant and Richard's favour to his turncoat friend may have been deliberately misleading to both Gloucester and Mowbray.

142 (1) cf. Armitage-Smith, *Op. cit.* 353–6.

(2) Probably 'the collar of SS' so frequently seen on the memorial brasses of Lancastrian knights. Its exact significance has never been determined.

(3) *Rot. Parl,* III 314a.

143 (1) Her sister was the Duchess of York, who had died two years before, and who was apparently as loose in her morals as Costanza was strict. One chronicler makes no bones about it – the Duchess of York was 'domina carnalis et delicata, mundialis et venerea'. The chroniclers add yet another death to the obituaries of 1394, the death of Sir John Hawkwood 'after almost incredible deeds' in Lombardy. He was the most famous of English *condottieri* and the leader of the White Company. His tomb is in the Duomo at Florence. According to one chronicler he began life as a poor apprentice to a London shoemaker. If the mediaeval poor boy had ambitions to break through the feudal crust he had to go abroad to do it, or else become a priest. cf *Higden,* IX 282.

(2) *Higden,* IX 243–5.

144 (1) *Adam of Usk,* 9 and 150–1.

(2) See especially *Annales,* 168.

(3) Steel, *Richard II* 204. See also 174–5 where modern psychiatry again seems to me to mar his invaluable analysis of the political scene.

145 (1) *Hist. Anglic,* II 215; *Annales,* 169 and 424.

(2) *Annales,* 166.

146 (1) See E. Curtis, *Richard II in Ireland,* Oxford 1927, *passim,* and also his *History of Mediaeval Ireland,* London 1938, 265–75.

(2) *Annales,* 172.

(3) In the library of Corpus Christi College, Oxford, is an illuminated Irish missal still to be seen in the leather satchel in which its monkish owner carried it about, thanks to the preservative qualities of the Irish bog in which he dropped it. It deserves wider fame and public exhibition.

257

NOTES

147 (1) cf Perroy, *Schisme* 97–128.

    (2) A Dublin parliament in 1385 had asked Richard to visit Ireland.

    (3) The best account is in *Annales* 172 ff., and cf Tout, *Chapters* III 485–6 and 488–9.

148 (1) *Froissart*, 430 *et seq.*

150 (1) See H. Nicolas, *Proceedings and Ordinances of the Privy Council* I 57–8; E. Curtis, *Proceedings of the Royal Irish Academy* XXXVII 276–303.

151 (1) *Statutes of the Realm*, 5 Ric. II, 2, cap v.

152 (1) *Knighton*, II 179–80 and 174 tells of the friends of Purvey who cared so little to 'hear the blessed mutter of the Mass, and see God made and eaten all day long' that they dismissed it as mere blabbering with the lips.

    (2) Langland, *The Vision of Piers Plowman* (Everyman edition) 71.

    (3) Langland, *Op. cit.* 131.

    (4) Langland, *Op. cit.* 98.

153 (1) Translated by Wyclif *'in Anglicam linguam non Angelicam'* says *Knighton*, II 152.

    (2) So-called because an earthquake of more than ordinary dimensions for England disturbed its sessions.

    (3) *Knighton*, II 191.

    (4) cf Stanley, *Memorials of Westminster Abbey*, London 1882, 123.

154 (1) For the Lollards under Richard II see *Knighton*, II 151–98; *Annales*, 174–82; *Hist. Anglic*, II 51–60, 157–9 and 188; *Fasc. Ziz, passim.*

    (2) If the Lollards' pacifism was justified by scripture, there was the less spiritual pacifism of a poet like Gower who, tired of perpetual warfare, complains in his *Confessio Amantis*, London 1889, 45:

> 'The wars are so general
> Among the Christians above all,
> That every man seeketh revenge
> And yet these clergy all day preach
> And say, good deeds may none be
> Which stand not upon charity.
> I know not how charity should stand
> Where deadly war is taken in hand'.

155 (1) *Annales*, 183.

156 (1) Adams & Stephens, *Op. cit.* 156–8. *Statutes of the Realm*, II 84.

    (2) Cardinal Wolsey was charged under the writ *'Praemunire facias'*. For the fourteenth-century attitude see *EHR*,

NOTES

Page

XXXVIII 173–205, and cf *EHR*, LX 316–48; *History*, VIII 289–92; Perroy, *Schisme* 332 ff.

(3) *Higden*, IX 221.

157 (1) See note on p 131 (1).

(2) *Hist. Anglic*, II 219; *Annales*, 184–5.

158 (1) *Froissart*, 423 *et seq.*

159 (1) Froissart received a silver goblet filled with a hundred nobles in return. For Froissart's compliment on Richard's French see note (1) to p 229.

160 (1) Froissart contrasts Gloucester with his brother of York, 'a Prince who loves his ease and little business, also he had a fair lady to his wife, daughter to the Earl of Kent on whom was all his pleasure'. *Froissart*, 429.

(2) The Continuator of the *Eulogium* chronicle states that he was formally recognized as Richard's heir in 1385, but this may have been a later Yorkist interpolation. See M. V. Clarke, *Fourteenth Century Studies* 107 note. *Eulogium*, III 361, and also 369–70, where there is the incredible story (unknown to Rolls or Records) of Gaunt demanding that his son Henry should be recognized as Richard's heir – cf Armitage-Smith, *Op. cit.* 359–62; and *Hardyng*, 353–4 notes.

161 (1) Tout, *Chapters* IV 1.

(2) Rymer, *Foedera* VII 811.

162 (1) cf Steel, *Richard II* 196–7.

163 (1) *Annales*, 188–94.

(2) In spite of their threats, the chronicles record that the Duchess of Gloucester and the Countesses of Huntingdon and Stafford joined with the new Duchess of Lancaster as ladies-in-waiting to accompany the new Queen to England. *Annales*, 192–3.

164 (1) Richard thanks Charles 'for so gracious and honourable a gift'! *Annales*, 193.

(2) Tout, *Chapters* IV 9.

CHAPTER VII

167 (1) And also the interpretation of the Kirkstall monk who seems to have written his version of the revenge as a loyalist and adjusted his tone with difficulty to the swift approach of the usurper. *Kirkstall*, 32–3; Clarke, *Fourteenth Century Studies* 99–144.

168 (1) In 1395 Richard had commissioned the beautiful tomb with its recumbent effigies of Anne and himself for Westminster Abbey. See p 187 and note 2 below.

259

NOTES

(2) See the learned note and the actual document in the article by N. B. Lewis in *EHR*, LII No 208, 662 *et seq*.

(3) '*Admirabilis et diuturna regalis paciencia*'; *Kirkstall*, 34.

169 (1) See *Adam of Usk*, 38 and 193; *Annales*, 213 for a contrary opinion.

(2) See Tout, *Chapters* IV 10–13 for the details, which he interprets in a way unfriendly to Richard.

(3) Tout's unkind phrase is 'strange recruits'.

170 (1) *Higden*, IX 94; *Adam of Usk*, 5 and 144–5; Wright, *Pol. Poems*, I 408–11; *Hist. Anglic*, II 224.

(2) See P. Shaw in *History*, XXIV 5; M. V. Clarke, *Op. cit*. 97–8; Stanley, *Op. cit*. 124 and note.

(3) *Annales* 208, *Hardyng* 346, and Trevelyan's *England in the Age of Wycliffe*, 289–90.

(4) *Kenilworth Chron*. by John Strecche (add. MS. 35295); Clarke, *Op. cit*. 98; *Traison* 293 note 1. cf note for p. 229.

172 (1) In 1407 Henry IV interpolated the phrase '*excepta dignitate regali*' into the Rolls of Parliament at a time when the brothers Beaufort were causing him jealous anxiety – the jealousy may have been of long standing.

(2) He was beheaded by an anti-Lollard mob at the Rout of Cirencester in 1400.

(3) *Adam of Usk*, 36 and 190.

173 (1) Richard was trying to keep a promise he had rashly made to Charles VI during the second wedding negotiations.

(2) See Stubbs, *Constitutional History* II 491–2.

174 (1) Lodge & Thornton, *Op. cit*. 69.

175 (1) It was an '*ex post facto*' offence, and therefore doubly unwise.

(2) Haxey was a dependent of Nottingham, and it is just possible that this added to Richard's exasperation. Was it also a warning to Nottingham?

(3) Bagot was no upstart. He was a sheriff of Warwickshire and Leicestershire and owned the castle of Baginton. He had been attached to both Gaunt and Nottingham, and, like Bushy and Green, had been on the Appellants' side in 1388. He became a King's knight towards the end of 1397, but was sufficiently discreet to entertain Hereford before the Lists of Coventry and perhaps therefore to avoid the fate of his friends at the final rebellion. Sir Henry Green was a Knight of the Shire in the Parliament of 1394, and was also in Gaunt's service. He became a King's knight in March 1397, and by the end of the year he and Bushy were earning a fee of £100 per annum for their services to Richard. All three are the subject of the

famous lampoon which has survived – it is a series of rhyming puns on the bush, the bag and the green bush helped out with the zoology of heraldry (see below pp 210–11 and Wright's *Pol. Poems*, I 363–6). All three were able gentry who were unlucky enough to be on the losing side in the rebellion of 1399.

176 (1) The Count Palatine and the Archbishop of Cologne were granted pensions of £1,000 per annum, and Rutland and Nottingham were sent to the Rhineland for negotiations which were finally abortive. The amount of the bribe, and the status of the Ambassadors, indicate that Richard was playing for what he and all men considered high stakes.

(2) Perroy, *Schisme* 341–3; *Annales*, 200–1.

(3) See *Hardyng*, 346–7 for a hearsay account of court extravagance which mentions 10,000 daily attendants, 300 kitchen hands, 300 launderers and grooms in cloth of silk; and see Trevelyan, *England in the Age of Wycliffe* 63 and Wright, *Pol. Poems*, I 153–234.

177 (1) *Annales*, 201.

(2) *Traison*, 119–21.

(3) *Traison*, 120–1.

178 (1) Three contemporary French chroniclers and a remark of the Lancastrian chronicler Usk, who was present at the succeeding Parliament, are the authorities for the conspiracy of St Albans and Arundel. No mention is made of it by the other English chroniclers. On the other hand, the Lancastrian chroniclers made the most of the story that Richard only captured the Earl of Arundel by employing his brother the Archbishop to invite him to conference under an oath of safe conduct which was promptly broken, and that Warwick was similarly tricked after dinner with the King. The French chroniclers had no cause to invent, the Lancastrians had: and Usk's reference to the confession of Warwick and a conspiracy hatched by the Abbot of St Albans and the Prior of Westminster gives substantially greater weight to the French version. The conflict of evidence is not of great significance – Richard was obviously determined on revenge by fair means or foul, and, in spite of Warwick's and Gloucester's confessions, he was content to base his official accusations on the misdeeds of the Merciless Parliament. The plot at Arundel was merely the trigger which finally launched him into action. I see no reason to dismiss the French chronicles (including Froissart's) as mere fabrications, and, on the whole, Steel

Page

(*Richard II* 230–3) supports me. Tout in *Chapters*, IV 21 of course takes the opposite view, and the *Annales*, 201–4 of course expatiate on Richard's 'treachery'. See *Traison*, 2–3 and 119–21; *Adam of Usk*, 16 and 161; Wallon, *Op. cit.* II 151.

179 (1) *Annales*, 206.

    (2) Steel's note (*Richard II* 232) on this point is that 'this in itself was perhaps the order of a not entirely sane man'. Vengeance is not a sign of mental health, but it is no proof of insanity. And what man is 'entirely' sane?

180 (1) 'Knights of Parliament who were not chosen by the Community as custom demanded but by the will of the King'. *Annales*, 209. Adam of Usk is an invaluable eye-witness of the whole proceedings; *Adam of Usk*, 9 *et seq.* and 152 *et seq.* And see H. G. Richardson, *Bulletin of John Ryland Library* XXII (April 1938).

    (2) *Rot. Parl*, III 379.

181 (1) See Steel, *Richard II* 238–9 for a useful summary of the available evidence (or lack of it) and the resulting academic disputes.

182 (1) This precedent was not followed, as it might have been, on the many occasions of 'judgments of blood' in the following century. The bishops therefore ceased to be peers and became mere 'Spiritual Lords of Parliament'.

    (2) *Adam of Usk*, 11 and 154.

    (3) *Monk of Evesham*, 134.

184 (1) The Lancastrian chronicler gives a moving description of the execution of a brave knight who scattered money to the lamenting crowds, who read the Service for the Dead with his confessor, who maintained his innocence to the last, who pardoned his executioner, who felt the sword and found it sharp enough, and who only begged for one good stroke to make a quick end. He goes on to describe the miracles that took place at his tomb. There is no question of Arundel's bravery, and his victories at sea certainly earned him popularity. But this picture of an innocent hero protests too much – Arundel deserves no sympathy from history even if his death became good propaganda for a usurping Lancastrian. The less Lancastrian chronicler of the Abbey of Kirkstall notes with significant satisfaction that Arundel was executed on the very spot where Sir Simon Burley had met his end. See *Annales*, 214–19; *Kirkstall*, 33; *Adam of Usk*, 13–15 and 157–9.

    (2) *Adam of Usk*, 16 and 161.

    (3) *Annales*, 220.

Page

(4) Steel in his *Richard II* 236–7 even suggests that the records were tampered with by the Lancastrians, but, while I agree with the rest of his inferences, his own footnote seems flatly to contradict his major suggestion – there is no sign on the Rolls of Parliament of any alterations at this stage.

185 (1) For a balanced assessment which sums up in favour of the theory that there was an unofficial deposition in 1386, and 'that both Richard and his enemies – he for his prestige and they from fear – would combine to check its circulation and force it into oblivion', see Clarke, *Op. cit.* 91–5, and cf *Rot. Parl*, III 379, and *EHR*, XXXVIII 249–51.

186 (1) *Annales*, 223.

(2) *Annales*, 223 states that this was done immediately after the new 'duketti' had been created, but there is Froissart's evidence that Richard made this gesture of piety to his favourite Saint when in Ireland in 1394. The *Annales* add the comment 'as though now he scorned all moderation'. cf Clarke, *Op. cit.* 274–6.

(3) Clarke, *Op. cit.* 103 and *Rot. Parl*, III 355–6.

187 (1) *Traison*, 11 and 140.

(2) The tomb of Richard and Anne was the work of Henry Yevele and Stephen Lote; the effigies in latten (a mixture of copper and bronze) richly engraved were the work of Nicolas Broke and Godfrey Prest, coppersmiths of London, and were commissioned in April 1395, for £400. See Rymer's *Foedera*, VII 795–6.

CHAPTER VIII

188 (1) *Adam of Usk*, 18 and 163.

(2) *Traison*, 11 and 140.

(3) For a fascinating commentary on this session see the poem of *Richard the Redeless* in Wright *Pol. Poems*, I 368–417. Here is criticism of royal luxury: 'For where was ever any Christian King that ye ever knew that held such an household by the half delle as Richard in this realm.' And here is criticism of Members of Parliament which carries a familiar modern ring: 'Than satte summe as siphre doth in awgrym, and somme slombrid and slepte and said but a lite and somme maffled with mouth and nyst what they ment . . .'

(4) *Rot. Parl*, III 368, No 75; Lodge & Thornton, *Op. cit.* 158–9. The peace-time royal revenue has been estimated at £60,000.

This special grant added £90,000 to the royal Exchequer, but that does not mean to the private pockets of the King.

189 (1) *Annales*, 263; *Adam of Usk*, 10 and 153; Tout, *Chapters* IV 31.

(2) For this spate of oath-taking see Clarke, *Fourteenth Century Studies*, 103 *et seq.*

190 (1) *Adam of Usk*, 19 and 164.

191 (1) For the detailed story see *Traison*, 12–14 and 141–7; cf *Adam of Usk*, 23–4 and 170–1; *Annales*, 225; *Hist. Anglic*, II 227.

192 (1) *Traison*, 14 and 145–6.

(2) Armitage-Smith, *John of Gaunt*, 402.

(3) Stubbs, *Constitutional History* II 521–4.

193 (1) K. H. Vickers, *England in the Later Middle Ages*, London 1921, 293.

(2) C. Oman, *The Political History of England 1377–1485*, London 1910, 141.

(3) cf J. E. J. Jolliffe, *Constitutional History of Mediaeval England*, London 1937, 433.

(4) cf Tout, *Chapters* IV 36, also *EHR*, XL 321–3.

194 (1) The best account of the Lists of Coventry is in *Traison*, 141–58.

195 (1) Accounts vary as to the precise method by which a duel could be stopped. The calling of 'Ho! ho!' by the King is preferred by the French chroniclers. It is probable that at such a crisis both gesture and command were used.

197 (1) cf *Traison* 156 note.

198 (1) There is record of the payment of 1,000 marks on Nov 14, 1398, and of £1,586.13.4. in June 1399. *Traison*, 160 note.

(2) *Calendar of the Patent Rolls*, 3 Oct, 22 Ric. II 1.

199 (1) *English Chronicle*, ed J. S. Davies (Camden 1856), 12, translating *Eulogium*, III 378; cf V. H. Galbraith, 'A New Life of Richard II' in *History*, XXVI 223–229.

(2) *Traison* 148.

(3) *Kirkstall*, 34 and note.

(4) *Annales*, 267–71.

201 (1) The Golden Bull of the Emperor Charles IV (1356) gives a good impression of what the Holy Roman Empire meant to the Middle Ages. See Henderson, *Documents* 220–61.

203 (1) See Clarke, *Op. cit.* 103–14 for this paragraph.

(2) For a summary of why Richard lost London and why Henry could count on it see *Traison*, xxxvi–xlv.

205 (1) See *Creton*, 21 note.

(2) *The Orygynale Cronykil of Scotland* by Andrew of Wyntoun, ed Laing, Edinburgh 1872, XIX 68–9.

206 (1) See Armitage-Smith, *Op. cit.* X 196–229.

NOTES

Page

(2) See J. G. Edwards in *EHR*, XL 321–33; Tout, *Chapters* IV 38; *EHR*, XLVII 276–80 and 453.

207 (1) *Annales*, 232–3; *Calendar of the Patent Rolls*, 1396–9 and 534–71; Tout, *Chapters* IV 53.

208 (1) *Annales*, 238.

(2) He later became one of Henry IV's Treasurers of the Exchequer and Archbishop of York.

(3) See S. B. Chrimes, *English Constitutional Ideas in the Fifteenth Century*, Cambridge 1936, 138; and cf *EHR*, XL 321–33.

(4) Oman, *Op. cit.* 145.

209 (1) See Tout, *Chapters* IV 39; Rymer, *Foedera* 77.

(2) *Traison*, 27 and 167.

CHAPTER IX

212 (1) See note (3) on p 175 above, and also *The Poem on the Deposition* by Richard of Maidstone (Camden) London 1838, *passim*.

(2) 'Richard failed because he refused to accept the first rule of the game – that a King should govern by the counsel and consent of his hereditary advisers. History therefore in the shape of the Tudors was on Richard's side. But the Tudors never made the mistake of confusing the substance of power with autocratic government on principle.' V. H. Galbraith 'A New Life of Richard II' in *History*, XXVI 223–39.

213 (1) *Annales*, 239 and Articles of Accusation No 23.

(2) In *Archaeologia*, II (1824) 1–423 where the translation and notes are valuable. See also Richard Beresford, *Glist'ring Phaeton*, Johannesburg 1945. The *Traison* makes great use of Creton's narrative.

(3) We know the names of three – William Byngley, William York, and Walterus de Lynne. See Rymer *Foedera*, VIII 78–9; and *Creton*, 21–2.

214 (1) 'Out of true and entire affection' says Creton, who witnessed the scene.

215 (1) For the movements of Henry in exile, and immediately after landing at Ravenspur, see *Traison*, Appendix E 287–94.

216 (1) See *Traison*, 179 for an example of Henry's ingenious and successful publicity methods working on the credulity of fishermen.

(2) *Traison*, 180–3.

(3) *Hardyng*, 350. But see J. M. W. Bean, 'Henry IV and the

Page

Percies', *History* XLIV 212–27 for a version much less friendly to the Percy family.

217 (1) *Traison*, Appendix E 292.

(2) *Traison*, 186.

218 (1) *Traison*, 187.

219 (1) The phrase is Creton's. For the details of events after Richard's landing I have relied on the admirable research of Miss M. V. Clarke and Prof Galbraith (Clarke, *Fourteenth Century Studies* 66–9) following on the discovery of the Dieulacres Chronicle and the tendency of modern research to test Lancastrian propaganda by reference to the French chroniclers.

(2) See Clarke, *Op. cit.* 73; Steel, *Richard II* 266. Both criticisms quote no evidence for their scorn.

220 (1) *Adam of Usk*, 26–7 and 175–7. Usk's report of the rapine of the Lancastrians is confirmed by *Dieulacres*, 49–50.

(2) *Annales*, 249–50; *Hist. Anglic*, II 234; *Rot. Parl*, III 416 for the official Lancastrian version.

(3) *Creton*, 125 *et seq.*; *Traison*, 46 and 195 *et seq.*; *Dieulacres*, 51 and the *Chronicle of Whalley* quoted by Clarke, *Op. cit.* 76.

221 (1) *Creton*, 140.

(2) *Annales*, 250.

(3) *Annales*, 251 and *Creton*, 177–8. Creton also mentions an attempt of Richard to escape from Lichfield by night, but this story is not mentioned elsewhere.

222 (1) *Traison*, 62 and 213.

(2) *Traison*, 63 and 214.

224 (1) *Adam of Usk*, 29–30 and 181–2.

(2) *Adam of Usk*, 30–1 and 182–4, and especially the notes, and cf *Hardyng*, 353.

(3) G. Lapsley, *Crown Community and Parliament*, Oxford 1951, VII and VIII, 272–373.

225 (1) *Rot. Parl*, III 415; and cf. T. F. T. Plucknett's edition of Taswell-Langmead's *English Constitutional History*, London 1946, 549–50.

226 (1) *Annales*, 254.

(2) *Adam of Usk*, 30 and 182.

(3) *Traison*, 65 and 216.

227 (1) *Dieulacres*, 51.

(2) Clarke, *Op. cit.* 78 *et seq.* The phrase is Miss Clarke's *Op. cit.* 89.

228 (1) *Annales*, 259–77, and *Rot. Parl*, III, 417–22.

229 (1) *Rot. Parl*, III, 422–3 and *Annales*, 281. Henry IV was the first of our mediaeval Kings to take care to use English in claiming

NOTES

Page

the throne. In the fourteenth century literacy still meant a knowledge of Latin, but this was mostly left to clerics. The court language was still Norman-French, but Richard was complimented by Froissart on his French (see above p 159) which was presumably *not* the French of Stratford-atte-Bowe. English had superseded French as the spoken language of the law courts in 1362, and it is significant of this transition period that Gower wrote in French, in Latin, and finally in English. Chaucer wrote for his royal and baronial patrons in English, and we are told that Richard talked to his Cheshire Archers *in materna lingua* (see above p 170). See V. H. Galbraith, *The Literacy of the Mediaeval English Kings*, British Academy Vol XXI, London 1935.

230 (1) *Rot. Parl*, III, 423 and *Annales*, 282, and for variants of this challenge and the preceding explanation cf *Evesham*, 209 and 212.

(2) *Adam of Usk*, 32 and 185.

(3) *Traison*, 70–1 and 221–2, as opposed to *Eulogium* III, 383–4, and see Clarke *Op. cit.* 86 *et seq.* And it is only fair to Shakespeare to refer the reader to Carlisle's speech in his *Richard II*, Act IV, Sc. i.

232 (1) *Annales*, 287.

(2) See Jolliffe *Constitutional History of Mediaeval England*, 486–9.

233 (1) *Annales*, 297–300.

(2) *Traison*, 75–6 and 227–8 and *Hardyng*, 356, but the *Annales* say that the place of imprisonment was secret.

234 (1) This is the version in the *Traison* which gives circumstantial evidence of the whole sequence of events, 77 and 229 *et seq.* The official version is in the *Annales*, 323 *et seq.*, and of course it suppresses the part played by Rutland. It is significant that Rutland in his will requests that, in all masses and prayers offered for him, mention is to be made of 'Richard II for whom he was in conscience obliged to pray'. See *Creton*, 402–4.

(2) The *Annales*, 323 mentions that the conspirators visited the young ex-Queen Isabelle at Sunning possibly in the hope of making her a rallying point.

(3) Oman *Political History of England*, 163, as a good military historian, points out that their 'wild ride' to the west was 'an astonishing march of some fifty miles' – which accounts for the poor military precautions at Cirencester.

(4) *Adam of Usk*, 42 and 198 reports that their 'bodies, quartered after the manner of the flesh of beasts taken in the chase,

267

Page

partly in sacks and partly slung on poles between men's shoulders, I saw carried to London and afterwards salted'. And there is a gory description of the execution of Sir Thomas Blount in *Traison*, 90–1 and 245–6 which equally illustrates the brutality of the times.

235 (1) *Minutes of the Privy Council*, I 42.
   (2) *Adam of Usk*, 42 and 199 and especially the lengthy note.
   (3) *Traison*, 94–5 and 248–51.
   (4) *Archaeologia*, XX 424–42 and VI 316. Also Stanley, *Op. cit.* 126.
   (5) Wallon, *Op. cit.* II 373–4.
236 (1) See Benjamin Williams' Preface to the *Traison*, l–lxxvi.
237 (1) It was Elizabeth who is said to have protested when Shakespeare's play was about to be produced at the time of Essex' rebellion 'I am Richard II, know ye not that?' See J. Palmer, *Political Characters of Shakespeare*, 118 *et seq.*
238 (1) See Jolliffe, *Op. cit.* 488.
   (2) Steel, *The Receipt of the Exchequer*, Cambridge 1954, 359.
239 (1) See Clarke, *Op. cit.* cap. VIII for a learned essay on the Wilton Dyptych (now in the National Gallery); and see *History* XXVI, 238 for the theory that it was probably a Ricardian 'ikon' dating from the early years of the following reign.
   (2) cf J. H. Harvey, *Henry Yevele*, London 1944, *passim*.
   (3) cf *Traison* Preface, 77; and the reproduction of the signed letter of Richard to Charles VI of France dated Sept. 30, 1395, printed as a frontispiece to the *Diplomatic Correspondence of Richard II*, ed E. Perroy (Camden 3rd series) XLVIII, 1933, and Intro xxxi. See colophon on p 240 above.
   (4) See Clarke, *Op. cit.* 117–18 quoting *Wardrobe Accounts*, 9–11, Ric. II, PRO. E. 101/401/15.
   (5) *The Forme of Cury*, 'a roll of ancient English cookery compiled about A.D. 1390 by the Master-Cooke of Richard the Second, presented afterwards to Elizabeth by Edward Lord Stafford.' R. Rankin, *Richard II*, London 1931, 129.

INDEX

INDEX

271

INDEX

225; abdication scenes, 226–7; challenges crown, 229–30; concessions to Parliament, 231–2; escapes from conspiracy, 234; Rout of Cirencester, 234–5; Richard's death, 235–7
Henry V, 213–14
Hereford, Bishop of, see Gilbert, John; Duke of, see Henry IV
Holland, Sir John, half-brother of Richard, 9, 66, 68, 93; Beverley Brawl, 98; to Spain, 101; Earl of Huntingdon, 122, 130; Chamberlain, 133, 135; Captain and Counsellor of Roman Church, 176; Duke of Exeter, 186; Captain of Calais, 192; to Ireland, 213, 220; reverts to Earl of Huntingdon, 223; conspiracy to save Richard, 233–4; slain at Pleshey, 234
Holland, Sir Thomas, the elder, half-brother of Richard, Earl of Kent, 9, 66, 68
Holland, Sir Thomas, the younger, nephew to Richard, third Earl of Kent, to Ireland, 148; king's friend, 162; Duke of Surrey, 186; bail for Hereford and Marshal, 192; to Ireland, 212; reverts to Earl of Kent, 223; conspiracy to save Richard, 233–4; slain at Rout of Cirencester, 234
Hood, Robin, 52, 75
Horne, John, Alderman of London, 64, 73, 77
Hotspur, see Percy, Henry, the younger
Hundred Years War, 7, 36–8, 42–3
Huntingdon, Earl of, see Angle, Guichard d', and Holland, Sir John
Huss, John, of Bohemia, 86–7

Ireland, Richard's First Expedition to, 145–50; Second Expedition to, 204, 209, 218. Duke of, see Vere, Robert de
Isabelle of France, daughter of Charles VI of France, second

Queen of Richard, 160, 163–4, 209

'Jacquerie', The, 58, 76
Joan of Kent, Princess of Wales, wife of the Black Prince, mother of Richard, 3–4; previous marriages, 3; supporter of Wyclif, 17; during Peasants' Revolt, 60 and n., 66, 69, 74, 85; reconciles Gaunt to Richard, 97; Beverley Brawl, 98; death, 99
John of Gaunt, third son of Edward III, Duke of Lancaster, at Nájera, 6–7; wicked (?) uncle, 14; v. Good Parliament, 15–16; defends Wyclif and quarrels with Londoners, 17–19; Palatinate for life, 19; at Coronation, 21; during Richard's minority, 26–8; St Malo, 42; Scotland, 61, 82, 91; Savoy Palace sacked, 65; quarrel with Percy, 82–83; Way of Portugal, 88–9, 90–1; Latemar 'plot', 92–3; John of Northampton, 95; de Vere's 'plot', 97; Richard's Scottish expedition, 98–100; Peninsular Expedition, 101; Lieutenant of Aquitaine, 122; Duke of Aquitaine, 126; ancestor to Peninsular monarchies, 126–7; welcomed home by Richard, 132; Palatinate hereditary, 133; peacemaker, 136–7; Cheshire Rising, 141; attacked by Arundel, 142; death of second wife Costanza, 143; to Gascony, 147–8, 157–8; Richard's second marriage, 161–3; marries mistress Catherine Swynford, 163; Beauforts legitimized, 171; bail for Hereford, 192; Parliamentary Committee of 1398, 193; death, 205–6
John of Northampton, Mayor of London, 95–6, 134
Judges, Questions to, 109–11

Kent, Earl of, see Holland, Sir Thomas, the elder and the younger

272

INDEX

Kilkenny, Statute of, 146
Knolles, Sir Robert, 61, 73, 77

Labourers, Statutes of, 124–5, 134
Lancaster, Duke of, see Henry IV and John of Gaunt
Lancastrian faction, 84
Langland, William, author of *Piers Plowman*, 52, 152, 212
Latemar, John, Carmelite friar, 92–3
Latimer, Lord William, 26
Latymer, Sir Thomas, of Braybroke, 152
Launcekron, Agnes, second wife of Vere, Robert de, 111
Law of Parliament, 117–19, 121, 189
Legge, John, 56, 59, 63
Lelinghen, Truce of, 137–8
Lichfield, Bishop of, see Burghill, John
Limoges, Sack of, 4 and n.
Lincoln, Bishop of, see Beaufort, Henry
Livery and Maintenance, 123, 133–4, 170–1
Loans, Forced, by Council, 45; by Richard, 176–7, 202–30
Lollards, 53; origins and beliefs, 151–152; petition to Parliament, 154–5
London, city of, welcome to Prince Richard, 17; quarrel with Gaunt, 17–19; appeal to Richard, 20–1; 'the Londoner's King', 22; guild factions, 95; supports Appellants, 114; for and against Brembre, 119; quarrel with Richard, 138–40; pro Gloucester, 179; reconciled to Richard, 187; welcome to Henry IV, 222. Bishop of, see Braybroke, Robert

MacMurrough, Art Oge, King of Leinster, 148, 189, 204, 214–15, 218
Maintenance, see Livery and Maintenance
Manorial System, 48–50, 77–8
March, Earl of, see Mortimer, Edmund and Roger
Mare, Peter de la, Speaker of Commons, 11–13, 15, 21, 27
Marsilius of Padua, 31, 200

Martin, Geoffrey, clerk to the Crown, 116
Maudeleyn, confessor and secretary to Richard, 221; conspires to save Richard, 233; executed, 234, 236
Medford, Richard, secretary to Richard, Bishop of Chichester, 85, 120; Bishop of Salisbury, 169, 213
Merciless Parliament, 115–22
Merke, Thomas, monk of Westminster, to Ireland, 148; Bishop of Carlisle, 169; to Ireland, 213; defends Richard, 230–1; conspires to save Richard, 233; exiled, 234
Mile End, 67–70
Molyneux, Sir Thomas, Constable of Chester, 113
Mone, Guy, Keeper of Privy Seal, 169; Bishop of St David's, 213
Montague, Sir John, 93; third Earl of Salisbury and king's friend, 172; Lists of Coventry, 194; to Ireland, 213; to North Wales, 218–19; imprisoned, 223; conspires to save Richard, 233; slain at Rout of Cirencester, 234
Montague, Sir William, second Earl of Salisbury, 63, 66–7, 70, 74
Mortimer, Edmund, third Earl of March, 26
Mortimer, Edmund, fifth Earl of March, heir presumptive, 204, 225
Mortimer, Roger, fourth Earl of March, 114; to Ireland, 148; Lieutenant of Ireland, 150; heir to Richard, 160; oath at Shrewsbury, 190, 204; slain at Battle of Kells, 204
Mortimer, Sir Thomas, illegitimate son of second Earl of March, 184–5, 188

Nájera, Rout of, 6–7
Neville, Ralph, Earl of Westmorland, 186, 216; Marshal, 223
Norbury, John, 223

273

INDEX